Storm Over the Constitution

D1282518

Storm Over the Constitution

Harry V. Jaffa

LEXINGTON BOOKS
Lanham • Boulder • New York • Oxford

LEXINGTON BOOKS

Published in the United States of America
by Lexington Books
4720 Boston Way, Lanham, Maryland 20706

12 Hid's Copse Road
Cumnor Hill, Oxford OX2 9JJ, England

Copyright © 1999 by Lexington Books

All rights reserved. No part of this publication may be reproduced,
stored in a retrieval system, or transmitted in any form or by any
means, electronic, mechanical, photocopying, recording, or otherwise,
without the prior permission of the publisher.

British Library Cataloguing in Publication Information Available

Library of Congress Cataloging-in-Publication Data

Jaffa, Harry V.
    Storm over the constitution / Harry V. Jaffa.
      p. cm.
    Includes bibliographical references and index.
    ISBN 0-7391-0040-8 (cloth : alk. paper). -- ISBN 0-7391-0041-6
(pbk. : alk. paper)
    1. Constitutional law--United States. I. Title.
KF4550.A2J34   1999
342.73'02--dc21   99-31693
                        CIP

Printed in the United States of America

♾™ The paper used in this publication meets the minimum requirements of American
National Standard for Information Sciences—Permanence of Paper for Printed Library
Materials, ANSI/NISO Z39.48–1992.

To the Memory of Francis R. Aumann
1902-1996

Francis Aumann was my colleague at Ohio State University, where I received my first tenure track appointment in 1951, and where I advanced to full professorship in 1959, the year I published *Crisis of the House Divided*.

To me, Columbus, after Washington, New York, and Chicago, was something of a culture shock. Most of the liberal arts faculty were Ivy Leaguers, of one kind or another, who regarded Columbus the way the Colonel Blimps of the British Empire, in the palmy days of Queen Victoria, regarded their stations on the outposts of civilization. Francis was a native Ohioan and, in a deeper sense, a son of the old Northwest Territory, who carried its history in his bones. His hero was his wife Katherine's father, Charles McCarthy, who had been a great athlete in his day, who founded the first legislative reference library in the country in Wisconsin, and who had been a Bull Mooser and friend of Theodore Roosevelt. But yesterday's Bull Moosers (like old New Dealers) are often today's conservatives.

I made my way across the political spectrum in the 1950s, changing my party registration from Democrat to Republican in 1962—at about the same time that Ronald Reagan changed his. I had worked for the Percy Committee in 1959 and 1960, and had a letter of appreciation from President Eisenhower. In 1963 I joined Ohioans for Goldwater, having earlier become faculty adviser to the Young Republicans at Ohio State. Meanwhile much of the department, and especially its younger members, were moving in an opposite direction, as the explosion of the later 60s showed. One with whom I had been especially close in my early years in Ohio would not speak to me after he learned I had become a Republican!

I soon discovered that I was in something like an academic foxhole. But I was not alone. Francis largely kept his own counsel, but he was unsparing in the comfort and support that he gave me in these years, and we grew ever closer. Francis had been a member of the Ohio State faculty since 1928, and he had many friends in the university administration as well as in the political community, many of them his former students. I discovered that I had a silent wall of nonacademic defenders, even as I acquired academic enemies.

Francis was a colorful character. His conversational style—which was also his lecturing style—was like the rambling reminiscences of an old frontiersman or river boatman, such as Mark Twain often featured. But he was a fount not only of folk wisdom but of classical learning. When your ear was properly tuned you could, as Yogi Berra might have said, "Hear a lot by listening." He recognized that I was bringing my own classical training to bear upon the understanding of the roots of America's greatness. In that project, no one except Leo Strauss gave me greater encouragement.

The Constitution, and the legal system as a whole, was Francis's special preoccupation. His love for the law, as it had evolved here, is demonstrated in *The Changing American Legal System*, published originally in 1940, and reprinted as a classic by the Da Capo Press in 1969. It traces the evolution of American law from the colonial origins to the Civil War, and from the Civil War until 1935. It has the depth and power of the historical scholarship that characterized American political science at its best, and before its descent into the nether regions of methodology and ideology in which it dwells today.

It is with gratitude and deep affection that I dedicate *Storm Over the Constitution* to Francis's memory.

Contents

Acknowledgments

The introduction was originally published as "Natural Right in the American Founding, Review Essay on *Original Intent and the Framers of the Constitution: A Disputed Question,* by Harry V. Jaffa," Vol. 23, No. 3 (Spring, 1996), INTERPRETATION: A JOURNAL OF POLITICAL PHILOSOPHY, pp. 457-475. "The Closing of the Conservative Mind," "Whatever Happened to the Emperor's New Clothes?," "Natural Law, the Constitution, and Robert Bork," "The Inkblot Constitution," and "Is the Constitution Good?" were originally published in *Storm Over the Constitution: Jaffa Answers Bork* (Claremont: The Claremont Institute, 1994). Lino Graglia, "Jaffa's Quarrel with Bork," was originally published in Vol. 4, No. 3 (Summer, 1995), THE SOUTHERN CALIFORNIA INTERDISCIPLINARY LAW JOURNAL, pp. 705-713; Jaffa, "Graglia's Quarrel with God" was published in the same issue at pp. 715-738. Charles Cooper, "Harry Jaffa's Bad Originalism" originally appeared in 1994 PUBLIC INTEREST LAW REVIEW, pp. 189-215. Jaffa's "Slaying the Dragon of Bad Originalism" appeared in a shorter version in 1995 PUBLIC INTEREST LAW REVIEW, pp. 209-219. All articles are reprinted with permission.

Preface

Larry P. Arnn

This book concerns a question of constitutional interpretation, the contemporary doctrine of "original intent." This term as used by some famous people requires that the judge, as judge, must bring no theory to the interpretation of the Constitution. In particular he must not look to the Declaration of Independence as a guide.

The argument concerns whether this sort of "original intent" is "original." The argument has been carried on with some acrimony, for which each side blames the other. The differences seem and are wide. Where the gulf exists, it is deep. But it does not quite run the whole length of the land. Harry Jaffa states definitely that he is a member of the original intent school, and that he would have the words of the Constitution be the controlling force over the judge. In an earlier volume of essays in this controversy, he wrote:

> Judge Bork and I begin with agreement on several points of the highest moment. First, we are equally opposed to liberal judicial activism, based upon the idea of a "living" or "evolving" Constitution. Second, we are agreed that a jurisprudence of original intent (sometimes called "original understanding" or "originalism") is the only alternative to allowing the justices to rewrite the Constitution according to their taste or preferences. Third we agree that the justices are properly confined, by the doctrine of original intent, to the text of the Constitution, and have no more warrant to emend or emend the text by reference to "higher law" principles, than to those of a "living" Constitution. Where we differ, is on the question of the place of higher law principles in the text itself.

If this assertion by Professor Jaffa is true, it eliminates one of the charges against him, namely that his theorizing would liberate the judge from the text of the Constitution.

The reader, in evaluating this part of the controversy, should bear in mind that Harry Jaffa is a follower of Abraham Lincoln in most things. No one admired the Declaration of Independence more openly, interpreted it more deeply, or implemented it more practically, than did Lincoln. No one opposed slavery with greater effect than Lincoln. But it was Lincoln's position that slavery was protected in certain provisions of the Constitution, and in those places he would not touch it himself, and he would resist others who attempted to do so. Moreover the Constitution gave the federal government an obligation to assist in the return of fugitive slaves—that is, to seize by force people who had risked their lives to reach the land of freedom, and to return them to the whips of their enraged "owners." Lincoln's devotion to the actual text of the Constitution was such that even here, in regard to this rank and ugly duty, he promised to fulfill his obligation completely, and he formed his whole political party upon the principle that this was right. Where the text of the Constitution commanded Lincoln, even in opposition to the principles of the Declaration, Lincoln thought it right to obey the Constitution. For taking these positions, abolitionists of his day, and liberals and some conservatives of our day, have condemned Lincoln as a friend of the slave power. Professor Jaffa has, for more than 40 years, defended Lincoln on these points.

If Professor Jaffa is in fact a true follower of Lincoln, as he claims to be, then this dispute does not concern whether the text of the Constitution is the supreme legal authority. What then is it about? The key, so far as it has to do with Robert Bork, may be found in his most recent book. There he writes more directly upon the principles of the Declaration of Independence, and there he makes his larger purpose plainer.

In *Slouching Toward Gomorrah*, Judge Bork writes many criticisms of the Founders generally and of the Declaration in particular. The sum of them amounts to this:

> The signers of the Declaration of Independence took the moral order they had inherited for granted. It never occurred to them that the document's rhetorical flourishes might be dangerous if that moral order weakened.

That is the point. In their drunkenness with liberty, the Founders forgot decency. In their orgy of liberated will, they failed in restraint. They forgot that if you get too excited about your rights, you will neglect your duties. Proclaiming a man's liberty will make him readier to cheat on his wife or steal from his partner. Looking about, Bork sees everywhere the infection of vice. It has festered because the Declaration of Independence broke our immunity. But perhaps to him the Founders did not mean to lay open our body politic to infection. They did not know what they were doing. The harm they were doing "never occurred" to them. They were rich kids, robust at birth, but never understanding the conditions of their health.

The trouble is that this statement, as an expression of the mind of the "signers of the Declaration," makes poor history. Read, to begin with, the Virginia Bill of Rights. This document was adopted by unanimous vote of the Virginia Convention on June 12, just 22 days before the adoption of the Declaration. Five members of that convention were "signers" of the Declaration. In the 15th article of the Virginia Bill of Rights, they wrote: "that no free government, or the blessings of Liberty, can be preserved to any people, but by a firm adherence to justice, moderation, temperance, frugality and virtue, and by frequent recurrence to fundamental principles." At least on that day, those five "signers" were not "taking for granted" the morality that they had "inherited." They were asserting it, as the necessary ground for freedom.

Such statements flow like a flood from the signers and their fellow founders, from the preachers of the revolution, from nearly every citizen who wrote about public matters. Of course they begin in the Declaration itself, where an argument—a deeply moral argument—is given to prove that the revolution is not merely possible, but also justified by a standard outside their own will. The very day upon which I write this, a national journalist has inquired of me where we got the idea of the "natural law." In the confirmation hearings of Justice Thomas, the whole Senate Judiciary Committee, Republican and Democrat, seemed to know nothing of it. Yet there it is, in the first sentence of the Declaration. It is placed there prominently, the first of four mentions of the Almighty, to provide the standard by which the Founders judged the English king, and by which they wished themselves to be judged.

Of course the great majority of those signers and the citizens who elected them were Christians, and they thought that their faith provided knowledge of morality that must command their behavior at the risk of their salvation. But the genius of the revolution is that it does not rest upon the high authority of revelation alone. Consider this statement by the preacher Samuel West, one of the most influential men of Massachusetts, speaking before the Massachusetts Council and House of Representatives in the same year the Declaration was adopted:

> The Deity has also invested us with moral powers and faculties, by which we are enabled to discern the difference between right and wrong, truth and falsehood, good and evil; hence the approbation of mind that arises upon doing a good action, and the remorse of conscience which we experience when we counteract the moral sense and do that which is evil. This

> proves that, in what is commonly called a state of nature, we
> are the subjects of the divine law and government; that the
> Deity is our supreme magistrate, who has written his law in our
> hearts, and will reward or punish us according as we obey or
> disobey his commands.

Here is laid the ground for a form of government that does not rest upon the authority of priests and kings standing upon divine right. It is a standard in full accord with revelation, but built upon the "rational perception of the divine and eternal truths." In this mating of reason and revelation upon a moral standard, America achieved the first religious and civil freedom that the world has known.

This achievement is the fulfillment of an old tradition, and the solution to an old problem. It gave rise itself to a tradition of civic understanding and of scholarship—a tradition closer in time to the founders and to that extent more "original." In this tradition the American experiment in freedom and popular government was distinguished especially in its moral seriousness. In this tradition the figure of George Washington is understood as the sum of the virtues that citizens must possess. In this tradition the pledge *these signers gave* of their "lives, fortunes, and sacred honor" is a moral pledge. These signers make this pledge "to each other." In that way they make a pact to face the danger, terribly apparent to every man in the room, of confronting a ruler who is at once oppressive and extremely powerful. Under the influence of this old tradition, this "original" tradition, children learned of the price paid by those signers for their courage. They learned of the wounds these signers suffered, of the farms they lost, of the loved ones who were captured or killed or left grieving when these signers themselves gave their lives in war.

In this older and better tradition, the courage of these signers was not seen as accidental to what they believed. When they appealed to the "laws of nature and of nature's God," they were thought to mean a standard of right, a standard by which the conduct of every man in every time was to be judged. Children were taught to cling to this standard. They were taught that to be an American was to be at once—and for the same reason—entitled to liberty and responsible for its use. They were taught sometimes that George Washington had owned up to an offense against the owner of a cherry tree, which perhaps he did not. But this little myth stood for them—too young to grasp the full and awesome achievement of the man—as an example. This is what their "father" did. By the goodness of his character he secured for them a blessing. And they owed something for that blessing. All the strength around them, all the decency, all the justice they saw stemmed from that blessing. And under this lesson they grew up straight and good themselves, both possessing and deserving of their liberty, sure that they could not possess it without deserving it. Perhaps George Washington did not chop the tree. But the record of his character still shines from the battlefields upon which he fought, across the city that he built, in each corner of the great nation that he raised up by his example. And yes, it shines too, if one will but read him a little, in the precepts that he taught right from his boyhood and to the edge of his grave. It was a fine thing to have the picture of George Washington hanging in every classroom in the land. Would Judge Bork hang it there?

This old tradition is not in fashion just now. That is the most dangerous fact confronting our nation today. This tradition has been systematically buried by generations of academics who set out with a will upon that task. They began early in this century to condemn the Declaration of Independence. They believed its principles were wrong, and they believed the institutions built under its influence were obsolete. To them this tradition, and the truth that lies behind it, was not an asset in their cause. It was an obstacle. The devotion it commanded made the people resistant to their new creed. And so they have been busy these many decades wearing down those institutions and obscuring those principles.

Setting out with a good purpose to resist them, Judge Bork has in his errors joined them. He has become another stage in the awful dialectic they have loosed upon the nation.

We at the Claremont Institute are and have been "conservatives." As the old and best tradition of our nation has gone out of fashion, so too has conservatism. Nonetheless we cling to it. We believe that American conservatism has something special to conserve. That something is formed around the Declaration of Independence. Yes surely, conservatives must devote themselves to the Constitution, because that Constitution is a marvelous thing in itself, and because it rests upon and protects with unprecedented success that basic ground of law, the right of every man to consent to the government under which he lives. If the Constitution is a wonderful structure, its foundation is the Declaration. Within that whole structure is sheltered the justice, the power, the success of this greatest of modern nations.

We seek to revive the tradition that reveres that whole structure. This book is part of the work.

Introduction: Harry Jaffa and Original Intent Jurisprudence

Edward J. Erler

A recent writer laments that the school of Leo Strauss has fallen into factious dispute regarding the character of the American regime. Some see the American political order as altogether modern and therefore defective. Some see it as not so bad because not so modern. Mostly, these implicitly reject the Straussian insistence on the partition between ancients and moderns. At first they claimed to be a kind of subset of Straussians, but now they openly speak of "Straussians" with the same bitterness and derision which characterized the earlier reactions of Marxists and behavioralists. A third group insists that the American scheme is wholly modern, but still good.

And, without the slightest trace of irony, a recent writer notes that "I have tended in this third direction."[1]

No one epitomizes the central position more than Harry Jaffa, who, more than any other student of Strauss, has devoted almost his entire career to uncovering and articulating the natural right foundations of the American regime. His frequent reliance on classical political philosophy in the explication of those foundations is particularly offensive to a recent writer because it rejects Strauss's "insistence on the partition between ancients and moderns." Jaffa answered a recent writer in the following terms:

> What Strauss taught about the modern break with the principles of antiquity—whether of reason or revelation—refers to the history of political philosophy. It does not refer to the history of politics, or of the incorporation, or nonincorporation, of principles, whether ancient or modern, in political regimes. Strauss was not an historical determinist. If his own belief in the superiority of pre-modern principles was

---

[1] *Crisis* (June, 1993), p. 55.

possible, why was it not possible in others, especially statesmen and legislators?[2]

Strauss, of course, wrote only obliquely about the American regime,
and in widely scattered places. The backdrop of his work was "the crisis
of the West" rather than "the crisis of America." Yet it would be difficult to believe that Strauss did not somehow see the crisis of the West
and the crisis of America as stemming from the same causes, namely,
the abandonment of natural right. The question that confronts us is
whether decent constitutionalism can be buttressed by teachings derived
from classic natural right. Although Strauss's works present daunting
problems for the interpreter—not the least of which is the fact that he
left many false trails and unmarked traps in his writings (amply attested
to by the recent works of Shadia Drury and Stephen Holmes, to mention
only two)—there can be little doubt that for him the study of classic
natural right was not merely a matter of antiquarianism. Jaffa quite reasonably expresses the conviction that "Strauss' entire work pointed toward rescuing the *political practice* of the modern world from the consequences of the *political theory* of modern philosophy," and that this
project would necessarily rely on "powerful support from . . . the premodern thought of our western tradition."[3]
On the issue of ancients and moderns, Strauss wrote in 1952 that

a modern phenomenon is not characterized by the fact that it is
located, say, between 1600 and 1952, because premodern traditions of course survived and survive. And more than that,

---

[2] *Crisis* (November, 1993), p. 2: "The Founding Fathers as one of the most exceptional
generations of political men who ever lived, are not to be understood as primarily Hob-
besians, Lockeans, or Aristotelians. They were rather phronemoi, morally and politically
wise men, the kind of characters from whom Aristotle himself drew his portraits of moral
and political virtues. And Aristotle understood what these virtues were, not from speculative thought as such, but from contemplating such actual examples of the virtues as
came under his observation. The source of his ability to recognize these virtues, was not
philosophy, but nature, the reality which was the ground of philosophy . . . . The vitality
of classical political philosophy—why it is so close to the spirit of the statesmanship of
the American Founding—is that it is grounded in the reality of political life itself." "Hu-
manizing Certitudes and Impoverishing Doubts," *Interpretation*, vol. 16, no. 1 (Fall,
1988), pp. 124-5.
[3] "The Legacy of Leo Strauss," *Claremont Review of Books*, vol. 3, no. 3 (Fall, 1984), p.
14 (quoting Strauss, "The Three Waves of Modernity," in Hilail Gildin, ed., *Political
Philosophy: Six Essays by Leo Strauss* [Indianapolis: Bobbs-Merrill Co., 1975], p. 98).

throughout the modern period, there has been a constant movement against this modern trend, from the very beginning.[4]

To say nothing of other considerations, there are significant points of agreement between ancients and moderns, most notably the modern premise "which would have been acceptable to the classics, that the moral principles have a greater evidence than the teachings even of natural theology and, therefore, that natural law or natural right should be kept independent of theology and its controversies.[5] The modern doctrine of the state of nature must be understood precisely in the light of this agreement.

Strauss, of course, emphasized the differences between classic natural right and modern natural right. Classic natural right is teleological; man's perfection must be understood in terms of his natural ends. Modern natural right rejects teleology in favor of beginnings. Men have rights; freedom rather than virtue is the proper goal of man. Classic natural right does not require consent of the governed to legitimate rule. Modern natural right is egalitarian; consent of the governed is necessitated by natural human equality. Classic natural right emphasizes prudence as a guide to political action. Scientific certitude replaces prudence in modern natural right. In short, modern natural right lowers the goals of political life in order to guarantee its actualization. Most importantly, however, modernity attempted to overcome the distinction between reason and revelation. It was within the context of the larger and more important distinction between reason and revelation that Strauss understood the quarrel between ancients and moderns. The revival of the quarrel was necessary to the preservation of both reason and revelation. In any case, the success of modern natural right means that classic natural right—if it is to be a force in modernity—must be presented by statesmen in the form or guise of modern natural right.

With the advent of Christianity, the question of political authority took on an entirely new dimension—one that could not have been anticipated by classical political philosophers. In classical political philosophy, the laws of particular polities are always supported by the gods of those polities. As Jaffa remarks, "divine sanction" is necessary for citizens even though "the intrinsic ground" of the authority of the laws

---

[4] "Progress or Return?" in Thomas L. Pangle, ed., *The Rebirth of Classical Political Rationalism* (Chicago: University of Chicago Press, 1989), pp. 242-43.
[5] *Natural Right and History* (Chicago: University of Chicago Press, 1953), p. 164.

"is its reasonableness. There must then be either immediate divine sanction for the laws, or a natural sanction translated from that form visible only to philosophers, to one that is intelligible to nonphilosophers." But the universalism of Christianity makes the appeal to particular gods as the ground or foundation of the laws of particular polities impossible. In this case, there must be "some way of translating the authority of a universal nature into the ground of particular laws. This . . . is exactly what the doctrine of the state of nature . . . accomplished. Moreover, it did so by defining nature itself in the light of the differences between man, beast and God. That is to say, it did so by a natural theology consistent with monotheistic revealed theology."[6] (One might add that this is precisely the way in which many—perhaps most—of the preachers of the colonial and constitutional periods understood the relation between natural and revealed theology.[7]) Jaffa concludes that the "necessary emendation" of Aristotle in particular was

> required not by any transformation in Aristotle's principles, but by the transformation of the human condition—and of political life—in which those principles are applied. The idea of the state of nature modifies and yet preserves the idea of man as by nature a political animal. Moreover the idea of the state of nature, by treating civil society as a voluntary association, lays a firmer foundation for the idea of the rule of law than in Aristotle's Politics.[8]

Thus the direct appeal to nature—unmediated by theological authority—provides the ground for the separation of church and state as well as the common ground of statesmanship, ancient and modern.

For Strauss, natural right in its classical understanding is always potentially demonstrable in the human condition. It is the ground of the

---

[6] "Equality, Wisdom, Morality and Consent," *Interpretation*, vol. 15, no. 1 (January, 1987), pp. 26-27; *Original Intent and the Framers of the Constitution*, pp. 314-15, 321, 322, 349, 355-56 (hereinafter cited in the text as *OI*).

[7] Some remarkable examples are John Tucker, "An Election Sermon," in Charles Hyneman and Donald Lutz, eds., *American Political Writing during the Founding Era, 1760-1805* (Indianapolis: Liberty Press, 1983), vol. 1, pp. 161-62; Samuel Cooper, "A Sermon on the Day of the Commencement of the Constitution," in Ellis Sandoz, ed., *Political Sermons of the American Founding Era, 1730-1805* (Indianapolis: Liberty Press, 1991), pp. 637, 639, 642, 656; John Leland, "The Rights of Conscience Inalienable," in *ibid.*, pp. 1084 ff.

[8] "Equality, Wisdom, Morality and Consent," p. 27.

most fundamental human experiences, those simple experiences of right and wrong, good and evil, and just and unjust.[9] If man is by nature political, then natural right is more or less a part of every regime. Or, to put it in slightly different terms, natural right is a part of political right, it has everywhere the same *dynamis* even though it is everywhere changeable. As Strauss remarked, "[t]he evidence adduced by conventionalism is perfectly compatible with the possibility that natural right exists and, as it were, solicits the indefinite variety of notions of justice or the indefinite variety of laws, or is at the bottom of all laws."[10] And if it is true that natural right is a part of political right, the political philosopher will come to sight first as a kind of umpire: "he tries to settle those political controversies that are both of paramount and of permanent importance."[11] It is true that Machiavelli "tried to effect, and he did effect, a break with the whole tradition of political philosophy,"[12] but Strauss's entire career seems to be a kind of proof that he did not believe that Machiavelli had succeeded in destroying the possibility of natural right.

In the role of "umpire," the political philosopher is indistinguishable from "a good citizen who can perform this function of the good citizen in the best way and on the highest level." Even though the political philosopher finds it necessary to look beyond the purview of the citizen, "he does not abandon his fundamental orientation, which is the orientation inherent in political life."[13] It almost goes without saying that the political philosopher as umpire is necessarily a "natural right teacher."[14] The task of such a teacher in the first instance would then be to uncover and build upon the natural right elements of his regime—indeed perhaps even magnify and adorn those elements—for politically salutary results.

---

[9] Strauss chose two passages from the Old Testament as epigraphs to *Natural Right and History*, even though there is "no knowledge of natural right as such in the Old Testament" (p. 81). While "knowledge" if natural is absent from the Old Testament, the experience of natural right is manifestly present. Cf. *Jerusalem and Athens*, pp. 17, 22-23; "Progress or Return," p. 256; "On Natural Law," in Thomas L. Pangle, ed., *Studies in Platonic Political Philosophy* (Chicago: University of Chicago Press, 1983), p. 138. The use of the epigraphs also shows that Strauss understood natural right in the light of the teachings of the Old Testament, i.e., in the light of revelation.

[10] *Natural Right and History*, p. 101.

[11] *What Is Political Philosophy?* (New York: The Free Press, 1984), p. 84.

[12] *Ibid.*, p. 40.

[13] *Ibid.*

[14] *Natural Right and History*, p. 99; Jaffa, *American Conservatism and the American Founding* (Durham, N.C.: Carolina Academic Press, 1984), p. 84.

Here the political philosopher must always be mindful of the "theological-political problem," the necessity of presenting his natural right
teachings in a manner consistent with the authoritative moral and religious views of his political community. But, if the political philosopher
is both "umpire" and "natural right teacher," he is also necessarily a
teacher of legislators, since "it is by being the teacher of legislators that
the political philosopher is the umpire par excellence." According to
Strauss, "Plato demonstrated this *ad oculos* in his dialogue on legislation, by presenting in the guise of a stranger the philosopher who is a
teacher of legislators."[15] And, the Athenian Stranger is the natural right
teacher par excellence.[16]

Awareness of the "theological-political problem" will, of course, entail the appropriate use of rhetoric, a rhetoric that will be animated by a
kind of "Socratic *kalam.*"[17] In our time, this Socratic *kalam* will derive
its rhetorical force from the twin roots that have animated the West, reason and revelation, both of which came under attack by modern philosophy. Today, the prospect of success is made exceedingly difficult not
only by the self-destruction of reason in modern philosophy but also by
the fact that "there is no traditional piety which can form the moral sub-
stratum for any such *kalam.*"[18] But, of course a difficulty is not an im-
possibility—the responsibility of the natural right teacher remains unaf-
fected by the prospects for success.

Strauss, of course, often wrote of the fundamental incompatibility of
the accounts of the human good given by reason and revelation.[19] He
nevertheless reiterated "that this unresolved conflict is the secret of the
vitality of Western civilization."[20] It is, of course, the duty of the defenders of Western civilization, i.e., the defenders of both reason and
revelation, to maintain the existence of this dialectic. The victory of one
or the other would be the death of both and, undoubtedly, the death of
the West.

Despite the opposition between reason and revelation, Strauss argued
that there is a crucial point of agreement between these conflicting views

---

[15] *What is Political Philosophy?*, p. 84.
[16] *Laws*, 631d.
[17] Jaffa, "The Legacy of Leo Strauss," p. 20; Harry Neumann, *Liberalism* (Durham, N.C.:
Carolina Academic Press, 1991), pp. 86-88.
[18] "The Legacy of Leo Strauss," p. 20.
[19] *Natural Right and History*, pp. 74-75; "Progress or Return?" p. 260.
[20] "Progress or Return?" p. 270.

of the human good: "the Bible and Greek philosophy agree in regard to what we may call, and we do call in fact, morality. They agree, if I may say so, regarding the importance of morality, regarding the content of morality, and regarding its ultimate insufficiency."[21] What divides the Bible and Greek philosophy concerns the "ultimate insufficiency" of morality or "the basis of morality," i.e., what "supplements or completes morality."[22] Jaffa surely captures the spirit of Strauss's understanding of Greek philosophy when he remarks that "as the founder of political philosophy, Socrates was also the founder of a new way of looking at the whole, that is to say, he became a refounder of philosophy." The consequence of this "refounding" is that the ground of philosophy itself becomes manifest—access to the being of things is through moral distinctions. "In Strauss," Jaffa writes, "the moral distinctions become the heart of philosophy. And statesmanship thus itself becomes part of philosophic activity" (*OI*, pp. 369-70).

It is true that we cannot turn to classical political philosophy for recipes for the resolution of the crisis of our time. "For the relative success of modern political philosophy," Strauss wrote,

> has brought into being a kind of society wholly unknown to the classics, a kind of society to which the classical principles as stated and elaborated by the classics are not immediately applicable. Only we living today can possibly find a solution to the problems of today. But an adequate understanding of the principles as elaborated by the classics may be the indispensable starting point for an adequate analysis, to be achieved by us, of present-day society in its peculiar character, and for the wise application, to be achieved by us, of these principles to our tasks.[23]

It hardly needs to be pointed out that the natural right of the American Founding is not classic natural right. With the success of Christianity, the only natural right that was available to the Founders was egalitarian natural right. But some of the Founders at least seemed to know—or divine—that natural law was the modern world's access to natural right and that natural law was therefore a kind of exoteric version of natural

---

[21] *Ibid.*, p. 246.
[22] *Ibid.*
[23] *The City and Man* (Chicago: Rand McNally & Co., 1964), p. 11.

right. In egalitarian natural right, consent necessarily takes precedence. It is the task of constitutional government—and the rule of law—to insure that consent is not merely the expression of the people's will but of their rationality.

Strauss remarked in an oft-quoted passage "that liberal or constitutional democracy comes closer to what the classics demanded than any alternative that is viable in our age."[24] Consequently, "wisdom requires unhesitating loyalty to a decent constitution and even to the cause of constitutionalism." Wisdom requires "unhesitating loyalty" to constitutional regimes because of their moderation and "moderation will protect us against the twin dangers of visionary expectations from politics and unmanly contempt for politics."[25] The loyalty will be to a moderate regime, but what of the character of the loyalty? Moderation is not a virtue of philosophy, although it is a "virtue controlling the philosopher's speech." The character of the rhetoric that provides the "unhesitating loyalty" will depend upon prudential considerations, i.e., the extent of the dangers threatening constitutionalism. The philosopher sees farther than the citizen and what may appear to the citizen—and the intellectual—as immoderate speech may in fact be the soul of moderation. If it is true that "[t]he United States of America may be said to be the only country in the world which was founded in explicit opposition to Machiavellian principles,"[26] then the fate of America may well determine the fate of both reason and revelation. Jaffa's unhesitating defense of the American regime is animated by his thoroughgoing conviction—as I believe it was also Strauss's conviction—that "the crisis of American constitutionalism" is "the crisis of the West"(*OI*, p. 42). And in defense of America and the West from "the superstitions of that relativism, positivism, and nihilism that are the reigning modes of thought in this new dark age" (*OI*, pp. 244, 252-53), moderation must surely be a vice.

In the mid-1980s, a remarkable debate surfaced in academic and legal circles concerning the principles of constitutional interpretation. At issue was the weight that should be given to the intentions of the Framers in interpreting the Constitution. As originally conceived by the Reagan administration's justice department, the argument in favor of "a jurisprudence of original intent" was specifically designed to restrain judicial

---

[24] *What Is Political Philosophy?*, p. 113.
[25] *Liberalism, Ancient and Modern* (New York: Basic Books, 1968), p. 24.
[26] *Thoughts on Machiavelli* (Glencoe, IL: The Free Press, 1958), pp. 13, 14.

activism. The defenders of judicial activism—most notably Justice Brennan, Justice Marshall, and the law-school professoriat—relied on arguments that envisioned the role of the Supreme Court as a kind of "continuing constitutional convention," specifically charged with reinterpreting the Constitution to meet the progressively evolving standards of "human dignity." The opponents of judicial activism—most notably Attorney General Edwin Meese, Chief Justice Rehnquist and Robert Bork—derived a jurisprudence of original intent from a strict adherence to the text, history, traditions, and logical structure of the Constitution.

The two sides, otherwise so different, agree on one thing: neither sees any need to return to first principles. This is the vacuum that Jaffa fills in his latest book, *Original Intent and the Framers of the Constitution: A Disputed Question.* This book consists of a foreword, "On Jaffa, Lincoln, Marshall, and Original Intent," by Lewis E. Lehrman, Jaffa's original essay "What Were the 'Original Intentions' of the Framers of the Constitution of the United States?" to which he has attached three appendices, a critique of Edwin Meese, a dissertation on the professional philosopher Leszek Kolakowski, and a critical appraisal of Chief Justice Rehnquist. There are three critiques of Jaffa's original essay: Bruce Ledewitz, "Judicial Conscience and Natural Rights: A Reply to Professor Jaffa"; Robert L. Stone, "Professor Harry V. Jaffa Divides the House: A Respectful Protest and a Defense Brief"; George Anastaplo, "Seven Questions for Professor Jaffa," with three appendices on various topics. Jaffa has responded to each of his interlocutors in turn and has added another appendix (on Robert Bork), an epilogue, and an afterword. The afterword consists of a prefatory note and four unanswered letters to Edwin Meese upbraiding him for refusing to become an interlocutor. This odd-appearing volume presents a sustained political polemic at the highest level.

Jaffa is not a partisan of either side of the debate, although he certainly supports a jurisprudence of original intent. It appears that Jaffa entered the fray merely as a partisan of first principles. He has reserved his considerable fire power, however, almost exclusively for the conservative proponents of original intent—his critique of Meese, Rehnquist and Bork is devastating. Why not make political common cause with them against the liberal judicial activists? Are they not the common enemy of sound constitutionalism? Surely this question has been asked by many who contemplate Jaffa's intention.[27]

Jaffa argues that, at bottom, the position of Meese, Rehnquist and Bork is indistinguishable from that of the liberal activists—they both share a kind of moral relativism rooted in the fact/value distinction. As Jaffa remarks, both sides "differ in the particulars of their 'value judgments,' but not in the subjectivity of what they propose as the ground of constitutional law" (*OI*, pp. 238, 49-50). Yet, because Meese, Rehnquist, and Bork profess at least a formal commitment to original-intent jurisprudence they would seem to be eminently more teachable than the liberal activists. And, besides other considerations no less important, one surely has more obligation to benefit and instruct friends than enemies. The partisans of original intent who have fallen under Jaffa's severe gaze here are opinion leaders (in former times they might have been called "gentlemen") who have been seduced by the false theories of modern philosophy, a danger from which opinion leaders and gentlemen are never immune—indeed, they "are nearly defenseless against false gods and false theories" (*OI*, pp. 313, 314-15, 319). The moral relativism of the right is no less pronounced than that of the left; this is especially evident in the positivism of Rehnquist and Bork. It matters little that Rehnquist makes decisions with which Jaffa mostly agrees. Rehnquist has no principled understanding of the Constitution and his opinions have more the character of accident than principle. What is vastly more important, in Jaffa's longer-term view, is not the particular decisions, but the articulation of the principles of the Constitution.

The major portion of Jaffa's career has been the explication of the principles of the Declaration of Independence. His point of departure was Strauss's remarks about the Declaration in the opening lines of *Natural Right and History*: "The nation dedicated to this proposition has now become, no doubt partly as a consequence of this dedication, the most powerful and prosperous of the nations of the earth. Does this nation in its maturity still cherish the faith in which it was conceived and raised? Does it still hold those 'truths to be self evident'?"[28] Strauss's answer, of course, was that the faith in the truth of these principles had

---

[27] Anastaplo, "Seven Questions for Professor Jaffa," questions 1 and 7; *OI*, pp. 172-73, 176-77; and Stone, "Professor Harry V. Jaffa Divides the House," *OI*, pp. 139 ff.
[28] *Natural Right and History*, p. 1.

been eroded by the combined onslaught of historicism and modern science. Strauss here issued an invitation to extend his analysis of natural right to the Declaration, and Jaffa took up the challenge in his extended analysis of Abraham Lincoln's political thought in *Crisis of the House Divided* (1959). Since then, Jaffa's understanding of the Declaration has matured and deepened. He is less inclined now to speak of the Declaration as "wholly a document of the rationalistic tradition" or the necessity of "a synthesis of elements which in Jefferson remained antagonistic." Jaffa sees a greater theoretical unity in the Founding than he did previously. The unity of the Founding is the principal theme of his latest work, a work that stands as the final prelude, as it were, for the sequel to *Crisis of the House Divided, The New Birth of Freedom*, a volume that is now, I am happy to report, more than half completed.

Jaffa has always seen the Declaration of Independence as filling the same function as the Athenian Stranger's prelude to the law code in Plato's *Laws*. It is a statement of regime principles, the ground not only of American constitutionalism but of the moral and political life of Americans. The natural law principles of the Declaration are embodied in the Constitution; thus "we do not look outside the Constitution but rather within it for the natural law basis of constitutional interpretation" (*OI*, p. 60). Meese, Bork, and Rehnquist, on the other hand, understand the Constitution as a purely positivist document, a procedural instrument that is indifferent to results. Thus, in their view, constitutional jurisprudence should be one of "neutral principles." In Bork's version, the intent of the Framers must be gleaned solely from "the text, structure, and history of the Constitution."[29] Any reference to "abstract theories" such as the Declaration of Independence simply opens the door to judicial activism—the substitution of the judge's own values for the values of the Framers. And these "values" have no ground in reason; they are merely the subjective product of "the social class or elite with which [the judge] identifies."[30]

Rehnquist makes an even bolder statement when he remarks that constitutional "safeguards for individual liberty . . . assume a general social acceptance neither because of any intrinsic worth nor because of any unique origins in someone's idea of natural justice but instead simply

---

[29] *The Tempting of America* (New York: The Free Press, 1990), pp. 162, 200.
[30] *Ibid.*, pp. 16, 31, 35, 43, 130, 145, 241, 242, 331.

because they have been incorporated in a constitution by the people."[31] For both Bork and Rehnquist, reason has no role to play in constitutional jurisprudence; reason is merely in the service of the idiosyncratic values of the so-called "reasoning class."[32]

Bork and his epigones have formulated a constitutional jurisprudence based solely on opposition to judicial activism, one that views the Constitution as "mere process without purpose" (*OI*, p. 294). Ignored entirely in Bork's account is the possibility of legislative tyranny, a problem that preoccupied the Framers more than any other constitutional is-

---

[31] "The Notion of a Living Constitution," *Texas Law Review*, vol. 54 (1976), p. 679 (quoted in *OI*, p. 85).

[32] *The Tempting of America*, p. 242; John H. Ely, *Democracy and Distrust: A Theory of Judicial Review* (Cambridge: Harvard University Press, 1980), p. 59. Ely, upon whom Bork relies, remarks that "'reason' as a source of fundamental values is . . . best stated in the alternative: either it is an empty source . . . or, if not empty, it is so flagrantly elitist and undemocratic that it should be dismissed forthwith." Neither Ely nor Bork indicates whether he believes himself to be a member of the reasoning class. Bork himself advocates a kind of judicial activism, however, when he argues that certain parts of the Constitution should be ignored because the text, history, and logical structure of these clauses cannot be understood—it is as if they have been rendered indecipherable by "inkblots" on the text. Those who assume that all parts of a written constitution must have force (i.e., that no part can be rendered inoperable or superfluous by interpretation) do so, according to Bork, on the abstract "theory that every part of the Constitution must be used" (p. 166). If it is possible to ignore parts of the Constitution that one does not like under the pretext that it is obscured by "inkblots," why is it not also legitimate to put into the Constitution clauses that one would like to have there? What is the essential difference? Bork makes his "inkblot" argument most forcefully in regard to the ninth amendment. He incorrectly asserts that there is "almost no history that would indicate what the ninth amendment was intended to accomplish" (p. 183). Madison made it clear, however, in his well-known speech before the House on June 8, 1789, that the amendment was designed to protect the unenumerated natural rights retained by the people. To Bork, however, any reference to natural rights propels us into the irrational realm of values and totalities. Like his liberal activist counterparts, Bork asserts the priority of society to the individual. Rights are conferred by government, they do not exist prior to the advent of government—thus there can be no "unenumerated rights." Bork's confusion is amply illustrated by his recent statement that "[i]t is particularly nonsensical to quote the Declaration of Independence's enunciation of a right to alter or abolish government. . . . Having established a representative government . . . the Founders proceeded to enact laws that denied any right of revolution on these shores" (*Commentary*, vol. 99, no. 5 [May, 1995], p. 15). Typically, Bork does not give any citations to the laws in question. *See* Erler, "The Ninth Amendment and Contemporary Jurisprudence," in Eugene Hickok, Jr., ed., *The Bill of Rights: Original Meaning and Current Understanding* (Charlottesville: University Press of Virginia, 1991), pp. 432-51.

sue. For Bork, legislative tyranny is a legitimate and positive expression of the democratic will of the people. "Our lack of consensus on moral first principles," Bork writes, dictates that questions of morality should be decided by democratic majorities.[33] Any "consensus" on first principles, of course, would simply be an accident, since value judgments are merely the idiosyncratic expression of class interests. In the absence of any rational basis or ground for morality, the will of the majority serves as the substitute for morality.

"The Madisonian dilemma," according to Bork, is the dilemma of how to reconcile the opposing principles of self rule—"that in wide areas of life majorities are entitled to rule, if they wish, simply because they are majorities"—and the protection of individual rights.[34] But as Jaffa cogently argues, there is no hint anywhere in Madison that majorities are entitled to rule "simply because they are majorities" (*OI*, pp. 285-6). Indeed, Madison, like Jefferson, argued from the opposite point of view, that a majority may do only those things "that could be rightfully done by the unanimous concurrence of the members." Thus, it is not simply the will of the majority that "rightfully" rules in a democracy, but the rational will of the majority (*OI*, p. 296). In the same vein, Jefferson wrote that "[i]ndependence can be trusted nowhere but with the people in mass. They are inherently independent of all but moral law."[35] Thus, it is clear that Madison and Jefferson viewed the people as a moral entity, not simply as a collection of discrete value-positing individuals. The positivism of both Bork and Rehnquist is predicated on a kind of moral relativism that ultimately leads to nihilism. In Jaffa's view, this is the direct consequence of attempting to sever morality and justice from their ground in nature or natural right. Jaffa argues that the "necessary presupposition" of Western civilization is that there is a "nonsubjective morality of man as man." And without this presupposition "[a]ny discussion of 'original intent' . . . is ultimately vain" (*OI*, pp. 89-90).

Much of the debate between Jaffa and the "originalists" concerns the issue of "substantive due process" and the *Dred Scott* case. According to Bork, *Dred Scott* "was the first appearance in American constitutional law of 'substantive due process,' and that concept has been used countless times since by judges who want to write their personal beliefs into a

---

[33] *The Tempting of America*, pp. 257, 259.
[34] *Ibid.*, p. 139.
[35] Letter to Spencer Roane, Sept. 6, 1819; *OI*, pp. 249, 287.

document that, most inconveniently, does not contain such beliefs."[36] The "substance" that Taney "poured" into the Constitution's purely procedural guarantee was that "slave ownership was a constitutional right." But, according to Bork, "[s]uch a right is nowhere to be found in the Constitution." Taney found it in the Constitution merely "because he was passionately convinced that it *must* be a constitutional right."[37] Yet, as Jaffa has demonstrated in excruciating detail,[38] Bork simply ignores the "text, history and logical structure" of the Constitution. While the Constitution does not use the word "slave" (preferring a variety of circumlocutions), it cannot be doubted that the fugitive slave clause, while not conferring a right to property in persons, certainly recognizes and protects that right. This, and the other clauses in the Constitution referring to slaves, are parts of the Constitution's compromises. Jaffa is quick to note that these compromises are ultimately in the service of emancipation. The compromises with slavery were made out of political expediency; without compromise, there would have been little prospect that any constitution would have emerged from the Constitutional Convention. And without a strong federal government, there would have been little prospect that slavery would ever have been put in the course of "ultimate extinction." But Jaffa rightly argues that it is impossible to distinguish the principles of the Constitution from its compromises without reference to the Declaration (*OI*, pp. 281, 21, 62, 71, 271, 293-4).

From Jaffa's point of view, the Founding was incomplete insofar as it departed from the principle of human equality in providing support for slavery. It was not until the adoption of the reconstruction amendments that the Constitution came into formal harmony with the principles of the Declaration. And, on the understanding that rightful sovereignty can be exercised only in the protection of inherent and unalienable rights, the thirteenth amendment would be an unrepealable expression of the Declaration's principle of the sovereignty of the people (*OI*, pp. 58-59).

The "originalists," on the other hand, maintain that the Constitution is only a procedural document that allows majorities to make decisions, restricted only by the specific guarantees in the Bill of Rights. Whatever "substance" the Constitution acquires must be determined by Congress acting as the representative of the will of the majority. In attempting to

---

[36] *The Tempting of America*, p. 31.
[37] *Ibid.* (emphasis original).
[38] Jaffa's critique of Bork continues in *Storm Over the Constitution: Jaffa Answers Bork* (Claremont: The Claremont Institute, 1994).

define property for purposes of the fifth amendment, Taney in *Dred Scott* was merely substituting his own values for those of the Congress. Jaffa, however, argues that *Dred Scott* was not a case of judicial activism since the Missouri Compromise Act forbidding slavery in the remaining portions of the Louisiana Purchase Territory had already been repealed by the Kansas-Nebraska Act of 1854. More importantly, in the Compromise of 1850, Congress had specifically allowed for appeals of any disputes regarding the status of slavery in the Utah and New Mexico territories directly to the Supreme Court. That is to say, Congress had specifically requested the Supreme Court to make the decision as to the issue of slavery in the territories. If *Dred Scott* is an example of "judicial activism," then it was "judicial activism" authorized in advance by the Congress!

The use of the concept of "substantive due process" is wholly anachronistic. None of the Framers ever used such terms or thought the Constitution was merely a procedural document that could be understood apart from its ends or purposes. The only question that animated the political debate surrounding the *Dred Scott* decision was whether a slave was a person or property and what the obligations of the federal government were in protecting persons and property. The Constitution itself is ambiguous; it refers to slaves as "persons" but also regards them as "property." Certainly an individual's "due process" rights under the fifth amendment are conditioned upon a prior determination of whether the individual is a "person" or "property." And this is impossible to determine within the "four corners of the Constitution." Bork, of course, would leave it for Congress to determine the issue: "The definition of what is or is not property would seem at least as an original matter, a question for legislatures."[39]

Madison, however, had argued, in his famous June 8, 1789, speech introducing the Bill of Rights in the First Congress, that the greatest

---

[39] *The Tempting of America*, pp. 30-31. Bork also seems to assert the fantastic idea that the federal government could have freed the slaves in states that allowed slavery under the "takings clause" of the fifth amendment as long as it provided the slave owners with compensation. But here Bork has succumbed to an interpretation of the Constitution not warranted by its text, history, or structure. The fifth amendment allows for the compensated taking of property only for "public use," not "public purposes." It would be difficult to imagine that anyone in 1857 believed that the "takings clause" could be used for such purposes. The Supreme Court for the last fifty years or so has interpreted "public use" to mean "public purpose," but a keen-eyed textualist such as Bork should know the difference between the Constitution and what the Court says it is.

danger to liberty resides in "the legislative, for it is the most powerful, and most likely to be abused, because it is under the least control." "Independent tribunals of justice," Madison concluded, "will consider themselves in a peculiar manner the guardians of those rights . . . expressly stipulated for in the constitution by the declaration of rights." Indeed, courts will provide an "impenetrable bulwark" against the violations of individual rights.[40] Here, Madison was merely echoing Hamilton's argument in *The Federalist*, number 78 (even to the extent of using the same language). If Madison and Hamilton are correct, it was not only appropriate, but absolutely necessary, for the Court to determine whether Scott was a person entitled to "life, liberty, or property": or whether he was merely a chattel, the property of another. Scott's due process rights—or conversely the rights of his master—were conditioned upon such a prior determination.

Unfortunately for the originalists, Taney also considered himself to be an originalist—and in fact was an originalist. The clauses of the Constitution, Taney argued in his *Dred Scott* opinion, must bear the same meaning that "they were intended to bear when the instrument was framed and adopted. . . . If any of its provisions are deemed unjust, there is a mode prescribed in the instrument itself by which it may be amended; but while it remains unaltered, it must be construed now as it was understood at the time of its adoption. . . . Any other rule of construction would abrogate the judicial character of this court, and make it the mere reflex of the popular opinion or passion of the day. This court was not created by the Constitution for such purposes" (19 How. 426 [1857]; *OI*, pp. 13-14). No originalist could possibly disagree with this statement of the jurisprudence of original intent. But while Taney stated the principles of interpretation correctly, he, like Bork and the whole tribe of "originalists," was unable to give an accurate account of the Framers' intentions.

Although Taney saw the necessity of confronting the Declaration, he utterly mistook its meaning. While he admitted that the language of the Declaration was capacious enough "to embrace the whole human family," he nevertheless believed that no one, given the historical circumstances of its adoption, could possibly conclude that the language of the Declaration was meant to include blacks of African descent. Indeed, it was "a fixed and universal" opinion, Taney wrote, "that the negro might

---

[40] 1 *Annals of Congress* (Gales and Seaton, ed., 1834), pp. 457-58.

justly and lawfully be reduced to slavery for his benefit" (at 407). Besides, "the conduct of the distinguished men who framed the Declaration of Independence would have been utterly and flagrantly inconsistent with the principles they asserted" had they intended to include blacks in the statement "all men are created equal" (at 410). Had the authors of the Declaration meant what they said, they would have at once emancipated slaves. Taney thus imputes to the authors of the Declaration a duty derived from a kind of categorical imperative—if they believed what they said, they would have acted on their belief; their failure to act is proof that they didn't believe that "all men are created equal." It is more than evident that Taney misunderstood the element of political prudence embodied in the Declaration's principles (*OI*, pp. 29, 239, 245, 281, 304-5). Lincoln accurately reflected this element in his famous "Dred Scott Speech" opposing Taney's decision. The authors of the Declaration, Lincoln stated,

> did not mean to assert the obvious untruth, that all men were then actually enjoying that equality, nor yet, that they were about to confer it immediately upon them. In fact they had no such power to confer such a boon. They meant simply to declare the *right*, so that the *enforcement* of it might follow as fast as circumstances should permit.[41]

Taney nevertheless concluded that under the "original" understanding of both the Declaration and the Constitution no black of African descent could ever be a citizen of the United States and the Constitution regards slaves as property with a status no different than any other form of property. Since slaves are property, the federal government has "the power coupled with the duty of guarding and protecting the owner in his rights" (at 452). Taney thus demonstrated that it is not enough merely to invoke the jurisprudence of original intent. Its invocation must be merely a prelude to determining what in fact the true intentions of the Framers were. Both Taney and Bork deny the relevance of the natural law principles of the Declaration in determining the question of whether a person can be property within the meaning of the Fifth Amendment. For Taney a kind of historicism is dispositive; for Bork, "it is a question for legislatures." Both fail to discern the intentions of the Framers.

---

[41] *Collected Works* (New Brunswick, N.J.: Rutgers University Press, 1953), vol. 2, p. 406 (emphasis original).

It is Jaffa's long-held position that "[i]n asking what were the original intentions of the Founding Fathers, we are asking what principles of moral and political philosophy guided them. We are not asking their personal judgments on contingent matters (*OI*, pp. 41-2). Jaffa points to evidence from a variety of sources indicating that it was the explicit intention of the Framers to base the Constitution on the natural law principles of the Declaration. Passages from *The Federalist*, from the Convention Debates, from the writings of Jefferson, Washington, Madison, James Wilson, Hamilton, numerous state constitutions, public proclamations, and sermons make this an indisputable point. Indeed, John Hancock, president of the Continental Congress, in his official letter transmitting the Declaration to the States remarked that since it would serve as the "Ground and Foundation" of any future government, the people should "be universally informed of it."[42] John Marshall certainly understood the extent to which the Constitution was animated by natural law principles. His decision in *Marbury v. Madison* (1803) is a primer on the social contract origins of civil society. Yet the plethora of historical evidence is disputed by Bork and his epigones; they find no evidence that the Framers relied on the Declaration in drafting the Constitution, nor any indication that they intended the Constitution to be interpreted in the light of natural law principles.[43] One must surely wonder when "We the people of the United States"—the creators of the Constitution—became a "people" if not by the constitutive act of the Declaration. Surely, the "one people" and the "good people" of the Declaration are the same as "We the people" of the Constitution.[44] Indeed, in light of

---

[42] Paul H. Smith, ed., *Letters of Delegates to Congress, 1774-1789* (Washington, D.C.: 1979), vol. 4, p. 396.

[43] *See* Charles J. Cooper, "Harry Jaffa's Bad Originalism," for a statement of one of Bork's supporters. Many of the sources that Cooper uses to demonstrate that natural law principles did not animate the Frames are actually paraphrases of the Declaration itself! For a particularly obvious example, *see* p.158 and Jaffa, "Slaying the Dragon of Bad Originalism," This volume, p.97

[44] Ken Masugi pointed out that Bork's "aversion to natural right" is so thoroughgoing that in reprinting the text of the Constitution in *The Tempting of America*, he deleted the Constitution's one specific reference to the Declaration in Article VII: "done in Convention by the Unanimous Consent of the States present the Seventeenth Day of September in the Year of our Lord one thousand seven hundred and Eighty seven and the Independence of the United States of America the Twelfth" (*Interpretation*, vol. 19, no. 1 [Fall, 1991], p. 89). It is necessary to add that Bork's bowdlerization of the text also leaves out the Constitution's only reference to "our Lord." One could thus say that both reason and revelation are excluded.

the evidence it would be difficult to deny that the Declaration occupied the "authoritative role . . . for the whole revolutionary generation, and most certainly for those who framed and those who ratified the Constitution of 1787" (*OI*, p. 26). Jefferson himself said that the Declaration was "intended to be an expression of the American mind."[45] Given its universal acceptance, it should not be surprising that extended dissertations and arguments were not published advocating the acceptance of its principles.

I believe that Jaffa has persuasively argued that "[a] jurisprudence of original intent would then of necessity have been—in decisive respects—a jurisprudence of natural law or natural right" (*OI*, p. 26). It is the principle of natural human equality that points to nature or natural right. The Declaration's statement that "all men are created equal" affirms the existence of a created universe in which rationality adheres in the very idea of nature itself.

> The equality of man proclaimed by the Declaration of Independence is to be understood first of all by comparison with the inequality that characterizes man's relationship with the lower orders of living beings. In comparison with this inequality there is nothing more evident, in the familiar words of John Locke, than that no human being is marked out by nature to rule, while others are marked out for subjection (*OI*, pp. 78-79).

Equality thus must be understood in the light of the "great chain of being." And it is in this light that equality becomes the ground of morality. As Jaffa notes, "the inequality of man and beast, and of man and God . . . implies an objective order of being, upon which is founded a prescriptive moral order" (*OI*, p. 323). And it is the existence of this "prescriptive moral order" that allows Jaffa to remark—correctly in my opinion—that "[t]he idea of 'the laws of nature and of nature's God' is derived from classical political philosophy" (*OI*, p. 355). In Jaffa's view Locke's explication of the laws of nature point to the classics. Jaffa no longer sees Locke as a radically modern influence on the American Founding. Among other things, it is clear that the Framers did not understand Locke as a radical modern. Rather, the exoteric Locke was easily reconcilable with an understanding of "the laws of nature and na-

---

[45] Letter to Henry Lee, May 8, 1825.

ture's God" as an expression of the objective order of being compatible
with the teachings of the classical political philosophers. A recent
scholar, however, has argued that it makes little difference whether the
Framers relied on the exoteric teachings of Locke or his radically modern esoteric teachings—the esoteric teaching will eventually undermine
and subvert any political practice premised on his seemingly traditional
view of the laws of nature.[46]

Equality is understood in the light of the inequality of man and God
on the one hand and man and beast on the other. This surely reminds us
of Aristotle's description of man in the *Politics* as the in-between being;
man is neither beast nor God. The providential rule of God over man,
because it would proceed from perfect wisdom, would not require the
consent of man. Similarly, it would be ludicrous to think that man's rule
over the beasts requires their consent, i.e., the consent of those without
rational will. Among men, consent is properly regarded as the reciprocal of equality—because by nature there are no natural rulers only consent can legitimate rule. It is true that virtue or human excellence does
give some the "right to rule"; but "[i]t is a right which comes to light by
virtue of the prior recognition of the equality of mankind and of the rule
of law constructed upon its premises" (*OI*, p. 79). The rule of law—in
Aristotle's terms the rule of reason without passion—is the substitute for
the rule of the wise. And the "fallibility of human reason" also requires
the institution of limited government with such constitutional devices as
the separation of powers. This is all designed to create the conditions
where it is possible for the "reason" of "the public . . . to control and
regulate the government." And while "the laws of nature and nature's
God" have their ultimate roots in classical political philosophy, Jaffa
clearly maintains that "[t]he classical political solutions are strictly
speaking only for the ancient city." Indeed, Jaffa argues,

> the Declaration addressed a problem peculiarly that of the Christian
> West, arising from the conflicting claims of reason and revelation.
> The idea of human equality, independent of sectarian identity, led
> to the idea of the enlightened consent of the governed as the ground
> of law. It enfranchised Aristotle's idea of law as "reason unaffected
> by desire" by removing from the jurisdiction of theology and theo-
> logians the judgment of rationality. It was no less pious for doing

---

[46] Michael P. Zuckert, *Natural Rights and the New Republicanism* (Princeton: Princeton
University Press, 1994), p. 288.

so, because it incorporated into the idea of enlightened consent respect for the rights with which all mankind had been endowed by their Creator. . . . . In the Declaration (and more generally in the American Founding) we find a principled ground for law that we cannot find in Aristotle. What we do find, however, is fully in accordance with Aristotle's intention, within a framework consistent with biblical religion (*OI*, p. 322).

Thus, the genius of the American Founding—and the basis for the rule of law understood in the Aristotelian sense—is the recognition of the claims of both reason and revelation. As Jaffa notes, the truth of the Declaration is "a truth no less of unassisted human reason than of divine revelation" (*OI*, p. 350).

It has been argued that the reliance on equality as the regime principle is misplaced because equality will inevitably degenerate into "permissive egalitarianism." As Anastaplo put it, "[d]edication to equality can no doubt contribute to justice and the common good . . . [b]ut it can also lead to an emphasis upon self-centeredness and upon private right—and these in turn can promote relativism, if not even nihilism, and hence another kind of tyranny." And in an idea made popular by Tocqueville, Anastaplo concludes that "[c]ertainly, mediocrity can easily become the order of the day when equality is made too much of."[47] "Permissive egalitarianism" is thus seen as the enemy of liberty as well as human excellence. For the Founding generation, of course, the words "liberty" and "equality" were virtually synonymous terms. Indeed, liberty found its ground in natural human equality. Tocqueville never saw the importance of the Declaration as a statement of regime principles; rather for him—and his modern-day followers—equality meant primarily an equality of condition. Liberty was opposed to equality because, for Tocqueville, liberty meant the cultivation of talents and abilities that would lead to an inequality of condition. But the Framers surely did not believe that there was an historically fated necessity that equality and liberty would become antagonistic elements of the regime. Those who argue that the principle of equality inevitably put the regime on the slippery slope to equality of results have succumbed to a kind of historicism that is expressly excluded from any proper understanding of natural human equality, i.e., equality understood in terms of the principles of natural right.

---

[47] "Seven Questions for Professor Jaffa," in *OI,* p. 174.

It has also been argued that egalitarian natural right requires too much "dilution" to be a genuine expression of natural right or the foundation of a decent politics. Indeed, one commentator has recently written that "a regime based on the self-evident half-truth that all men are created equal will eventually founder because of its disregard of the many ways in which men are created unequal. Even if such a regime seems powerful at the moment, it will be subject to revolution by the partisans, in this case those of the few, whom it ignores." This analysis is said to be derived from the Aristotelian point of view that regimes are vulnerable and subject to revolution because they are "partial and partisan. Although they claim to advance the common good, in fact they represent the good of a party, typically the party of the few or of the many."[48] Thus the Framers' notion that the principle of equality, properly understood as the equal protection of equal rights, could provide the common ground for the few and the many is merely an illusion—or perhaps a deception. But the principle of distributive justice inherent in the idea of natural equality is equal opportunity, that there are no preordained class or caste barriers to the expression of natural inequalities.

Indeed, the genius of the American experiment was to replace pseudo-aristocracy with natural aristocracy. Jefferson, in an oft-quoted letter to John Adams, remarked that

> the natural aristocracy I consider as the most precious gift of nature for the instruction, the trusts, and government of society. And indeed it would have been inconsistent in creation to have formed man for the social state, and not to have provided virtue and wisdom enough to manage the concerns of the society. May we not even say that that form of government is the best which provides the most effectually for a pure selection of these natural aristoi into the offices of government? The artificial aristocracy is a mischievous ingredient in government, and provision should be made to prevent its ascendancy.[49]

Both the partisans of the few and the many can support this principle of natural justice which reconciles both the claims of equality and the claims of inequality—equality of opportunity and the legitimacy of the inequality of results. Surely this is the meaning of Madison's famous

---

[48] Harvey C. Mansfield, Jr., "Returning to the Founders: The Debate on the Constitution," *The New Criterion*, vol. 12, no. 1 (Sept., 1993), pp. 50-51.
[49] Letter to John Adams, Oct. 28, 1813; *See What Is Political Philosophy?*, p. 86.

statement in *The Federalist*, number 10 that "[t]he protection of different and unequal faculties" is "the first object of Government." It is only with some hyperbole that one could call this "the truest and best equality"—"the natural equality given on each occasion to unequal men."[50]

It is true that Strauss, on occasion, argued that "natural right or natural law must be diluted in order to become compatible with the requirements of the city."[51] This observation has less force, of course, if the natural right principles have the support of the regnant morality and religion. In any case, Strauss makes an exception for Aristotelian natural right where "there is no fundamental disproportion between natural right and the requirements of political society, or there is no essential need for the dilution of natural right."[52] As far as the necessity of "dilution" in Platonic natural right, Strauss makes reference, not only to the obvious case of the *Republic*, but also to Plato's "most political work" ("even . . . his only political work"),[53] the *Laws* (756e-758a).[54] The Athenian Stranger teaches that the regime should always aim at the mean between monarchy and democracy, two regimes animated by incompatible notions of equality. It is necessary sometimes to blur the distinction between the two forms of equality if civil war is to be avoided. The "blurring" principally involves the assignment of equality by lot—or as we might say today, equality of result. Among a host of other considerations, it is clear that this kind of "dilution" was no part of the American experiment. The classics generally aimed at a kind of mixed regime, a regime not wholly incompatible, as Strauss notes, with the one described in *The Federalist*.[55]

In any case, the analysis of Plato and Aristotle was predicated on a regime of scarcity—the few wealthy who had leisure to acquire virtue and education and the many poor. The Framers, however, explicitly looked forward to the end of the regime of scarcity and all that this implied for the establishment of constitutionalism and the rule of law. Strauss noted that "[i]t is a demand of justice that there should be a rea-

---

[50] *Laws*, 757d.
[51] *Natural Right and History*, p. 152; "On Natural Law," pp. 139 ff.; *Liberalism, Ancient and Modern*, p. 15.
[52] *Ibid.*, p. 156; "On Natural Law," pp. 139-140.
[53] *The Argument and Action of Plato's Laws* (Chicago: University of Chicago Press, 1975), p. 1; *What Is Political Philosophy?*, p. 29.
[54] *Natural Right and History*, p. 153; "On Natural Law," p. 139.
[55] *Liberalism, Ancient and Modern*, p. 15.

sonable correspondence between the social hierarchy and the natural hierarchy. The lack of such a correspondence in the old scheme was defended by the fundamental fact of scarcity." The "old scheme" was thus exposed for what it was: oligarchy masquerading as aristocracy. The doctrine of natural equality, "that all men have the same natural rights" is the foundation of natural justice "provided one uses this rule of thumb as the major premise for reaching the conclusion that everyone should be given the same opportunity as everyone else: natural inequality has its rightful place in the use, nonuse, or abuse of opportunity in the race as distinguished from at the start. Thus it becomes possible to abolish many injustices or at least many things which had become injustices."[56]

As Jaffa's many protagonists surely know—especially the conservatives—he is strident in his efforts to articulate a natural right ground for the American regime that will serve as an antidote to the corrosive effects of modern philosophy's assault on both reason and revelation. The triumph of moral relativism grounded in nihilism will inevitably lead to tyranny. Nihilism is the belief that the metaphysical freedom of man is merely a delusion. Strauss, however, made it clear that he believed the human mind was at home in the universe: "By becoming aware of the dignity of the mind, we realize the true ground of the dignity of man and therewith the goodness of the world, whether we understand it as created or as uncreated, which is the home of man because it is the home of the human mind."[57] But it is a very short step indeed from the denial of man's metaphysical freedom to the denial of his moral and political freedom. At bottom, the denial of man's metaphysical freedom is a denial of man's nature. What is called "nature" is either the epiphenomenal product of history or simply a self-willed delusion. Standing against these currents of contemporary nihilism are the natural law and natural right principles of the Declaration of Independence.

---

[56] *Ibid.*, p. 24; "The Crisis of Political Philosophy," in Harold J. Spaeth, ed., *The Predicament of Modern Politics* (Detroit: University of Detroit Press, 1964), pp. 93-94.
[57] *Liberalism, Ancient and Modern*, p. 8.

The Closing of the Conservative Mind:
A Dissenting Opinion on Judge Robert H. Bork

It is difficult to remember when conservatives have been so nearly unanimous in according a book something approaching a neo-scriptural status, as they have been with respect to Judge Robert H. Bork's *The Tempting of America: The Political Seduction of the Law*. (Bork himself has invited the scriptural analogy, by speaking of the "creation" of the Constitution, and of an ensuing "temptation" by the apple of natural law and substantive due process, followed by a "fall" into judicial activism.)[1] The December 8, 1989 *National Review* featured as its main cover article, "Our Captive Courts: How Political Judges Have Perverted the Constitution," which the editors have described as Judge Bork's own adaptation of his book.

There is also, however, a second article by Judge Bork, encapsulated within the first in the same issue, entitled "Why Do the Liberals Rage?" One can summarize the two articles together by saying that the liberals rage because Judge Bork says that judges should stick to the law—including the law of the Constitution—in their judging. He thinks—or so he says—that judges should not substitute their opinions of what the law *ought* to be. It is emphatically their job—whether they like the results or not—to say what the law *is*.

The liberals assert however that there is nothing but ambiguity and uncertainty in many key phrases of the Constitution (e.g. "general wel-

---

[1] Judge Bork's analogy between natural law and the forbidden fruit of the Garden of Eden is not however original. Consider the following:

> I do not propose to argue questions of natural rights and inherent powers; I plant my reliance upon the Constitution. . . . When the tempter entered the garden of Eden and induced our common mother to offend against the law which God had given her through Adam, he was the first teacher of that "higher law" which sets the individual above the solemn rule which he is bound, as part of every community, to observe. . . . Why then shall we talk about natural rights? Who is to define them? Where is the judge that is to sit over the court to try natural rights? . . . I say then I come not to argue the questions outside of or above the Constitution, but to plead the cause of right of law and order under the Constitution.

Jefferson Davis, in the Senate, May 9, 1860. *Jefferson Davis, Constitutionalist: His Letters, Papers, and Speeches*, ed. Dunbar Rowland, Vol. IV, pp. 253, 254.

fare," "due process," or "equal protection"). No one really knows what they "originally" meant, and even if one did know, one could find little guidance in applying them in present-day circumstances. They insist therefore that there is no alternative but to say what the Constitution ought to mean, here and now, rather than what it might have meant, when it was framed and ratified. The favorite liberal posture is to call for a "living Constitution," freed from the "dead hand" of the past, one which "evolves" over time, adapting itself to new circumstances in and through the "creative" interpretations by judges sensitive to the needs of society.

In point of fact, Judge Bork replies, these judges, by discovering judicial remedies for what different interest groups claim to be "injuries," but which are really problems of society at large, are usurping powers proper to the political branches of government, and subverting the right of the people to be governed by their elected representatives.

Judge Bork has indeed presented his case against liberal jurisprudence cogently and passionately. He has convinced his conservative followers—and up to a point he has convinced me—that it is unanswerable. He has moreover convinced his followers that the campaign of vicious misrepresentation against him—especially during the fight over his nomination to the Supreme Court—is due mainly if not solely to the fact that they cannot meet him on the ground of the argument. That argument, in a nutshell, is that judicial activism is usurpation, denying to the political processes of democracy their rightful role in governance. His disciples believe—quite rightly—that the American public, by and large, still thinks that the function of judges is to interpret the law, not invent it. His critics on the Left supported their war against him by appealing to highly organized and highly motivated interest groups—especially advocates of group rights (especially those of race, color, and sex) which are not recognized by the Constitution—as opposed to the rights of individuals, which are. These critics blinded the public to the nature of their attack, by declaring Judge Bork to be "out of the mainstream." His votaries are confident that the public would have been mightily indignant at his critics had they known the real character of the attack upon him.

In the minds of Judge Bork's partisans—and no doubt in his own mind—he has taken on something of the status of a martyred saint of conservatism. The tone of triumphant martyrology is particularly marked in Senator Orrin Hatch's hosanna in the December 8, 1989 *Na-*

tional Review, the issue following the publication of Judge Bork's two articles. Hatch's review begins:

> When President Reagan nominated Robert H. Bork to the Supreme Court in the summer of 1987, a carefully staged firestorm of opposition erupted, although no question was ever raised about Judge Bork's qualifications. But those who would manipulate the law to their own political ends knew that they would have no friend in Bob Bork were he confirmed. Their misrepresentations of his record denied Bork a seat on the Court, but their short-term victory is Pyrrhic. Bork is back.

The theological implications of the review might have been better rendered by "Bork is risen." Hatch ends as follows:

> It is rare that those at the center of history happen also to be great scholars or writers of a talent sufficient to explain momentous events. Churchill is the outstanding exception to the rule. Now we know that Judge Bork is another.

Surely hyperbole can go no further! Comparing Bork's prose to Churchill's is approximately on a level with comparing Andy Warhol's Campbell's soup can to da Vinci's Last Supper.

That Judge Bork was treated ill by his critics on the Left may certainly be granted. But the March 8, 1988 *National Review* carried an article by the present writer entitled "Judge Bork's Mistake." In it I had accepted everything Judge Bork had said about the necessity and desirability of a constitutional jurisprudence of "original intent." But I denied that what Bork had *called* "original intent" *was* "original intent." I referred my readers to a monograph I had published in the *University of Puget Sound Law Review*, Spring 1987, entitled "What Were the 'Original Intentions' of the Framers of the Constitution of the United States," where I had argued at great length and with copious documentation that a genuine jurisprudence of "original intent," with respect to the Constitution would have to recognize the principles of the Declaration of Independence as the principles of the Constitution. The Constitution, as every beginning student knows, is a bundle of compromises. There is no way, from the text of the Constitution alone, that one can distinguish those provisions which are consistent with its principles, and which implement those principles (e.g. the provisions for the election of Congress and president), from those that are compromises with those same principles (e.g. the security given to property in human chattels). This distinction between the principles of the Constitution and its compromises is one Judge Bork has studiously ignored. His critics have exploited the fact to persuade the general public—not without reason—that Judge Bork really has no principles. That judges should be neutral interpreters of the law is one thing: but to say that the law itself is essentially neutral—that it is mere process without purpose—is another. Judge Bork's position can be well summarized by saying that he rejects, root and branch, the following resolution of the Republican Party Platform of 1860, upon which Abraham Lincoln was elected president of the United States.

> Resolved, That the maintenance of the principles promulgated in the Declaration of Independence and embodied in the Federal Constitution, "That all men are created equal; that they are endowed by their Creator with certain unalienable rights; that among these are life, liberty and the pursuit of happiness; that, to secure these rights, governments are instituted among men, deriving their just powers from the consent of the governed," is essential to the preservation of our Republican institutions.

Judge Bork's book begins with a discussion of the 1798 case of *Calder v. Bull*, in which Justice Samuel Chase, in a concurring opinion, had appealed to "the great first principles of the social compact" (which meant the principles of the Declaration of Independence), as possible grounds for judicial limitation of legislative power. According to Bork, here was the first time that a justice of the Supreme Court would "cast covetous glances at the apple that would eventually cause the fall."

But what Chase had to say about the "social compact" was not different from what James Madison said on countless occasions. It was not different from what Chief Justice Marshall would say in 1819, in the case of *Ogden v. Saunders*. Commenting upon Article I, Section 10 of the Constitution, which declares that no State shall "pass any law impairing the obligation of contracts," Marshall said that

> These words seem to us to import that the obligation is intrinsic, that it is created by the contract itself, not that it is dependent on the laws made to enforce it. When we advert to the course of reading generally pursued by American statesmen in early life, we must suppose that the framers of our constitution were intimately acquainted with the writings of those wise and learned men, whose treatises on the laws of nature and nations

have guided public opinion on the subjects of obligation and contract. If we turn to those treatises, we find them to concur in the declaration that contracts possess an original intrinsic obligation, derived from the acts of free agents and not given by government.

Later, in the same opinion, Marshall spoke of how the excesses of the state legislatures, before the adoption of the Constitution, had caused

mischief . . . so great [and] so alarming, as not only to impair commercial intercourse . . . but to sap the morals of the people and destroy the sanctity of private faith.

A major purpose of the Constitution, said Marshall, was "to guard against the continuance of [this] evil . . . " It would do this by imposing "restraints on state legislation." And Marshall left no room for doubt that it was a proper function of the courts to impose such restraints.

It cannot be emphasized too strongly, not only that Marshall (unlike Bork) believed in "an original intrinsic obligation . . . not given by government," as the ground of some of the most important provisions of the Constitution, but that he believed that this belief informed the understanding of the framers and of the public opinion that ratified their work. A jurisprudence of original intent would then of necessity have been—in decisive respects—a jurisprudence of natural law or natural right. Judge Bork is of course perfectly free to reject natural law and natural right— as he does—but he cannot consistently call his rejection of original intent, original intent. He cannot have it both ways.

Judge Bork did not always think about original intent as he does now. In "The Supreme Court Needs a New Philosophy," published in *Fortune* of December 1968, he wrote:

A desire for some legitimate form of judicial activism is inherent in a tradition that runs strong and deep in our culture, a tradition that can be called "Madisonian." We continue to believe there are some things no majority should be allowed to do to us, no matter how democratically it may decide to do them. A Madisonian system assumes that in wide areas of life a legislative majority is entitled to rule for no better reason than that it is a majority. But it also assumes there are some aspects of life a majority should not control, that coercion in such matters is tyranny, a violation of the individual's natural rights. Clearly the definition of natural rights cannot be left to either the majority or the minority. In the popular understanding upon which the power of the Supreme Court rests, it is precisely the function of the Court to resolve this dilemma by giving content to the concept of natural rights in case-by-case interpretation of the Constitution.

Bork's notion of a "Madisonian system" here is less than perfect since, according to Madison, there is never an area of life in which "a legislative majority is entitled to rule for no better reason than that it is a majority." No aphorism is more characteristically Madisonian, than that "all power in just and free government is derived from compact." And, as Madison wrote in his famous essay on "Sovereignty," a majority may do only those things "that could be *rightfully* done by the unanimous concurrence of the members." The word "rightfully," underscored by Madison himself, emphasizes the fact that a natural moral law underlies and undergirds all the constitutionalism of original intent. According to Madison, in the same essay,

> the reserved rights of individuals (of conscience for example) in becoming parties to the original compact [are] beyond the reach of sovereignty, wherever vested or however viewed.

This means—in flat opposition to the Bork of today—that the free exercise of religion is a constitutional right, whether or not it is written into the Constitution. In the "Madisonian system" (as in that of John Marshall) the understanding of the nature of "the original compact" is the key to all constitutional interpretation.

However imperfect Bork's understanding of "the Madisonian system" in 1968, we venture to say that, had he enunciated it at his hearings, he would almost certainly have been confirmed as a justice of the Supreme Court. I am the more persuaded of this because in the same article he wrote that

> Legitimate [judicial] activism requires, first of all, a warrant for the Court to move beyond the limited range of substantive rights that can be derived from traditional sources of constitutional law. The case for locating this warrant in the long-ignored Ninth Amendment was persuasively argued by Justice Arthur J. Goldberg in a concurring opinion in *Griswold v. Connecticut.*

In Judge Bork's new book, there is a chapter entitled "The Madisonian Dilemma and the Need for Constitutional Theory." What had been called the "Madisonian system" in 1968 is now called the "Madisonian Dilemma." And the "concept of natural rights" disappears altogether from his discussion. In short, the "system" became a "dilemma" when natural rights—that is to say, genuine original intent—disappeared. The dilemma however is Bork's, not Madison's.

The Bork of 1990 no longer recognizes the possibility of a "legitimate form of judicial activism." All judicial activism is now seen as the fruit of original sin. The principal vehicle for such activism, according to Bork, has been "the concept of 'substantive due process.'" And, says Bork, substantive due process was introduced into constitutional jurisprudence by Chief Justice Taney, in his opinion for the Court in the case of *Dred Scott* (1857). Bork's accusation against Taney for gratuitously inventing the doctrine of substantive due process, is the linchpin of the entire argument of his book.

Dred Scott had sued for his freedom in the slave state of Missouri, where he had returned, after having been taken by his master to live in Minnesota Territory, in which slavery had been prohibited by the Missouri Compromise legislation of 1820. Scott claimed his freedom on the ground that he had been taken by his master to reside (he was not a runaway), and had resided, in a federal territory. But Taney's opinion declared that the 1820 legislation had been unconstitutional, because Congress had no lawful power to deprive a slaveowner of his property, merely because he had exercised his constitutional right to migrate to a United States territory. To do so would violate the Fifth Amendment's prohibition against of depriving a person of his property "without due process of law." Congress had no power over slavery in the territories, said Taney, other than "the power coupled with the duty of guarding and protecting the owner in his rights." According to Bork, however,

> The definition of what is, or is not property would seem, at least as an original matter, a question for legislatures. How then [Bork asks] can there be a constitutional right to own slaves where a statute forbids it?

According to Bork, Taney's "transformation of the due process clause [of the Fifth Amendment]" was an obvious sham, it was a momentous sham, for this was the first appearance in American constitutional law of the concept of "substantive due process," and that concept has been used countless times since by judges who want to write their personal beliefs into a document that, most inconveniently, does not contain those beliefs.

Bork says that "Taney was determined to prove that the right of property in slaves was guaranteed by the Constitution." He quotes Taney saying that no one would presume that Congress could make any law in a territory—for example, establishing a religion—that it is forbidden to make by the First Amendment. "All well and good," Bork comments, adding however that

> there is no similar constitutional provision that can be read with any semblance of plausibility to confer a right to own slaves. It may well have been the case that the federal government could not then have freed slaves in states where the laws allowed slavery without committing a taking of property for which the Fifth Amendment to the Constitution would require compensation.

Among Bork's innumerable errors in dealing with this case (and it would take at least fifty pages to explain them all) is the foregoing reference to the federal government freeing slaves, and then compensating their owners. Under the antebellum Constitution, however, the federal government had no power whatever either to free slaves in the slave states, or to compensate their owners. The same Republican platform that resolved that the principles of the Declaration of Independence were the principles of the Constitution, also resolved

> That the maintenance inviolate of the rights of the States, and especially the right of each State to order and control its own domestic institutions according to its own judgment exclusively, is essential to that balance of powers on which the perfection and endurance of our political fabric depends.

This was common ground to the free soil movement and to the most ardent advocates of slavery. In 1862—in the very midst of the Civil War— Lincoln attempted to provide for compensation for loyal slave owners, who were losing their slaves by the mere attrition of the war. He did so by recommending a series of constitutional amendments, authorizing the federal government to make payments to states that undertook programs of compensated emancipation. It never even occurred to Lincoln that the "takings" clause of the Fifth Amendment might authorize the federal government itself to buy and free slaves, or even to pay for slaves that had run away.

We return, however, to Bork's amazing assertion that there is nothing in the Constitution that can be said "with any semblance of plausibility to confer a right to own slaves." He repeats this even more emphatically when he asks,

> How did Taney know that slave ownership was a constitutional right? Such a right is nowhere to be found in the Constitution. He knew it because he was passionately convinced that it *must* be in the Constitution [emphasis original].

Well, the answer is that, although the Constitution does not "confer" a right to own slaves, it most assuredly recognizes such a right. Moreover, it recognizes that right as arising, not from the action of judges, but of legislatures. Here is the text of Article IV, Section 2, para. 3:

> No person held to service of labor in one State, under the laws thereof, escaping into another, shall, in consequence of any law or regulation therein, be discharged from such service or labor, but shall be delivered up on claim of the party to whom such service or labor may be due.

This is the fugitive slave clause. The original Constitution never uses the words "slave" or "slavery," preferring euphemisms in their place. Article I speaks of "adding to the whole number of free persons . . . three fifth of all other persons." Can it be doubted that the "other persons" are unfree, that is, slaves? Or that their slavery is regarded by the Constitution as lawful? But the Constitution, in Article IV, not only recognizes the lawfulness of the right to own slaves—a lawfulness arising from the actions of the legislatures of the slave states—but it pledges the full power of the federal government to making that right secure, whenever the slave shall escape from his master into a jurisdiction where slavery is forbidden. The phrase "shall be delivered up" is categorical, and implies an obligation on Congress to pass enabling legislation, if such should be necessary. So far as I know, no one, in two hundred years, has ever made the fantastic assertion that Bork makes, that the right to slave ownership "is nowhere to be found in the [original] Constitution." In short, it was not Taney who read the right to slave ownership *into* the Constitution; it is Judge Bork who has read it *out* of the Constitution. Judge Bork was so passionately convinced that Taney's opinion represented a reading of his personal beliefs into a Constitution that did not contain such beliefs, that he was blind to the extent to which the Constitution actually did embody those beliefs.

It is clear moreover—from Article IV—that Taney did not form his opinion in *Dred Scott* on the basis of the due process clause of the Fifth Amendment alone. The substantive element also rested in part on Article I, Section 9, in which it is said that

> The migration or importation of such persons as any of the States now existing shall think fit to admit, shall not be prohibited by the Congress prior to the year one thousand eight hundred and eight.

This clause is an exception made to the power granted to Congress in Section 8, "to regulate commerce with foreign nations," as well as that "to establish a uniform rule of naturalization." No one has ever doubted that, however ponderous the euphemism, Congress was prohibited thereby from interfering—for twenty years—with the buying of slaves on the west coast of Africa, where they could be obtained much more cheaply than in any of the States. Taney held—not unreasonably—that this concession to business profit was evidence of a "right to traffic" in slave property as "an ordinary article of merchandise and property." Taney could more plausibly have referred to it as extraordinary rather than ordinary. If however one puts together—as Taney did—the substantive and substantial consideration given by the Constitution in these several places to the profit and security of slave property and the slave trade, it was not unreasonable for him to conclude that it was unconstitutional to deprive a person of such valuable considerations merely because he took them with him into a United States territory. Or, to be more precise, it was not unreasonable for him to conclude as he did, if one draws one's inferences concerning the intent of the Constitution, from the text of the Constitution alone, in the manner commended by Judge Bork. In any event, it is certainly the case that Judge Bork makes his case against Taney only by the most shameless expurgating and bowdlerizing of the Constitution's text.

What then was wrong with Taney's opinion in *Dred Scott*? Let us recall that in all the places in the Constitution in which slaves are referred to euphemistically, they are called "persons." And we must recall that in the Fifth Amendment the Constitution says that

> No person shall . . . be deprived of life, liberty, or property, without due process of law.

Now the persons held to service or labor, in Article IV (like those imported under Article I, section 9) were so held (or imported), not as persons but as chattels. But a person, qua person, is possessed of a rational will. And a chattel, qua chattel, is a piece of movable property without a rational will. Under the law of slavery slaves were always regarded as human persons for some purposes—e.g. by being held responsible for their actions under the criminal law—while at the same time they were regarded as chattels, mere extensions of their master's will, like a horse or a dog or an ox. Hence they could not make contracts, for which reason there was no legal marriage among them. That the law of slavery at once regarded the slaves as persons and as chattels—notwithstanding the fact that, in reason and in nature, a person cannot be a chattel, and a chattel cannot be a person—was what made slavery indeed a "peculiar institution." In the slave states themselves, the character of a chattel always took precedence of the person in the slave. But what happened when he was taken to a territory? Why should the positive law of slavery follow him? Looking within the four quarters of the text of the Constitution, Taney inferred that Negroes (whether free or slave) were regarded by the Framers as

> beings of an inferior order . . . and so far inferior, that they had no rights which white men were bound to respect; and that the negro might justly and lawfully be reduced to slavery for his benefit.

These are the decisive words in Taney's opinion—ignored by Bork. They justified Taney, in his own mind, in deciding that when the master took his slave into a territory, the master was the "person" who could not be lawfully deprived of his property. But Lincoln and the Republican Party, looking to the words of the Declaration of Independence, said that the slave was equally a human person with the master. Under "the laws of nature and of nature's God" the right to liberty took precedence of the right to property. This was because, underlying the positive law of property, was the natural right—the natural liberty—of every human being to own himself. This was also the ground of the right of contract, referred to by John Marshall. The positive law of slavery might overrule the law of nature in the slave states, but it could not extend beyond their boundaries, except for the reclaiming of fugitives.

The case of Dred Scott can only be understood if one realizes that in it the chatteldom of slavery and the personhood of the slave have come into uncompromising contradiction. That contradiction can be resolved only by recourse to the principles of natural right and natural law, as embodied in the Declaration of Independence. For this purpose, Judge Bork's conception of "original intent" is perfectly useless. But if it is useless here, it is useless everywhere: for the reason that in this case the distinction between the compromises of the Constitution and the principles of the Constitution is brought into sharper focus than anywhere else. It is because the Civil War amendments (to which one might add the Nineteenth Amendment) have eliminated the most evident contradictions between the Constitution and its principles, that the question of what those principles are, has become more obscure. Yet, as I believe it can be proved, the meaning of the Fourteenth Amendment, and in particular the meaning of its "due process" and "equal protection" clauses, depends in the highest degree upon the correct understanding of where Taney went wrong in *Dred Scott*. And of that Judge Bork has not an inkling.

March 11, 1990

Whatever Happened to the Emperor's Clothes?
Jaffa Replies to Bork

Judge Bork concludes his discourse in the February 7, 1994 *National Review*, as follows:

> Written in dyspeptic prose, *Original Intent and the Framers of the Constitution* is one of the least coherent, least consequential, and most disingenuous pieces of constitutional theorizing on record: incoherent because Mr. Jaffa offers conclusions that cannot possibly be tortured out of constitutional text, history, or structure; inconsequential because, so far as is apparent, his argument has applicability only to one pre-Civil War case; disingenuous because he misrepresents not only that case but the Constitution itself. This may sound unduly harsh. I have tried to show that it is only duly harsh.

I have been writing for *National Review* for nearly thirty years, and I believe its readers are sophisticated enough to tell a critique of a book with which one disagrees from a temper tantrum. No one before has pronounced my prose "dyspeptic," although clearly it has given Judge Bork heartburn. It is not difficult to know why.

The July 9, 1991 issue of *National Review* published an article entitled "The Closing of the Conservative Mind: A Dissenting Opinion on Judge Robert H. Bork." In it I offered a critical analysis of the central thesis of Judge Bork's then recently published book, *The Tempting of America: The Political Seduction of the Law*.[1] In the two and a half years that have intervened Judge Bork has studiously ignored that critique, but now that it is incorporated in *Original Intent and the Framers of the Constitution*, he has condescended to notice it.

Bork's book is built around the proposition that liberal judges write their own subjective opinions into constitutional law. They attribute to the Constitution rights that are the judges' own invention, and then devise remedies on the ground that the Constitution requires them. Judge Bork and I are agreed that when that happens, it is wrong and bad. I don't like liberal judicial activism any more than he does.

---

[1] The Free Press, 1990. Hereafter cited as *Tempting*.

According to Bork however (in *Tempting*) the first such case in which this occurred was that of *Dred Scott v. Sandford*, in which Chief Justice Taney, in his opinion for the Court, discovered a constitutional right of slave ownership, which "right is nowhere in the Constitution." Because of this alleged right, says Bork, Taney pronounced the Missouri Compromise ban on slavery, or any prospective congressional ban on slavery in any United States territory, to be unconstitutional. According to Bork

> this was the first appearance in American constitutional law of "substantive due process," and that concept has been used countless times since by judges who want to write their personal beliefs into a document that, most inconveniently, does not contain such beliefs.

The only trouble with this assertion, is that Taney did *not* invent a right to slave ownership that is "nowhere to be found in the Constitution." The recognition of the right of slave ownership is massively present within the Constitution of 1787. Taney did not, as Bork says, read a right of slave ownership *into* the Constitution. It is Bork who has read the right *out* of the Constitution.[2] And it is just as illegitimate for a conservative to deny rights that are recognized by the Constitution as it is for liberals to invent rights that are not recognized by it. I wrote that no one, so far as I knew, in two hundred years (that is, before Judge Bork) had ever denied that the Constitution of 1787 recognized the lawfulness of slave property. This why I said that Bork had bowdlerized the text of the Constitution.

Judge Bork now asserts that

> The Constitution certainly recognized that slaves were held pursuant to the laws of some states, but the Constitution most emphatically did not guarantee such a right.

---

[2] This is not the only example of Bork rewriting the Constitution to suit his purposes. He does the same thing to the Ninth Amendment, which reads: "The enumeration in the Constitution of certain rights shall not be construed to deny or disparage others retained by the people." Professor Douglas Kmiec, of Notre Dame University Law School, and former Head of the Office of Legal Counsel in the Meese Justice Department, takes Bork to task for arguing that these words "are a meaningless 'inkblot.'" He writes that "Bork's inkblot assertion cannot stand. If the Constitution is law, no part of it can go unenforced." Kmiec also writes that "Madison . . . perceived the Ninth Amendment as incorporating natural law . . . " which is of course why Bork de-incorporates it from the Constitution. So much for the advocate of a jurisprudence of "original understanding"! Kmiec, *The Attorney General's Lawyer: Inside the Meese Justice Department* (New York: Praeger, 1992), pp. 35-37.

It bears repeating that in *Tempting* Judge Bork asserted categorically that recognition of a right of slave ownership was "nowhere to be found" in the Constitution. Now he says that the Constitution of 1787 "certainly recognized" such a right. But he does not admit that he was "certainly wrong" previously.

However, Judge Bork compounds his error, even while pretending that he had not made it. He says that the Constitution "most emphatically did not guarantee a right" in slave property. But consider the words of Article IV, Section 2, para. 2:

> No person held to service or labor in one state, under the laws thereof, escaping into another, shall, in consequence of any law or regulation therein, be discharged from such service or labor, but shall be delivered up on claim of the party to whom such service or labor may be due.

Bork writes of the "obligation of states to return fugitive slaves." But the Constitution does not say whether fugitives are to be returned by state or federal authority. A good indication of the "original understanding" of this clause is the fact that the first federal fugitive slave law was passed in 1793, and remained in effect until a much more stringent law was passed in 1850. Returning fugitive slaves was therefore recognized as a federal responsibility during almost all of the period between the adoption of the Constitution and the adoption of the Thirteenth Amendment. Even after the Emancipation Proclamation the fugitive slave law continued in effect—legally if not practically—in slaveholding counties that were loyal to the Union. Persons "held to service or labor" in the slave states were held, not as persons, but as chattels. But no similar provision was made for returning runaway horses or dogs or beef cattle. This "peculiar" form of chattel property could not be maintained without elaborate police provisions, both within the slave states, and across their borders. One of the major grievances of the slave states in 1860, was the personal liberty laws that had been passed by a number of free states. Any interference with the execution of the fugitive slave law had been declared unconstitutional by the Supreme Court, and federal authority was practically unchallenged in its enforcement. Nevertheless, President Buchanan, in his last annual message, declared that the free states must

> repeal their unconstitutional and obnoxious enactments. Unless this shall be done without unnecessary delay, it is impossible for any human power to save the Union.

That is some indication of how important the federal constitutional guarantee to the security of slave property was regarded, Judge Bork to the contrary notwithstanding. Judge Bork should know, furthermore, that the fugitive slave act of 1850 did not permit an alleged fugitive any benefit of the writ of *habeas corpus*, or any legal representation in the trial before the federal commissioner appointed to decide his fate. The slaveowner could summon witnesses, but the accused runaway could not. Finally, the commissioner would receive ten dollars if he decided in favor of the slaveowner, and five dollars if he decided for the alleged runaway! The personal liberty laws were intended in part to prevent free persons of color from being carried away into slavery. Yet for the Congress that passed the 1850 law, and for three presidents thereafter, the liberty of persons of color, whether free or not, was considered insignificant compared with the Constitution's pledge that fugitives from slavery "shall be delivered up." It is absurd for Judge Bork to deny that the Constitution of 1787 made the federal government an active agent in preserving, protecting, and defending the system of chattel slavery.

Bork writes that the "three fifths clause [Article I, Section 2] was designed to limit slave state representation." But consider: a man in antebellum Pennsylvania owns property in land and buildings and livestock. Another man, in Virginia, only a few miles to the south, owns property of the same value. But the Virginian's property is invested in part in five slaves. The Virginian in effect casts one vote for himself and three more for his five slaves.[3] And these additional votes were registered in representation in the Electoral College as well as in the federal Congress. If Judge Bork had read any of the antebellum debates over slavery, he would have found this to be one of the leading free state grievances, and one of the reasons for their opposition to adding more slave states to the Union.

Judge Bork writes that

> The importation clause [Article I, Section 9] was a compromise that delayed a federal ban on the importation of slaves for twenty years.

This article merits more notice than Judge Bork's passing glance. Taney relied upon it when he wrote that under the Constitution of 1787

---

[3] Of course, the Virginian would have liked to have had five more votes, rather than three. Perhaps this is what Judge Bork meant by limiting slave state representation! All the Virginian had to do to have his slaves counted as whole persons, rather than three-fifths of a person, was to free them. But then they might have asked for the right to vote for themselves!

the negro . . . was bought and sold and treated as an ordinary article of merchandise and traffic, when ever a profit could be made by it.

Consider that, contrary to Judge Bork, the Constitution says nothing about delaying a ban. Article I, Section 9 only forbids a ban. This clause constitutes an exception to the power of Congress "to regulate commerce with foreign nations and among the several states. . ." And it is a powerful exception, so powerful that Article V of the Constitution says that this clause may not be amended. It is true that when the twenty years had elapsed, the *foreign* slave trade was in fact banned. But the *interstate* slave trade was never banned. Despite the fact that the words of the Constitution grant power—without exception—to regulate commerce among the several states, the "original understanding" of the commerce clause in fact exempted the interstate commerce in slaves from any regulation whatsoever. Despite repeated efforts of antislavery societies to promote legislation requiring humane treatment of the Negroes transported in interstate commerce, every such attempt was rejected as hostile to the constitutional sanctity of slave property. Moreover, at least one reason why the foreign slave trade was banned in 1808 was that states like Virginia and Kentucky were exporting their surplus slaves to newer slave states which could more profitably employ them. Cheap African imports lowered the price at which they could sell their homegrown products on the domestic market.[4] The banning of the foreign slave trade in 1808 was a protectionist measure as well as a humanitarian one. And despite the ban, slaves continued to be imported from Africa right up until the Civil War.[5] The only slave trader ever executed for piracy was hanged as a result of a warrant signed by Abraham Lincoln. In short, throughout the antebellum period the interstate slave trade went a long way towards justifying Taney in holding that, according to the "original understanding" of the Constitution, slaves were ordinary articles of commercial property.

---

[4] The conflicting economic interests involved in Article I, Section 9, can be seen in the provision that a duty may be imposed on each imported slave, "not exceeding ten dollars for each person." Obviously there were those who wanted no duty laid, and others who did not want any limit placed upon such a duty.

[5] The problem of preventing the importation of slaves from Africa before the Civil War was not unlike the problem of preventing the importation of illegal drugs from Latin America today. Slaves were brought from Africa to Cuba, and then smuggled into the United States.

Judge Bork has now admitted what he had previously denied, viz., that at least three conspicuous clauses of the Constitution of 1787 recognize a right of slave ownership. But, he says,

> How any of this adds up to justifying Taney's invention of a constitutional right to own slaves in federal territory remains a complete mystery.

Bork then asserts that

> Congress has legislative power over territories more complete than a state legislature has over its state, for the state legislature may not interfere with the exercise of federal power. There can be nothing constitutionally wrong therefore if Congress defines what may or may not be property within a federal territory. In the Missouri Compromise Congress said that persons could not be property in a designated part of federal territory. That is why *Dred Scott* was a usurpation of congressional power accomplished, Mr. Jaffa to the contrary notwithstanding, through Taney's invention of substantive due process.

Judge Bork writes as if Taney's opinion in *Dred Scott* was merely a judicial idiosyncrasy. Indeed, he writes as if he, Judge Bork, but not the American people who elected Congresses and presidents in antebellum America, knew what were then the powers of Congress over slavery in the territories. In fact, Taney's opinion was an outcome of the firestorm over slavery in the territories that began during the Mexican War and that culminated in the Civil War. Judge Bork says that there "can be nothing constitutionally wrong . . . if Congress defines what may or may not be property within a federal territory." In the generation before the Civil War, however, the political process was dominated by those who categorically denied that there could be anything constitutionally right in Congress defining what might be property within a federal territory. It is unhistorical, if not plainly absurd, for Judge Bork to denounce Taney for not holding a constitutional opinion that had been rejected repeatedly by the political process. No resolution embodying Bork's view could have passed the United States Congress in the years leading up to *Dred Scott*. During the Mexican War, an antislavery majority in the House of Representatives attempted regularly to pass just such a resolution. It was called the Wilmot Proviso. For Judge Bork's information, the Wilmot Proviso declared that in all the territory to be acquired from Mexico as a result of the war, slavery would be prohibited. The Proviso repeatedly passed the House and just as repeatedly was defeated in the Senate. Abraham Lincoln said—somewhat hyperbolically—that as a member of

Congress he had voted for it "as good as forty times." The 1862 law that finally banned slavery in all United States territories passed during the Civil War only because the representatives of eleven slave states had withdrawn from the Congress.

Long before Taney joined the Supreme Court, the Missouri Compromise ban of 1820 was widely denounced in the South as unconstitutional.[6] It was permitted to pass, however, as a concession necessary to have Missouri admitted as a slave state. Moreover, at the time it appeared to be a settlement of all outstanding constitutional questions in regard to slavery. With the acquisition of vast new territories conquered from Mexico—adding (with Texas and California) about 40 percent to the land area of the United States—all previous concessions with regard to the congressional exclusion of slavery from the territories were regarded by the proslavery South as null and void. In the 1850 territorial laws for Utah and New Mexico, Congress could not agree either to permit or to ban slavery. It provided that any state formed from these territories might be admitted into the Union, with or without slavery, as their constitutions might prescribe. But the crucial question was: What would be the status of slavery in the territories *before* the time for adoption of a state constitution? This would be the determining factor as to whether such constitutions would or would not sanction slavery. And on this question the Congress, like the country, was irreconcilably and irrevocably divided. Hence it was written into the territorial laws of 1850 that any dispute as to the status of slavery in those territories could be appealed directly from the Supreme Court of the territory to the Supreme Court of the United States. In short, it was Congress itself, and not any merely gratuitous intervention by the Court, that handed over to the Court the question of the constitutional status of slavery in the territories. It makes no sense at all for Judge Bork to tell us that *his* mind is made up *now* as to what were the powers of Congress in the antebellum Constitution, when the American people, and their elected representatives, were unable *then* to make up *their* minds.

In 1854 Congress passed the Kansas-Nebraska Act, which said that the Missouri ban of 1820 was inconsistent with the policy of the 1850 laws, and was therefore "inoperative and void." Senator Douglas, the author of the Kansas-Nebraska Act, always claimed that the policy of the

---

[6] "Sir, let me say a word as to the [Missouri] compromise line. I have always regarded it as a great error—highly injurious to the South, because it surrendered, for mere temporary purposes, those high principles of the constitution upon which we ought to stand. I am against any compromise line." John C. Calhoun, in the Senate, February 19, 1847. *Union and Liberty: The Political Philosophy of John C. Calhoun*, Ross M. Lence, ed. (Indianapolis: Liberty Fund, 1992), p. 519.

1850 laws was one of congressional non-intervention. The hard line Southerners, who had a dominating influence on both the presidents who preceded Lincoln, as well as on the Senate during the same period, were not satisfied with Douglas's "popular sovereignty," which left the decision on slavery in each territory up to the local inhabitants. They wanted federal guarantees that slave property, no less than any other kind of property, would have whatever protection it needed. When Taney wrote that the only power conferred by the Constitution on Congress in the territories, "is the power, coupled with the duty of guarding and protecting the owner in his rights" they finally got what they wanted.

On the eve of the decision in March 1857, both the outgoing and the incoming presidents (Pierce and Buchanan) exhorted the American people to accept the forthcoming decision of the Supreme Court as a final resolution of the question of the status of slavery in the territories. There is little doubt that these "doughface" presidents[7] were in some kind of collusion with Taney, as well as with some other members of the Court. When therefore the Court acted as it did, it attempted to cut the Gordian knot which had immobilized the political process. The decision, and Taney's opinion, were evidence that the Southern Democrats at that moment dominated the Presidency, the Senate, and the Supreme Court. But the rising tide of Republicanism marked the imminent end of that dominance. *Dred Scott* was a desperate attempt to prevent the Republicans from coming to power by taking the territorial question out of the political process by judicial fiat. But it was political, not legal forces, that produced the result. "Substantive due process" had absolutely nothing whatever to do with it.

Judge Bork finds it a "complete mystery" how the constitutional recognition of the right of slave ownership "adds up . . . to a constitutional right to own slaves in federal territory." What is a mystery to Judge Bork is however transparent to anyone who understands that the antebellum debate over slavery in the territories was also a debate between two great theories as to the nature of the Union and of the Constitution. It was also a debate between two rival and conflicting opinions as to the "original intent" or "original understanding" of the Constitution. The Civil War itself was nothing more than, or less than, a continuation of that debate, "by other means."

The architect of the Southern view of the Constitution was John C. Calhoun. Although he died in 1850, he is rightly regarded as the Moses of the Confederacy, the lawgiver who showed the South the promised land where slavery would be unmolested and unchallenged. Jefferson

---

[7] In antebellum politics, a "doughface" was a Northern man with Southern principles.

Davis was his disciple. Roger B. Taney was his disciple. [8] Public opinion in the states that seceded in 1860 and 1861 was influenced decisively by Calhoun. It is difficult, perhaps impossible, to imagine the Civil War except in the light of the mind of the South as it had been shaped by Calhoun.

Calhoun's idea of state rights was the cornerstone of his constitutional architecture. Each state, he held, became a member of the Union under the Constitution of 1787 solely by virtue of its ratification of the Constitution. The Constitution was a "compact" among the states so ratifying. Each state was an equal partner in this compact. The territories of the United States belonged equally to all the states. The federal government was their agent, deriving all its authority from their acts of ratification. It had no power to govern the territories, except as that power had been delegated to it by the states in the Constitution. The constitutional equality of the states forbade the Congress, as the common agent of the states, to discriminate between or among the property rights recognized as lawful by any of the states. It had therefore no lawful power to discriminate against slave property, or to offer it less protection than any other kind of property. Hence the Missouri law was unconstitutional. This was the Calhounian theory behind Taney's opinion. [9]

This is a powerful argument, so powerful that eventually 300,000 Americans died to maintain it, and another 300,000 died to oppose it. If one grants its premises, then one would have to grant that the Missouri law was unconstitutional, and that Taney was correct in saying that anyone who was deprived of his slave property because of it, and who had committed no punishable offense, would be deprived of that property without due process of law. "Substantive due process" simply does not enter into the argument.

Consider the following present-day elucidation of Calhoun's premises:

---

[8] In *National Review*'s history, Willmoore Kendall, Frank Meyer, Garry Wills (as he once was), Mel Bradford, and Russell Kirk, are among those who have subscribed to the view of Calhoun as the supreme sage of American constitutionalism.

[9] "I am a Southern man and a slaveholder—and none the worse for being a slaveholder. I say, for one, I would rather meet any extremity upon earth than give up one inch of our equality—one inch of what belongs to us as members of this great republic! What acknowledged inferiority! The surrender of life is nothing to sinking down into acknowledged inferiority!" Calhoun, ibid. p. 520. The equality of which Calhoun speaks is state equality. Calhoun would prefer death to admitting what Judge Bork thinks is the incontestable meaning of the Constitution.

> If . . . a society adopts a constitution and incorporates in that constitution safeguards for individual liberty, these safeguards indeed do take on a generalized moral rightness or goodness. They assume a general social acceptance neither because of any intrinsic worth nor because of any unique origins in someone's idea of natural justice but instead simply because they have been incorporated in a constitution by the people.[10]

This statement of legal positivism grounded upon moral relativism was made by the present chief justice of the United States. Applying it to the Constitution of 1787 we would certainly observe the incorporation of safeguards for individual liberty. But we would also observe safeguards for chattel slavery. According to Mr. Justice Rehnquist, as according to John C. Calhoun, both kinds rest upon an identical foundation. To emphasize this Mr. Justice Rehnquist adds that

> It is the fact of their enactment [i.e. ratification] that gives them whatever moral claim they have upon us as a society, however, and not any independent virtue they may have in any particular citizen's own scale of values.

If constitutional safeguards derive their authority solely from the "fact of their enactment" and not from any idea of "intrinsic worth" or of "natural justice," it follows—as the night the day—that the moral status of constitutional safeguards of liberty and of slavery must be the same. This is exactly what Calhoun contended, and explains why the South was morally indignant at the moral condemnation of slavery within the free states. They found it intolerable that the morality of one part of the Constitution, which had particular reference to their "domestic institutions," should be held in lower regard than any other parts of the Constitution.

Judge Bork has never been quite as lucid as Justice Rehnquist in expressing the pure positivism that informs his conception of a jurisprudence of original intent. However, he "rejoices" at being placed in the company of Mr. Justice Rehnquist, but cannot understand why they are considered "disciples of the late, unlamented John C. Calhoun." I trust that no one, with the possible exception of Judge Bork, will remain in any doubt upon this point.

---

[10] William H. Rehnquist, in the ninth annual Will E. Orgain Lecture, delivered at The University of Texas School of Law, March 12, 1976. Reprinted in *Taking the Constitution Seriously*, Gary L. McDowell, ed. (Dubuque, Iowa: Kendall/Hunt, 1981), p. 77.

Let us however ask Judge Bork and Justice Rehnquist, do they think that the positive laws of the slave states conferred upon slavery a moral goodness that placed the slaves themselves under an obligation of obedience? Could the slaves themselves be expected to observe the "moral goodness" that emanated from a process of ratification or adoption in which they had no part?

Judge Bork, in his review of *Original Intent*, quotes the statement of principles in the Declaration of Independence, beginning "We hold these truths to be self-evident . . . " "These are," he says, "noble words, words of high aspiration, but it is unclear what they add to our reading of the Constitution." What they add to our reading of the Constitution is a flat denial of the legal positivism grounded upon moral relativism that we find equally in Calhoun and Rehnquist/Bork. The principles of the Declaration provide a firm basis for discriminating the safeguards for liberty from the safeguards for slavery, pronouncing the one to be principled, and the other to be compromises with principle, justified—if they can be justified—only on grounds of prudence.

Having called the words of the Declaration "noble," Judge Bork asks how the doctrine of unalienable rights is consistent with laws that contemplate the deprivation of both liberty and life. It is embarrassing to have to instruct Judge Bork in these the simplest elements of the political philosophy of the American Founding. That philosophy was expressed by John Locke, when he wrote that

> Political power [is the] right of making laws with penalties of death, and consequently all lesser penalties, for the regulating and preserving of property, and of employing the force of the community in the execution of such laws.

So far is the doctrine of unalienable rights from protecting thieves or murderers, that it is formulated with the precise purpose of explaining how governments may act justly in punishing them. The right of political power in the community is derived from the unalienable right that each human individual possesses "to punish the offender and be the executioner of the law of nature." By the social contract (or compact), citizens have transferred to their governments the task of securing their unalienable rights. It is for this reason that governments come to possess the lawful power to punish transgressors—whether foreign or domestic—against these rights. The Americans of the Revolution denied that God or nature or history had given kings or ruling classes any power inherent in themselves to define crimes or punish them. All such power was derived, whether directly or indirectly, from the people. Because all men are equally endowed by God and nature with these rights, a legitimate government guarantees to all citizens, without discrimination, the "equal protection of the laws."

Judge Bork writes that

so far as the Constitution is concerned, these rights are unalienable unless society has reason to take them away.

Let us note, however, that the Declaration of Independence says that it is

to secure *these* rights [among which are "life, liberty, and the pursuit of happiness"] that governments are instituted among men, deriving their just powers from the consent of the governed.

Governments may exercise only such powers as have been delegated to them by the people through the Constitution. Legitimate political power is limited by the purposes for which, by the laws of nature, governments are instituted. Society *may not*, for example, take away the free exercise of religion, because it *cannot* have any reason, under the laws of nature, to do so. Nor can it enact *ex post facto* laws, or bills of attainder. If such things are done by governments, they are done inconsistently with the doctrine of unalienable rights. Although the doctrine of the equal and unalienable rights of man has as its corollary the doctrine of popular sovereignty, that does not mean that the people have a plenary or unlimited right to govern. Writing to Spencer Roane in 1819, Jefferson asserted that

Independence can be trusted nowhere but with the people *en masse*. They are inherently independent of all but moral law. [11]

Contrary to Mr. Justice Rehnquist, the morality of law is not derived from the fact of enactment. On the contrary, the legitimacy of government is derived from its conformity with the laws of nature, including that law of nature that requires the consent of the governed.

* * * * *

Judge Bork complains because I take him

---

[11] *The Works of Thomas Jefferson*, edited by Paul Leicester Ford (New York: Putnam, 1905), Vol. XII, p. 137.

severely to task for having said that "our constitutional liberties, arose out of historical experience . . . they do not rest upon any general theory." Citing the Declaration once more and a number of state constitutions asserting that all men are born free and equal, etc., [Jaffa] wonders whether I have "ever read a single document of our Founding." Well, I suppose the Constitution qualifies as one.

Certainly the Constitution qualifies as one. But we must ask whether Judge Bork's reading of the Constitution qualifies *him*, since we found him unable to recognize in it any recognition of a right of ownership of slave property. Nor did he improve his qualifications when, after conceding such recognition, he denied that the fugitive slave clause constituted any guarantee of slave property. But can the Constitution of 1787 (or 1791) be read as a self-contained document? If a state that ratified the Constitution proclaimed a certain general theory as the foundation of its own state constitution, is it not reasonable to assume that in ratifying the federal constitution, it was doing so upon the same premises?

In fact, we have high authority for this assumption. In 1825 Jefferson asked Madison to recommend the books or documents that should supply the *norma docendi*—the instructional principles—to guide the law faculty of the new University of Virginia. The Father of the Constitution thereupon advised the Father of the University (who was also the Author of the Declaration of Independence) that, of the *best* guides to the principles of the governments of Virginia and of the United States, the *first* was "The Declaration of Independence as the act of union of these states."[12] It was a matter of course to the third and fourth presidents of the United States, if not to Judge Bork, that the general theory of the Declaration, should guide the education of young Virginians, in the laws of the constitutions, of both Virginia and the United States. To what better place would Judge Bork turn to discover the principles of that "republican form of government" that the Constitution says (Article IV, Section 4) the United States shall guarantee to every state in the union? The Constitution itself does not tell us. If we look at the text alone would we not be driven to accept slavery as perfectly consistent with republicanism? Have we not seen that reason and nature tell us that a chattel cannot be a person, and a person cannot be a chattel, however much the positive law says that they are one and the same? If the

---

[12] See Harry V. Jaffa, *How to Think about the American Revolution* (Durham: Carolina Academic Press, 1978), pp. 103, 104. Madison's advice was taken, and incorporated into a resolution of the Board of Visitors of the University.

republican form of government is one whose principles require the consent of the governed, then we learn from the Declaration of Independence that certain clauses of the Constitution constitute compromises with its principles, and should be read as such. Yet Judge Bork says it is "unclear what [the words of the Declaration] add to our reading of the Constitution!" Will someone please tell him!

Judge Bork continues the passage just cited, as follows:

> The liberties to be found [in the Constitution] clearly derive from historical experience with the British Crown and the states' fear of the new federal power. The First Amendment's prohibition of the establishment of religion reflected not only the fact that various denominations feared a federal choice of one but that six states had established religions which they did not want Congress to supplant.

One may concede that the fears Judge Bork mentions may have played some role in the drafting of the First Amendment's religion clauses. But that role was slight, and ultimately inconsequential, compared with the impact of the theories of civil and religious liberty embraced by the Declaration of Independence (1776) and the Virginia Statute of Religious Liberty (1786). The latter was the result of a tremendous political struggle in Virginia, led by Madison's "Memorial and Remonstrance," and consummated in Jefferson's Statute. As the Declaration points towards that republican form of government in which governments derive their just powers from free elections, so does the statute point toward a citizen body that is not divided politically by sectarian religious differences. The historical experience of intolerance during the wars of religion had demonstrated to the Framers and Ratifiers of the Constitution the necessity for extirpating religious passions from politics, and political passions from religion. They knew that government of majority rule and minority rights, government by elections, was impossible, given the presence of religious passions in the political process. And they knew that genuine religion was not possible in the presence of political passions. They knew therefore that, as Jefferson said, a republican constitutional order was impossible, unless it was accepted that a man's civil rights had no more dependence upon his religious opinions, than upon his opinions in physics and geometry. How was it that the same historical experience had not taught the same lessons anywhere else? The doctrine of religious liberty, Judge Bork to the contrary notwithstanding, does not reflect historical experience alone. It reflects rather the intrusion of a non-historical philosophic wisdom into history. Because of it, President Washington, in 1790, in his letter to the

Hebrew Synagogue in Newport, Rhode Island, greeted the Jews of the congregation as his equal fellow citizens. Never before in all human history had Jews ever been addressed in this way by a non-Jewish head of state. But Washington was explicit that they were equal in their civil and political rights *because* they were equal in those natural rights that had been set forth in both the Declaration of Independence and the Virginia Statute of Religious Liberty.

Virginia's Statute of 1786 was of course binding only upon Virginia. As Washington demonstrated however, the terms of the argument advanced by Madison and Jefferson in Virginia were intrinsically applicable to any and all republican governments, foreign or domestic, state or federal. In 1787 a version of the doctrine of religious liberty was incorporated—along with a ban on slavery—in the Northwest Ordinance, setting the pattern for the states to be formed therefrom. Eventually—but inexorably—as the general theory of religious liberty spread its beneficent influence, disestablishment and free exercise became the law throughout the United States.

It must not however escape our attention (as it has Judge Bork's) that the influence of the theory of religious liberty is manifest in the body of the Constitution *before* the First Amendment. Article VI declares that there shall never be any religious test for any office under the government of the United States. That clause cannot be fobbed off as something to do with state rights. Nor can it be put down to any cause other than the philosophical one, as expounded in Virginia by Madison and Jefferson. The conflicts of interest that were resolved by their arguments for religious freedom had been present in human society throughout human history. That those arguments prevailed at that time, never having prevailed before, cannot be set down merely to their utility. The decisive historical fact is that those non-historical arguments prevailed first in the minds of Jefferson and Madison, and that they subsequently prevailed in the minds of others, like George Washington. And the reasons why those arguments prevailed in those minds were the reasons that they gave. That is why Judge Bork needs to do more reading than the Constitution alone in order to understand the Constitution.

* * * * *

Judge Bork continues his polemic against the thesis that our constitutional liberties rest upon any "general theory," as follows:

> The Second Amendment's right to bear arms was supposed to protect against any tyrannizing tendencies of the central government. The Third Amendment's prohibition of the

quartering of troops in private homes in peacetime was a reaction to the British practice in the colonies, as was the Fourth Amendment's ban of unreasonable searches and seizures and general warrants. And so it goes. One wonders, for example, what natural law theory produced the Seventh Amendment's guarantee of a jury trial in common law suits involving more than twenty dollars.

The Second, Third and Fourth amendments, by Judge Bork's own account, are intended to supply protection against "tyrannizing tendencies." But what are tyrannizing tendencies and how do we know them? The greatest of all denunciations of tyrannizing tendencies is the Declaration of Independence, which supplies us both with a general theory by which to distinguish tyrannical from non-tyrannical government, and particular instances of tyrannical violations. Certainly the experience recorded in the indictment of the King and Parliament is historical, but it is seen through the eyes of the mind trained in the "the laws of nature and of nature's God." Like Molière's character who did not know he was speaking prose, Judge Bork, speaking of "tyrannizing tendencies," does not know he is himself speaking the language of natural law.

Judge Bork thinks he is particularly clever in asking "what natural law theory" was responsible for the requirement in the Seventh Amendment that the right of trial by jury should be preserved in common law suits in which the "value in controversy" shall exceed twenty dollars. Now Judge Bork might as well have asked what natural law theory is responsible for the right hand rule of the road, or the 65 mile an hour speed limit on interstate highways. I think there is a natural necessity, that if there are roads, and they are heavily traveled, that there be rules of the road. There is no natural law dictating a left hand rule, or a right hand rule. But there must be one or the other, and once a decision is made, it is natural to require everyone to abide by it. Speed limits, or suit limits, are judgments of prudence, serving public requirements for safety and justice, requirements which do indeed devolve upon civil society from the laws of its nature.

Judge Bork then writes:

Nor is the original Constitution much more help to the proponent of a general theory of human liberty. The writ of habeas corpus is guaranteed and bills of attainder prohibited, again based on historical experience. The ban on state laws impairing the obligation of contracts reacted to the practice of relieving debtors of their obligation to repay. There is simply no point in nattering on about freedom and equality as though they constituted a general theory of liberty that was written into the Constitution. They don't and it wasn't.

There is nothing wrong in saying that bills of attainder, like *ex post facto* laws, are prohibited by the Constitution because of what historical experience has revealed about them. But history is not a set of banners or bumper stickers, fluttering down the corridors of time, with "Read Me" inscribed upon them. Is it not wrong, everywhere and always, to convict someone of a crime without a trial? Is it not wrong, everywhere and always, to convict a man of a crime for doing what was not a crime when it was committed? To answer those questions in the affirmative is to say that they are in violation of natural law. The writ of *habeas corpus* certainly revealed its utility in the records of history. What it revealed however was that it was a necessary instrument in preventing kings from perverting the administration of justice for tyrannical purposes. And tyrannical purposes, like tyranny itself, are condemned by the natural law. And if Judge Bork had actually read my book he would have seen that I quote Chief Justice John Marshall as saying that "contracts possess an original intrinsic obligation, derived from the acts of free agents, and not given by government" (p. 282). According to the great chief justice, the obligation of contracts is derived from the natural law, and the Constitution recognizes that fact.

Judge Bork writes that,

It is not at all clear how the tenet that all men are created equal would bear upon such issues as women in combat, abortion, homosexual rights, affirmative action, the death penalty, or other topics that vex us and the courts today.

Although Judge Bork does not know it, all of the above topics are discussed in my book, except women in combat. They are all difficult, but none of them can be addressed intelligently, unless they are addressed from the perspective of natural law. The question of women in combat involves the more general question of how the genuine distinction that nature has made between men and women justifies, or requires, discrimination in the kinds of hazards to which they may be subjected in their lawful occupations. Sodomy has always—hitherto—been regarded as an unnatural act, and a violation of natural law. The dispute about abortion is about when the unborn child acquires the nature of a human person, and thereby becomes entitled to the same protection of law as any other human person. That is eminently a question about natural law. If affirmative action means "counting by race" in governmental allocation of privileges or benefits then it certainly can be judged wrong as a violation of the Constitution because it is a violation of the natural law principle of equality of rights. I defend the death penalty in my book (pp. 262, 263), as I have already done above, in the discussion of unalienable rights.

* * * * *

Judge Bork has said that the argument of my book "has application only to one pre-Civil War case." This is untrue. Both Bork and I in our respective books discuss what we find wrong in Chief Justice Warren's opinion for the Court in *Brown v. Board of Education*. Both of us say that it abandoned any idea of grounding it in the original intent of the Fourteenth Amendment. Both of us object to the fact that Warren frankly asserted what he thought the amendment ought to mean, whether it actually meant it or not. And Judge Bork and I agree that the consequences of that opinion have been disastrous for the law. In *Original Intent* (pp. 259, 260) I tried to show how the chief justice could have written a much different and much better opinion had he followed the canons of original intent as I outlined them.

Judge Bork attempts to do the same: to show how the Court's opinion in *Brown* could have been consistent with his understanding of original intent. We have here a basis for a direct comparison of the application of our two different conceptions of a jurisprudence of original intent. Judge Bork writes: [13]

> By 1954 when *Brown* came up for decision, it had been apparent for some time that segregation *rarely if ever* produced equality. Quite aside from any question of psychology, the physical facilities provided for blacks were not as good as those provided for whites. . . . Since equality and segregation were mutually inconsistent, *though the ratifiers did not understand that*, both could not be honored. When that is seen, it is obvious the Court must choose equality and prohibit state-imposed segregation. The purpose that brought the Fourteenth Amendment into being was equality before the law, and equality, not separation, was written into the text. (emphasis added)

Since throughout his book "original understanding" is the touchstone of constitutional interpretation, we here see Judge Bork rejecting his own

---

[13] *Tempting*, p. 82.

criterion. It is true that he has rejected it here because he says that it leads to self-contradictory results, and one must choose between these results. However, in making such a choice, he reserves to the judge precisely that kind of freedom that his jurisprudence is supposed to prevent. He chooses equality over segregation, he says, because equality is in the text of the amendment. But if the Framers and Ratifiers thought that equality and segregation were perfectly consistent with each other, what right has Judge Bork—on his own premises—to say that they are not consistent with each other?

Now let us go back a step. Judge Bork writes that "for some time . . . the physical facilities provided for blacks were not as good as those provided for whites . . . " *This is Judge Bork's only ground for saying separate is not equal.* By saying that segregation "rarely if ever" produces the constitutionally required "equality" he implies that segregation *can* produce such equality.[14] There is then no inherent reason why the physical facilities provided blacks in a segregated system could not be made equal, or even superior, to those provided for whites. Hence there is no reason, on Judge Bork's premises, why separate could not be made equal to satisfy the requirements of the original intent of the Fourteenth Amendment. The fact that separate physical facilities had not been equal in the past, did not mean that they could not be equal in the future. The white South, in 1954, was more than willing to be put to the test. There is no reason, on Judge Bork's premises, why the Court could not have ordered the equalization of physical facilities instead of desegregation.

Let us now look at our alternative. We begin by noting that Taney in *Dred Scott* had declared that Negroes, whether free or slave, could not be citizens of the United States. The Thirteenth Amendment, while abolishing slavery, did not overrule this part of Taney's opinion. It was however overruled by the first sentence of the Fourteenth Amendment, which reads:

> All persons born or naturalized in the United States and subject
> to the jurisdiction thereof, are citizens of the United States and of
> the State wherein they reside.

If now we ask why Taney said that free Negroes could not be citizens of the United States, we find a leading reason to be that they were allegedly not comprehended within the meaning of the proposition of the Declaration of Independence, "that all men are created equal." Taney conceded that the words, in themselves, would include Negroes, but that

---

[14] Indeed, by granting that segregation can produce equality, Judge Bork reveals the boundless irrationality to which "historical experience" unenlightened by any "general theory" can lead.

the intentions of the Framers cannot be construed to mean what their words actually mean, because of the degraded position that Negroes, whether free or slave, occupied in the world of the Framers and Ratifiers. But Taney was wrong in his premises, as Abraham Lincoln pointed out then and thereafter. The Signers of the Declaration intended by their act to elevate the condition of mankind (and womankind), whether free or slave, and not to consign it to whatever conditions of inequality prevailed in the world as they knew it. These purposes of the Declaration became then part of the intention of the Framers and Ratifiers of the Fourteenth Amendment. Thus the second sentence of the Fourteenth Amendment:

> No state shall make or enforce any law which shall abridge the privileges or immunities of citizens of the United States; nor shall any state deprive any persons within its jurisdiction the equal protection of the laws.

Is it not clear that the second sentence is designed to remove the possibility that Negroes be denied the benefits—or any of them—of that citizenship conferred on them by the first sentence? In repealing Taney's denial of citizenship to Negroes, the amendment intended to repeal as well the reasons for that denial, viz., that Negroes were not included in the proposition that all men are created equal. In repealing Taney's denial, the Fourteenth Amendment tacitly affirmed the Negroes' inclusion in the famous proposition, and by that inclusion affirmed the ground for Mr. Justice Harlan's famous colorblind Constitution. Only if the Constitution is color blind can we properly say that any form of discrimination on the basis of color is unconstitutional. Nor are the principles of the Fourteenth Amendment to be limited—as Judge Bork's idea of original intention would limit them—by reason of the practices of segregation in 1868, any more than the principles of the Declaration of Independence are limited by the existence of slavery in 1776. Warren's opinion in *Brown* does not declare discrimination on the basis of color to be unconstitutional, which is why we have been flooded with race based remedies ever since. *Nor does Bork's emendation of Warren.* Neither of them reverses *Plessy.*[15] By grounding the constitutional jurisprudence of the Fourteenth Amendment in the Declaration of Independence, we do.

March 3, 1994

---

[15] In the matter of whether *Brown* reverses *Plessy*, see Edward J. Erler, "Sowing the Wind: Judicial Legislation and the Legacy of *Brown v. Board of Education*," *Harvard Journal of Law and Public Policy*, Vol. VIII, Spring 1985, pp. 399-426.

Appendix to
Whatever Happened to the Emperor's Clothes?

I have not hitherto commented on certain passages in Judge Bork's review of *Original Intent* because frankly I could not assign any intelligible meaning to them. I believe I now understand them well enough to make the following observations.

I.

Judge Bork writes:

> The most that can be made of the unexpurgated and unbowdlerized text is that the Constitution did not of its own force forbid slavery. That is why it is startling to see Mr. Jaffa reverse his field and, in a mirror image of Taney's opinion, pour his own substance into a purely procedural provision in order to state that the due process clause of the Fifth Amendment accomplished just that. Taney went wrong, he says, because that clause prevents a person from being deprived of liberty without due process of law, which slaves were not afforded.

Judge Bork is entirely correct here in saying that mine is a "mirror image of Taney's opinion." Taney held that a congressional exclusion of slavery from a United States territory would deprive the person who is a slaveowner of his property without due process of law. I agreed with the Republican position that a permission of slavery in a United States territory would deprive the person held as a slave of his liberty without due process of law. There was agreement between the proslavery and antislavery parties that the Fifth Amendment ought to govern the status of slavery in the territories. In what way it ought to govern depended, however, upon which took precedence: the right of property in the person who claimed ownership of the slave, or the right of liberty in the person held as a slave.

In opposition to the foregoing, Judge Bork, be it noted, says that "the Constitution did not of its own force forbid slavery" in a territory. Judge Bork is famous for maintaining unrelentingly, as he does here, that the due process clause of the Fifth Amendment is "a purely procedural provision," completely neutral as between slavery and freedom. Taney was wrong, he holds, in thinking that it favored the property rights of the slaveowner, and the antislavery parties (and Jaffa) were just as wrong in thinking it favored the liberty of the person held as a slave.

In exhibiting a "mirror image" of Taney—in agreeing that due process is substantive and not merely procedural—I am only following the authority of what was in this respect an undivided constitutional tradition. Consider this passage from Don E. Fehrenbacher's *Slavery, Law, and Politics: The Dred Scott Case in Historical Perspective* (Oxford University Press, 1981), pp. 67-68.

> The principal antislavery imperatives were pro-slavery arguments turned upside down [i.e. mirror images!]. Thus the due process clause of the Fifth Amendment, to which Southerners occasionally appealed, with emphasis on the word *property*, could be invoked by northern radicals, with emphasis on the word *liberty*. "Slavery," wrote Salmon P. Chase in 1844, "never has lawfully existed in any territory of the United States since the adoption of that amendment which declares that no person shall be deprived of liberty without due process of law." This argument was incorporated into the platforms of the Liberty Party in 1844, the Free Soil Party in 1848, and the Republican Party in 1856 and 1860.

It is worth noting that Chase was the chief justice who succeeded Taney. They were in agreement that the due process clause was not the merely procedural provision that Bork says it is.

II.

According to Bork, [Jaffa's] understanding of the due process clause

> produces two preposterous conclusions. If a slave and his owner entered Northern territory where slavery was forbidden by the Missouri Compromise, the due process clause would have no effect whatever because that clause forbids only the federal government from depriving a person of liberty. It has no application to private individuals. Thus Dred Scott, who was not deprived of liberty by any federal law, could not have been freed by the due process clause. Mr. Jaffa's position collapses. He has transformed a prohibition of government action into a prohibition of private action.

The mental confusion in the foregoing is boundless. It is sufficient here to remind the reader that the position Bork attributes to me is not one that

I invented. It was, as Don Fehrenbacher noted, in the Republican platform of 1860, and was presumably shared by everyone who voted for Lincoln in that year.

No one in the antebellum free soil movement ever expected any slave to be freed by the due process clause alone. This would have been possible only if a majority of the Supreme Court justices had shared Chase's and Lincoln's understanding of the Constitution. By the time that happened, the Thirteenth Amendment made the question moot. It was however important to the antislavery movement, as it pursued its ends through the political process, to insist that the conjunction of the natural law of freedom, in the Declaration of Independence, and of the due process clause, in the Constitution, meant that the Constitution, of its own intrinsic force, made slavery unlawful. Remember that the Garrisonian abolitionists had burned the Constitution as "an agreement with Hell" because of its compromises with slavery. It was the association of the due process clause with the Declaration of Independence that led men like Lincoln and Frederick Douglass to disagree with the radical abolitionists, and insist that the Constitution, notwithstanding its compromises, was essentially antislavery. This argument was critical to the eventual political success of the antislavery movement under the Republican banner.

Judge Bork's diatribe then continues as follows.

> Mr. Jaffa's argument [also] means that if Scott had been taken to a Southern territory where the Missouri Compromise allowed slavery, he would have been able to claim freedom under the due process clause because the compromise was federal law that deprived him of liberty. Thus the Missouri Compromise was unconstitutional, not as Taney thought, because it barred slavery in the northern part of the Louisiana Territory, but, following Mr. Jaffa's argument, because it allowed slavery in the southern part. Not even Lincoln made that claim. But perhaps he did not understand the Constitution's incorporation of the Declaration of Independence as well as Professor Jaffa does.

In the first place, the Missouri Compromise did not allow slavery in the southern part of the Louisiana Territory. The law or laws comprising the Compromise had reference only to land lying north of 36 degrees 30 minutes, the southern border of the Missouri. In 1819, before the Missouri Compromise went into effect, Congress had organized the Territory of Arkansas, without any restriction of slavery. Secondly, it must be repeated that what Bork is pleased to call "Mr. Jaffa's argument" is *Lincoln's* argument, and represents *Lincoln's* incorporation of the Declaration of Independence into constitutional jurisprudence. The Gettysburg Address means nothing less. Does Bork really think that the politicians of the Republican Party in 1860—lacking Bork as their legal adviser—didn't know what they were doing?

III.

We come at last to this concluding effusion:

> Again and again, Mr. Jaffa quotes Jefferson, Madison, and others about the principles of equality, liberty, and natural rights. "No one can at one and the same time be a legal positivist and an adherent of the original intentions of the Framers. For the Framers were very far from being either moral skeptics or legal positivists. Their commitment to the natural rights and natural law doctrine of the Declaration of Independence represented the most profound of their original intentions." That observation is simply silly. The Framers were not legal positivists for the very good reason that no one who makes law can be. The lawgiver must have ideas of right and wrong that antecede the law he makes. *The Framers wrote law, presumably embodying as much of their thinking on natural rights as prudence allowed, and the judge is bound to follow the law no matter what he thinks of its correspondence to natural law.* That means that, in his judicial capacity, though in no other, the judge must be a legal positivist. Which further means, contrary to Mr. Jaffa, that only a legal positivist judge can be an adherent of the Framers' original intent.

If Judge Bork understands correctly the words I have italicized, and really believes them, he and I have nothing to differ about. Our continuing differences turn apparently on what he understands by legal positivism. On this question we repeat the words of that fountain of authority, Mr. Justice Rehnquist:

> If . . . a society adopts a constitution and incorporates in that constitution safeguards for individual liberty, these safeguards do indeed take on a generalized moral rightness or goodness. They assume a general social acceptance neither because of any intrinsic worth nor because of any unique origins in someone's idea of natural justice but instead simply because they have been incorporated in a constitution by the people.

Does Bork believe, with Rehnquist, that the moral authority of freedom is derived from the positive law? Or that the moral authority of the positive law is derived from the nature of human freedom? According to Rehnquist, there is no objective rational moral order independent of human will, by which the will of the legislator—or the judge interpreting that will—ought to be guided. According to Rehnquist "the ideas of right and wrong" that guided the Framers, whether they called them natural rights or something else, were "value judgments," with no reasoned justification. Does Bork too regard the natural rights enshrined in the Constitution as arbitrary preferences, or the rational principles the Framers believed them to be? Consider, for example, a judge confronted with a demand for the recognition of an equal constitutional right of single sex marriage. It makes all the difference whether that judge thinks of marriage as entirely a creation of positive law, or as having an antecedent existence in natural law.

I agree with Judge Bork, that it is the Framers' idea of natural law, and not any other, that should guide the judge. But how can a legal positivist be faithful to the intention of the Framers if he does not believe in the existence of the moral order that the Framers believed the Constitution was designed to implement? Where can such a judge turn to deny that a right claimed under the Ninth Amendment by a liberal activist is not a genuine constitutional right? The moral reasoning of the natural law tradition is stringent. Positivism in itself neither admits nor requires reasoned justification. All it needs is votes.

I believe I have now answered every point made against me in Judge Bork's review of *Original Intent and the Framers of the Constitution.*

March 19, 1994

Natural Law, the Constitution, and Robert Bork

In "Natural Law and the Constitution" (*First Things*, March 1992) Judge Bork declares that Justice Clarence Thomas's "past writing" embraces the view that "justices could use natural law to alter the Constitution." He also attributes to Professor Hadley Arkes the same opinion, when he writes that according to Arkes

> moral reasoning . . . may properly be employed by judges to create new constitutional principles. A natural law judge would make positive laws out of his own perception of universal moral principles. Those moral postulates would then become just as binding on the polity as the written law of the Constitution. That is where we legal positivists get off.

Judge Bork attributes similar views to Messrs. Russell Hittinger and William Bentley Ball. I do not speak for any of these gentlemen, but I do not believe that any of them hold anything like the opinion that Bork attributes to them. Bork is attacking a straw man of his own invention.

Since citations to my publications occur in the writings of Mr. Justice Thomas, I assert categorically that I regard the notion that the justices of the Supreme Court may in any way alter or amend the law of the Constitution by importing into it ideas or principles drawn from outside the Constitution itself is utterly abhorrent to sound jurisprudence. Like Judge Bork, I am devoted to the principle that the justices of the Supreme Court are bound unqualifiedly by the positive law of the Constitution, and that the positive law of the Constitution is to be understood in terms of the original intent of those who framed and those who ratified it. Where Judge Bork and I differ, is in our answer to the question, What was the original intent of those who framed and those who ratified the Constitution?

The classic statement of the idea of a jurisprudence of original intent is the following:

> No one, we presume, supposes that any change in public opinion or feeling . . . should induce the court to give to the words of the Constitution a more liberal construction . . . than they were intended to bear when the instrument was framed and adopted. Such an argument would be altogether inadmissible in any tribunal called upon to interpret it. If any of its provisions are deemed unjust there is a mode prescribed in

the instrument itself by which it may be amended; but while it remains unaltered, it must be construed now as it was understood at the time of its adoption. It is not only the same in words, but the same in meaning . . . it speaks not only in the same words but with the same meaning and intent with which it spoke when it came from the hands of its framers, and was voted on and adopted by the people of the United States.

What is remarkable about this unexceptionable dictum, is that it occurs in Chief Justice Taney's opinion in the case of *Dred Scott*. I believe that Judge Bork would agree with me that the meaning of the words of the Constitution were never more disastrously misunderstood than by Chief Justice Taney in this opinion. This proves, if proof were necessary, that being committed to a jurisprudence of original intent is not a sufficient condition for a jurisprudence of original intent. During the Senate hearings on Judge Bork's nomination to the Supreme Court, Senator Metzenbaum read this passage from Taney's opinion to Judge Bork, and asked his comment. Judge Bork replied that the Devil could quote Scripture. By this Judge Bork admitted that these words of Taney, taken by themselves, were Scriptural. Why it was the Devil quoting them, however, Judge Bork did not explain to Senator Metzenbaum. Elsewhere however Judge Bork has told us where Taney went wrong in *Dred Scott*. In so doing he has demonstrated as complete a misunderstanding of the Constitution as Taney himself.[1] He has done so precisely because he has failed to grasp the manner and sense in which natural law principles are present *within* the Constitution, as elements of the *positive law* of the Constitution, and in accordance with the *original understanding* of those who framed and those who ratified the Constitution.

If we ask how and where natural law enters the text of the Constitution, our answer is, with its very first words, "We the people . . . " Who is this people? Whence did it derive the authority to "ordain and establish" the Constitution? The answer is that the people in question became the people of the United States when they

---

[1] Judge Bork seems utterly incapable of understanding that the issue in *Dred Scott* was not whether Congress or the Court should decide the legal status of slavery in the territories. Congress in the territorial laws of 1850 had made any dispute as to the status of slavery directly appealable to the Supreme Court. The fundamental question was whether or not the Constitution, as it applied to the territories, was to be interpreted in the light of the fact that the Negro was by nature a human person, and not a piece of property belonging to the irrational order of being.

assume[d] among the powers of the earth, the separate and equal station to which the law of nature and of nature's God entitle[d] them . . .

In short, it was because of the authority of the laws of nature, that the American people had the right, first of all, to "ordain and establish" the Constitution. Before exercising such a right, it was necessary for them

to dissolve the political bands which [had] connected them with another . . .

Only then might they

institute new government, laying its foundations on such principles and organizing its powers in such form, as to them shall seem most likely to effect their safety and happiness.

But where did the people gain the authority, first to separate themselves from Great Britain, and then to institute new governments for themselves? In the famous second paragraph of the Declaration of Independence, the essential and axiomatic ground in natural law of the authority of the people is set forth.

We hold these truths to be self-evident: that all men are created equal, that they are endowed by their Creator with certain unalienable rights, that among these are life, liberty, and the pursuit of happiness. That to secure these rights, governments are instituted among men, deriving their just powers from the consent of the governed.

Because all men are created equal, no man is by nature the ruler of another man—as any man can be said to be by nature the ruler of any dog—so that legitimate political authority can be said to be grounded in consent. The Massachusetts Bill of Rights is more explicit as to how this takes place:

The body politic is formed by a voluntary associations of individuals; it is a social compact by which the whole people covenants with each citizen and each citizen with the whole people that all shall be governed by certain laws for the common good.

The people "covenant" with each other to form a people, before they have the authority to dissolve or reestablish political authority. The origin of the authority of the people, taken as a whole, lies in the rights with which each individual, has been "endowed by [his] Creator," rights which are better secured by governments than they possibly can be by individuals acting alone. But "the people" consists of human individuals who have agreed among themselves to be a people, in order to have the protection that government can offer. From the people are derived "the just powers" of government. Not *any* powers, only *just* powers. The government cannot derive from the people powers that individuals did not consent should be exercised on their behalf. In Jefferson's words,

> The error seems not sufficiently eradicated, that the operations of the mind, as well as the acts of the body, are subject to the coercion of the laws. But our rulers can have no authority over such natural rights, only as we have submitted to them. The rights of conscience we never submitted, we could not submit.

While Jefferson had primarily in mind the free exercise of religion, it is certainly the case that the "operations of the mind" extend to everything that is the subject of contemplative reason and discursive speech. Limited government in general, and the freedoms of the First Amendment—but not only of the First Amendment—are clearly grounded in and derived from the natural rights of individuals.

Governments—that is to say, legitimate governments, not governments based upon force or fraud—are instituted "to secure these [aforementioned] rights." Whenever any form of government "becomes destructive of *these ends*, it is the right of the people to alter or abolish it." The right of the people to alter or abolish governments is not unqualified. The right of overthrowing governments, and of instituting new ones, is not a right *ad libitum*, a right that may be exercised for any purpose whatever. The people have a right to overthrow only governments destructive of certain ends, and to institute new governments only as they are conducive to the same ends. Those ends however are fixed by the nature of man. The people are at full liberty to deliberate as to what means conduce to those ends, but they do not deliberate as to the ends themselves.

As Jefferson wrote in another context, the people are themselves subject to the moral law. They are not a gang of robbers. Because—but only because—they are a "good people" they may confidently appeal "to the Supreme Judge of the World, for the rectitude of [their] intentions."

Judge Bork, we know, denies any constitutional status to the Declaration of Independence. But this is in direct opposition to the authority of the Father of the Constitution. In 1825 Jefferson asked Madison to recommend works that ought to be considered authoritative for the law faculty of the new University of Virginia. Madison recommended, and Jefferson agreed, that of the "best guides" to "the distinctive principles of the government of our own state and of that of the United States," the *first* is, "The Declaration of Independence, as the fundamental act of Union of these States." To speak of the Declaration as the "act of Union" means of course that it is the first law of the United States, the law which is constitutive of the American people as a legal person among the nations. The Declaration was therefore not only an instrument of separation of the several colonies from Great Britain—but of combination of the states with each other. The principles enunciated in the Declaration are therefore not only those justifying separation, but also those by which the union of the states will be governed. The more perfect union under the Constitution will therefore be one more perfectly embodying these principles. The natural law doctrines to which constitutional interpreters ought to turn are not any that anyone might turn to, as Judge Bork suggests. They are the principles endorsed by the generation that framed and ratified the constitution itself. The positive law of the Constitution cannot be understood without them *because they are the ground of that positive law*.

April 21, 1992

The Inkblot Constitution

In "Beside the Law" (*National Review*, October 19, 1992) Judge Robert H. Bork continues to display his virtuosity as a critic of judicial tyranny, but he does not seem to be aware that there is any other kind. Certainly the Supreme Court has threatened us—notably but not exclusively in *Roe v. Wade*—with a usurpation of powers by an unelected minority. But those who framed and those who ratified the Constitution of the United States were even more concerned with the elected tyranny of the majority. In the tenth *Federalist* the greatest of all concerns expressed by Madison is that, in popular governments "measures are too often decided, not according to the rules of justice and the rights of the minor party; but by the superior force of an interested and over-bearing majority." In the *Notes on Virginia*, Jefferson thundered, "An *elective despotism* was not the government we fought for . . ." And in the Kentucky Resolutions, he asked "if it be not a tyranny which the men of our choice have conferred on our President, and the President of our choice has assented to" in the enactment of the Alien and Sedition acts.

Justices O'Connor, Souter, and Kennedy, deserve all the scorn that Bork pours upon them for refusing to overturn *Roe*. He cites the following language, by which the three upheld the continuing alleged constitutional right to an abortion.

> [T]he most intimate and personal choices a person may make in a lifetime, choices central to personal dignity and autonomy, are central to the liberty protected by the Fourteenth Amendment. At the heart of liberty is the right to define one's own existence, of meaning, of the universe, and of the mystery of human life.

As Judge Bork rightly observes, "This is New Age jurisprudence, and from it a judge can go anywhere."

The *novus ordo seclorum*[1]—the new order of the ages—that attended the birth of a nation in 1776 had little in common with the pretentious rhetoric quoted above. The United States of America did however become independent by virtue of an appeal to "the laws of nature and of Nature's God." One's right "to define one's own

---

[1] The motto on the obverse of the Great Seal of the United States. The motto on the reverse is *e pluribus unum*. For verification, see your local friendly dollar bill!

existence" was not understood to be merely idiosyncratic. As Jefferson said, the people are independent of all "but moral law." The moral law, however, defines the people, the people do not define the moral law. The Constitution was framed and ratified by those who believed that all positive law had as its purpose, to give effect to the natural rights that human beings possessed under the natural law. Because Judge Bork denies this, his jurisprudence has little in common with the original intent of those who framed and those who ratified the Constitution.

Consider Judge Bork's view of the due process clause of the Fifth and Fourteenth amendments. "The original purpose of the clause," he writes, "was to guarantee just procedure in the application of a law's substance . . . the due process clause gives *no slightest hint* of what liberties may not be curbed by legislation" (emphasis added). But suppose a law requires Jews to wear yellow badges. Suppose that someone convicted under this law appeals to the Supreme Court. Would Judge Bork have the Court limit the scope of due process only to the questions of whether the defendant a) was a Jew and b) had gone out without his badge? Would "judicial restraint" forbid the justices to ask whether the law itself was substantively constitutional? It is quite possible that the next Congress will pass a "freedom of choice" act, whose purpose will be to restore *Roe* to its pristine vigor. Where in the Constitution is the enumerated, or necessary and proper power of Congress, authorizing such a law? Would Judge Bork call it judicial activism for the Court to inquire into the constitutional morality of such a law?

In his book, *The Tempting of America*, Judge Bork wrote approvingly of the Supreme Court's decision in the notorious *Slaughterhouse Cases* (1873), upholding the constitutionality of a Louisiana law granting a monopoly requiring all butchers in the New Orleans area to pay for the use of one company's abattoir. It is a fair assumption that the legislature had been bribed, and that its members were splitting the company's monopoly profits. Is not the authorizing of monopolies for no valid public purpose (or for one which is a transparent pretext), levying a tax without the consent of the governed? Mr. Justice Field, the last of Abraham Lincoln's appointees to the Court, wrote a brilliant dissent, grounded in the equal natural rights of the citizens, which Judge Bork however denounced as an attempt at illicit judicial activism.

Professor Douglas Kmiec of the University of Notre Dame Law School—formerly head of the Office of Legal Counsel in the Meese Justice Department, the same that brought forward Judge Bork's nomination to the Supreme Court—has commented as follows about Bork's conception of the due process clause:

> [I]t is analytically silly not to recognize that, at some point, procedure is substance and that appropriate procedures must include a check against arbitrary governmental actions. [2]

Judge Bork's nomination to the Supreme Court foundered on his refusal to recognize a constitutional right of privacy. It was this, and not the propaganda campaign of the Left that was decisive against him. In 1968, however, Judge Bork had found "persuasive" the concurring opinion of Mr. Justice Goldberg, in *Griswold* (1965). Goldberg had cited, in support of a constitutional right of privacy, the Ninth Amendment, which says that

> The enumeration in the Constitution, of certain rights, shall not be construed to deny or disparage others retained by the people.

In 1987 and still today, Judge Bork has denied that the Ninth Amendment is the source of any constitutional rights that the Court ought to protect. Professor Kmiec quotes Bork as arguing that the words of the Ninth Amendment "are a meaningless 'inkblot' . . ." [3] But, Kmiec says, "Bork's inkblot assertion cannot stand. If the Constitution is law, then no part of it can go unenforced." Kmiec quotes Madison, speaking of the proposed rights in the Bill of Rights, that

> [i]f they are incorporated into the constitution, independent tribunals of justice will consider themselves in a peculiar manner the guardians of those rights; they will be an impenetrable bulwark against every assumption of power in the legislative or executive.

Kmiec notes that "Madison's assumption that the Bill of Rights, including the Ninth Amendment, would be judicially enforced directly rebuts Bork, who claims that the role of judges in this regard went 'wholly unmentioned.'" [4]

Since the Ninth Amendment speaks of "rights retained by the people," it is obvious that the Constitution itself assumes that the people possess rights antecedently to the Constitution. But what can be the source of these rights? They cannot be rights under positive

---

[2] Kmiec, *The Attorney General's Lawyer*, p. 42.

[3] *Op. cit.*, p. 35.

[4] *Op. cit.*, p. 37.

law, and hence must be rights under natural law. According to Professor Kmiec, the "only credible source of right having any meaningful influence on the Founders is natural law." As long as Judge Bork continues his radically unhistorical and positivist view of the Constitution, much more of it than the Ninth Amendment will remain only an "inkblot" to him.

October 14, 1992

Is the Constitution Good? (And If So, Why?)

Good and being are convertible terms.
Thomas Aquinas

The intensity of the Bork/Jaffa debate may have left *National Review* readers somewhat bewildered by the details of the arguments, and wondering what was really at stake. I thought I would rescue them from their perplexity by an objective overview, like that of the man who wrote "An Impartial History of the War between the States from a Southern Point of View."

The first thing that needs to be said is that Judge Bork did not write a review of my book, *Original Intent and the Framers of the Constitution: A Disputed Question*. The only portions of the book that attracted his attention were the ones that bore on him personally. It is important to recall that in the July 9, 1991 issue of *National Review*, I had published a critique of Judge Bork's book, *The Tempting of America*, entitled "The Closing of the Conservative Mind." The thesis of that book can be encapsulated in the proposition that activist judges invent rights, nowhere to be found in the Constitution, and then invent judicial remedies for violations of those rights, creating constitutional law that has no constitutional foundation. That thesis is one in which I concur: it is mine no less that Judge Bork's. The question remains, however, How does one go about discovering what rights are genuinely in the Constitution? That resolves itself in the end into the question of, What were the original intentions of the Framers and Ratifiers of the Constitution?

In *Tempting* Judge Bork argued that "substantive due process" was the means by which judges invented imaginary rights, and that the first example, and fatal precedent, was in Chief Justice Taney's opinion in *Dred Scott* (1857). There, said Bork, Taney had invented a right to slave ownership that was "nowhere in the Constitution." Bork made this assertion the cornerstone of the argument of his entire book. It was unfortunate that he did so, because the lawfulness of slave ownership is recognized in the most conspicuous way in at least three distinct places in the Constitution of 1787, above all in the fugitive slave clause of Article IV. Because of this utter disregard of the actual text of the Constitution, Bork's argument collapsed like a house of cards.[1]

---

[1] In his rebuttal of my reply in the March 21, 1994 *National Review*, Bork threw in the towel when he said that the recognition of the right to own slaves in the antebellum

Judge Bork never denied this gross and fatal error. Instead he launched a campaign of invective, attempting to camouflage the shambles of his book, by using his authority to discredit me. My intention here is not to go over old ground, but rather to explain as simply as possible, why our differences are far more important than the reputations of either Judge Bork or myself, why they are more important than any question of public policy now being discussed in the pages of *National Review*, or of any other journal. Our differences go to the question of, What are the ultimate principles, the ultimate sources of obligation, of the Constitution of the United States? Or, put even more simply, Why is the Constitution good?

My answer to that question is that of Abraham Lincoln. The Constitution is good because it is the embodiment, to the greatest extent possible in 1787, of the principles of the Declaration of Independence. What follows are excerpts from a meditation by Abraham Lincoln on Proverbs 25:11. "A word fitly spoken is like apples of gold in pictures of silver."

> All this is not the result of accident. It has a philosophical cause. Without the *Constitution* and the *Union*, we could not have attained the result; but even these are not the primary cause of our great prosperity. There is something back of these, entwining itself more closely about the human heart. That something, is the principle of "Liberty to all"—the principle that clears the *path* for all—gives *hope* to all—and, by consequence, *enterprise* and *industry* to all.

> The expression of that principle, in our Declaration of Independence, was most happy, and fortunate. *Without* this, as well as *with* it, we could have declared our independence of Great Britain; but *without* it, we could not, I think, have secured our free government and consequent prosperity. The assertion of that *principle*, at *that time*, was the word, *"fitly spoken"* which has proved an "apple of gold" to us. The *Union*, and the *Constitution*, are the *picture* of *silver*, subsequently framed around it. The picture was made, not to *conceal*, or *destroy* the apple; but to *adorn* and *preserve* it. The *picture* was made *for* the apple—*not* the apple for the picture . . . [emphasis original].

Constitution "rests entirely upon a few provisions . . . " Indeed! Upon how many provisions of the Constitution does the right to the free exercise of religion rest? Or freedom of speech? Or freedom of the press?

According to Lincoln, the essential relationship of Union and Constitution to the principles of the Declaration is one of means to ends. Lincoln argued that the purposes of the words of the Constitution must be found in their purest form, not in the Constitution, but in the Declaration. Even the concessions to slavery had to be looked upon in this way. Under the Articles of Confederation there would have been no Union government strong enough to contain the growth and expansion of slavery. The concessions to slavery in the Constitution of 1787, Lincoln argued, were ultimately in the interest of the slaves themselves, because they made possible a government that could, in Lincoln's words, place slavery "in the course of ultimate extinction." That it fell to Lincoln to preside over that "ultimate extinction" was no accident. Lincoln's presidency, like the growth and prosperity of the Union, both before and after his presidency, had "a philosophical cause."

The statement of principles in the Declaration of Independence is a compressed summary of "the laws of nature and of nature's God." It represents the convictions of those we still call the Founding Fathers. It consists in an articulation—and, I would contend, a perfection—of a natural law tradition that goes back at least to Aristotle, and that embodies the ethical core of the Judeo-Christian tradition as well. Although Judge Bork gives no hint of it, there is in my book a concise, systematic, comprehensive exposition of the political and constitutional doctrine of the Declaration. In it, I gave an extended explanation of why Madison and Jefferson called the Declaration the *first* of the *best guides* to the principles of the governments of both Virginia and the United States, and *why they required the professors of law at the University of Virginia to teach this.* (Judge Bork could not have accepted appointment to this faculty.)

There is no space here to recapitulate all of what I have written in *Original Intent.* But I remind my readers that the *constitutional status* of the proposition "that all men are created equal" is one that Lincoln inherited from Madison and Jefferson, and for this reason, at Gettysburg he said the nation had been dedicated to it at its birth. Here is an excerpt from my gloss upon that greatest of all political texts.

> The equality of mankind is . . . to be understood in the light of this two-fold inequality: the inequality of man and the lower order of Creation, on the one hand, and the inequality of man and God, on the other. The contemplation of the very differences between man, beast, and God, instructs us in what it is that makes man by nature the master of beast. But the contemplation of the same differences instructs us in man's imperfections. Man's wisdom, goodness, and rectitude [unlike

God's] are forever limited by the fact that his passions are often at war with his reason, and his self-interest with his goodness and rectitude. Hence no man is good enough, in Lincoln's words, to govern another without his consent. For consent is the reciprocal of equality. And in the reciprocity of equality and consent we find that ground of morality that Lincoln found in the great proposition. The consent arising from equality assures . . . that those who live under the law will share in making the law they live under, and that those who make the law must live under the law that they make. Constitutions are devices—inventions of prudence—to carry into practice these principles. (Op. cit., p. 81.)

Thus the goodness of the Constitution is rooted in the goodness of the created universe. The equality of man and man is rooted in the inequality of man and beast, on the one hand, and the inequality of man and God, on the other. No man has the right to play God, or treat his fellow men as beasts. This is the ground in nature of the denunciation of tyranny, and the moral necessity of the rule of law. It follows from this that there is no more right in a majority than in a minority, to rule others without their consent. And no distinction among human persons can be drawn on the basis of race or color that is not morally and constitutionally irrelevant.

The principles of the Declaration alone permit us to make the indispensable distinction in the 1787 Constitution between its principles and is compromises. It was because of his inability to admit the necessary role of these principles in constitutional interpretation, that Judge Bork simply read the compromises with slavery out of the Constitution. Yet without this distinction, we cannot understand the role of the Civil War amendments, and in particular of the Fourteenth Amendment, in constitutional jurisprudence today. For the word "equal" enters the Constitution in the Fourteenth Amendment, and by its presence indicates that the equality of the Declaration, which could not find full expression in the antebellum document, now has assumed its rightful role. If Chief Justice Earl Warren, in his opinion for the Court in *Brown v. Board of Education* (1954) had grounded his interpretation on the Declaration of Independence, as the source of the meaning of the "equal protection" clause, he would have declared the Constitution to be color blind, as Justice Harlan had done in his dissenting opinion in *Plessy*, in 1896. Disregarding the philosophical meaning of equality at the root of the equal protection clause, Warren turned instead to modern "psychological knowledge" to define the wrongfulness of segregated schools. Yet in 1954, as in 1994, one could find psychologists to give expert testimony to support any thesis whatever that might find its way into a court of law. Warren could have found innumerable psychologists to testify against the ones he cited. Because of the arbitrary way he arrived at his conclusion we have been visited ever since by a plague of race-based "remedies," in which "equal" (and the Constitution) means whatever the judge wants it to mean. And Judge Bork, as inhibited as Warren and his judicial progeny from looking to the philosophical ground in nature of human equality, is no better able than Warren to pronounce the Constitution color blind.

* * * * *

The crisis in contemporary jurisprudence is identical in principle with what Leo Strauss called the crisis of the west. It represents an alienation from the philosophical tradition of natural law, as well as from the ethical tradition of the Bible.

In *Original Intent* I found this alienation represented far more lucidly by Chief Justice Rehnquist than by Judge Bork. In his celebrated essay, "The Notion of a Living Constitution"—about which I wrote at length— Justice Rehnquist takes to task those who

> ignore . . . . the nature of political value judgments in a democratic society. If such a society adopts a constitution and incorporates in that constitution safeguards for individual liberty, these safeguards do indeed take on a generalized moral rightness or goodness. They assume a general social acceptance neither because of any intrinsic worth nor because of any unique origins in someone's idea of natural justice but instead simply because they have been incorporated in a constitution by the people.

This is a clearer statement of legal positivism than any by Judge Bork, but I believe that he agrees with it. What is notable is that "safeguards for individual liberty"—e.g. freedom of speech, freedom of the press, freedom of religion, freedom from arbitrary arrest or imprisonment—are said not to possess "*any intrinsic worth.*" They are said to derive whatever "moral rightness or goodness" they are held to possess, not because of any rights with which we have been "endowed by [our] Creator," but merely because of the arbitrary will embodied in the act of adoption or incorporation. However, if we look again at the Constitution of 1787, together with the amendments of 1791, we see not only safeguards of individual liberty, but safeguards of slavery. Thus Mr. Justice Rehnquist, no more than Judge Bork, has any way of distinguishing the principles of the Constitution from its compromises. According to Mr. Justice Rehnquist's legal positivism, the safeguards of slavery and those of individual liberty, possess the *identical ground* of "moral rightness or goodness." Now this was exactly the position taken by John C. Calhoun, and by all the seceding states in 1860-61. They seceded, and fought the Civil War, because they denied any right of the free states (e.g. by their personal liberty laws) to draw any *moral* distinction between the guarantees of slavery, and any other constitutional guarantees.

According to Mr. Justice Rehnquist, the distinction between freedom and slavery is a moral judgment, and all moral judgments, he tells us, are "value judgments," and no one can, he says, demonstrate the superiority of one value judgment to another. Constitutions, resting as they do upon moral judgments, are therefore acts of will, not of reason. Just as no non-arbitrary moral distinction can be drawn between the safeguards of slavery and the safeguards of liberty in the Constitution of 1787, so no non-arbitrary distinction can be drawn between the American Constitution, and a Nazi or Communist or any other constitution.

It is to little effect that Bill Bennett, or other "cultural conservatives," attempt to promote the virtues of virtue, if public figures of the eminence of Rehnquist and Bork assert that what anyone (e.g. Bill Bennett) calls "virtue" is no more than an emotional expression of an idiosyncratic preference.

April 3, 1994

Graglia's Quarrel with God: Atheism and Nihilism Masquerading as Constitutional Argument

How you, men of Athens, have been affected by my accusers, I do not know; but I, for my part, almost forgot myself, so persuasively did they speak; and yet there is hardly a word of truth in what they have said.

Plato, *The Apology of Socrates*

Professor Graglia's basic charge against me is that of heresy. He denounces my critiques of the jurisprudence of Judge Robert H. Bork and of Chief Justice Rehnquist in *Original Intent and the Framers of the Constitution* and in *Storm Over the Constitution* as a "campaign of vilification" that is "both sad and shabby." He rejects them because, as a "hard core political conservative" I should not have called into question the authority of these high priests of judicial conservatism. There is alas much in Graglia's accusation that resembles not only those against Socrates, but those made against heretics throughout the ages. It is however unusual to be accused of heresy by an atheist, unusual but not unprecedented: there is the case of the Grand Inquisitor.

Let me say however that I do believe that in the context of a free society with a democratic form of government, the quest for consensus in a major political party justifies many concessions for the sake of the larger goals of political partisanship. I supported Judge Bork's nomination, and contributed money to his cause. And even today I believe he would have made a better justice than Kennedy, Souter, or O'Connor. But Rehnquist[1] and Bork[2] (together with former attorney general Meese[3])

---

[1] See, e.g., William H. Rehnquist, "The Notion of a Living Constitution," in *Taking the Constitution Seriously,* Gary L. McDowell, ed. (Dubuque, Iowa: Kendall/Hunt Publishing Co., 1981), p. 72.: "A mere change in public opinion since the adoption of the Constitution, unaccompanied by a constitutional amendment, should not change the meaning of the Constitution."

[2] See, e.g., Robert H. Bork, "Original Intent: The Only Legitimate Basis for Constitutional Decision Making," *Judges Journal* (Summer 1987), p. 12.

[3] See, e.g., Edwin Meese, III, "Toward a Jurisprudence of Original Intent," 11 *Harvard Journal of Law & Public Policy* (1988), p. 5.

have identified themselves with a jurisprudence of original intent. I share with them the conviction that only such a jurisprudence can counteract the inroads of the liberal judicial activism that like a cancer is eating away the substance of our constitution. I have however proved—beyond I think a reasonable doubt—that what they call original intent is not that of those who framed and ratified the Constitution. They identify original intent—as does Graglia—with a legal positivism that is completely alien to the thought of the Founding generation. I do not think that any good purpose can be served by acquiescing in an error of such magnitude.

While I may agree with what Bork or Rehnquist may say (or decide) concerning particular cases, such agreement may be nothing more than an agreement on results. I do not believe that legal positivism, grounded in moral relativism and philosophical nihilism, can effectively counteract that very same legal positivism when it appears in the form of liberal judicial activism. A result oriented conservative jurisprudence does not differ in principle from a result oriented liberal jurisprudence. Alienation from the genuine principles of the American Founding, whether by those calling themselves conservatives or by those calling themselves liberals can undermine fatally, not only constitutional law, but the loyalty and conviction of the citizens themselves, upon which everything else depends.

The core of Graglia's disagreement with me concerns the status of the principles of the Declaration of Independence in their relationship to the Constitution. These are the principles of the natural law, as the Founding generation understood them. Graglia's abhorrence of the idea of the presence of the principles of the Declaration in the Constitution is rooted in his abhorrence of the Declaration itself. He writes that:

> The Declaration . . . consists largely of a lengthy indictment of King George III for a series of alleged misdeeds. It is hardly the sort of thing you would expect to find in a nation's constitution.[4] What it is, of course, is a document meant to justify revolution, that is, illegal action. Having no real law to rely on—being in defiance of law—revolutionaries necessarily

---

[4] Actually, in the indictment of the British king and Parliament, nearly every element of American constitutionalism is presented, in the denunciation of its violation. E.g., interfering with the independence of the judiciary, violating separation of powers, rendering "the military independent of an superior to the civil power," "depriving us in many cases of the benefits of trial by jury," "imposing taxes on us without our consent," etc. The Declaration is a very textbook of constitutionalism. Graglia should read it some time.

come to rely on the law of God, God being so marvelously unprotesting.

And again: "The American colonies separated from Great Britain not because they had "authority" to do so—they were acting in defiance of authority—but simply because they had the power to do so." Graglia's contempt for the argument put forth by the American people on July 4, 1776—and celebrated as the birthday of the nation ever since—is boundless. It is hard to tell whether that contempt is greater for the natural law to which they appealed, or for the God to whom it is attributed. With the demise of the U.S.S.R. it is extraordinary to find such militant atheism today outside the ranks of liberal academics. Graglia's quarrel is with the American people who for more than two hundred years have regarded the Declaration of Independence as an authentic expression and justification of their identity as a free and independent people.

Graglia denies that natural law is "real law." He does not deny that the Signers of the Declaration, and the American people, then and since, believed it to be real law. Nor does he deny the seriousness with which the American people had, before 1776, regarded their obligation to the laws of Great Britain. Nor does he deny that—in their own minds—the Americans of 1776 could not have renounced that obligation without the gravest justification, and without appealing to God for the "rectitude of [their] intentions." Graglia not only thinks that what they did was illegal, but that the American Revolution represented nothing but the successful use of force. According Graglia, force, not right, lies at the foundation of our independence, and of our Constitution. He recognizes no moral distinction between, for example, the American Revolution and the Bolshevik Revolution, between a revolution based upon the principles of the Declaration of Independence and one based upon the principles of the Communist Manifesto.

Graglia's reserves his greatest derision for the following:

Jaffa's statement that "the goodness of the Constitution is rooted in the goodness of the created universe" is not a statement of fact, testable and falsifiable, but an expression of mystical feeling to which only another mystic can respond. It is meant not to communicate thought, but to impart a religious emotion. If taken as meant to convey meaning, one would have to ask whether "goodness" or even "created" are words that can properly be applied to the universe. I think Wittgenstein would see the need for some drastic philosophical therapy, probably shock treatment.

Nothing is more revealing than Graglia's doubt whether "goodness" or "created" can "properly be applied to the universe." Let me introduce him to the Bible, and to Genesis, chapter 1, verse 1: "In the beginning God created the heavens and the earth." The same chapter ends, verse 31, "And God saw everything that he had made, and behold, it was very good." For most of us, "goodness" and "created" are understood primarily and essentially, as well as properly, as applied to the universe. For most of us, all other meanings of "goodness" and "created" are derivative from this. Graglia's private beliefs are irrelevant, but within the context of western civilization, and certainly within the context of American civilization, the meaning of these words is drawn from the Bible.

Graglia finds meaningless the appeal to God in the Declaration. Undoubtedly he would find equally meaningless the proposition upon which Jefferson grounded the argument of the Virginia Statute of Religious Liberty, that "Almighty God hath created the mind free. . ." He would also consider meaningless that final purpose of the Constitution, as set forth in the Preamble, to "secure the blessings of liberty, to ourselves and our posterity." What did the American people mean by a blessing, except something good in the eyes of God, something in the gift of God, something that one prayed that God might think you deserved? In the words of the late Justice William O. Douglas, "We are a religious people, and our institutions presuppose a Supreme Being."[5] To repeat, Graglia's private beliefs are of no concern to us whatever, but he has no right to interpret the Constitution in the light of his beliefs, rather than of those who framed and ratified it.

The very first sentence of the Declaration of Independence appeals to "the laws of nature and of nature's God" as justification of our separation from Great Britain. Everything that follows is an elucidation of what is meant by this appeal. The rights to life, liberty, and the pursuit of happiness are rights with which, under the laws of nature, we have been "endowed by [our] Creator." The violations charged to the British crown and parliament are not merely violations of positive law, but of those provisions of positive law that were regarded as implementations of the natural law. In the *Summary View of the Rights of British America* of 1774—whose composition led to his selection by the Continental Con-

---

[5] *Zorach v. Clauson*, 343 U.S. 300, 313 (1952).

gress as draftsman of the Declaration of Independence—Jefferson told the King that "our properties shall [not] be taxed by any power on earth, but our own. The God who gave us life, gave us liberty at the same time: the hand of force may destroy, but cannot disjoin them." Certainly no more unconditional commitment to the idea of a non-arbitrary standard of political right is imaginable, a standard in nature to which positive law is subject. Jefferson, unlike Graglia, did not think that might makes right. Here is Graglia's opinion of those who use such language:

> Perhaps nothing better or more concisely illustrates the difference between believers and skeptics regarding natural law than their reactions to such a pronouncement: believers get a thrill of profound insight, and skeptics hear only meaningless noise. Believers think some deep thinker has announced an important discovery; skeptics realize that another pedant has become so fascinated by the magic of language that he has forgotten its function or limits.

In his famous letter to Henry Lee of 1825, Jefferson said of the Declaration of Independence that it was "intended to be an expression of the American mind," and so it has ever been regarded.

But is Graglia really the skeptic he thinks he is? He says that he believes only in concepts that are "testable and falsifiable," that is to say, empirically verifiable, as approved by Wittgenstein's epistemology. But what if it turns out that this positivism is itself based upon assumptions—acts of faith—as indemonstrable as any he attributes to the believers in God or natural law?

Is the existence and identity of Lino Graglia a verifiable fact? Can he prove to us that he is possessed of an identity, that makes him, and not someone or something else responsible for the checks he signs, the books he writes, the children he fathers? (We are reminded by the "bed trick" in Shakespeare's *Measure for Measure* that either partner can be deceived as to who the other is!) Graglia's identity does not consist in his body, since his body, like that of any living organism, is merely a metabolic process continually replacing its material components. The human body—like all living bodies—is a stream that is never the same, like the river of Heraclitus, into which one cannot step twice. But does not the metabolic process retain identity in its form, even as it replaces matter? Just look at any old photograph of oneself, to see that one's form is also continually changing. But is there not resemblance? Certainly, but resemblance is not identity. Some resemblances to others may be greater than to our former selves. What about memory? Of all means of identification, this is certainly the most treacherous. Names of course are mere externals. We may make the greatest efforts that our names be respected, or honored. But our names are not ourselves. Names represent something other than themselves, but are not themselves the identity of what they represent. What then is there that verifies our identities? The answer, certified by no less verified a philosopher than David Hume, is nothing.[6] Every attempt to verify our own existence or identity presupposes that existence or identity. The existence or identity cannot itself be proved or verified in any way.

Should we then abandon the conviction that we are who we think we are, because we cannot verify ourselves? To do so would mean quite literally, to become insane. Without firm belief in personal identity, the world is reduced to chaos. No one can be more responsible than anyone else for anything that happens. Law becomes impossible. Lino Graglia does not want to admit into the discussion of law anything that he does not think is verifiable. But who will verify the verifiers?

Are we faced with a dilemma? Certainly not. We cannot prove our identities, but we must believe in them nonetheless. An assumption that is the *sine qua non* of all rationality must itself be regarded as rational. There is a prescientific rationality, which is no less rational for being prescientific. Scientists themselves are compelled to employ it when they communicate with each other. They do not even think about verifying each other's identities when discussing the verification of their experiments. The truth is that the rationality of positivism, legal and otherwise, is a subdivision of human rationality. The truth is that Graglia, like Molière's character Mr. Jourdain who was talking prose without knowing it, has depended upon an unconscious act of metaphysical faith all along.

* * * * *

In an earlier version of the article printed in this volume, Graglia declared that he does "not subscribe or have access to any metaphysical or supernatural system of thought . . . [and hence is] unable to participate in discussions of such matters." To speak of the "metaphysical or super-

---

[66] *See* David Hume, 1 *A Treatise of Human Nature,* p. 252 (L.A. Selby-Bigge, ed., 1941). "I may venture to affirm of . . . mankind, that they are nothing but a bundle or collection of different perceptions . . . and are in a perpetual flux and movement."

natural," as Graglia does, implies a claim to know the boundaries that divide the natural and the physical from the supernatural and metaphysical. But can he validate this claim? Let us then consider what is implied in knowing nature. Indeed, let us consider what is implied by the ordinary experience of knowing itself. Since Graglia has been so kind as to refer me to Wittgenstein for instruction, I will here present him with a simplified, or perhaps over simplified, course in Aristotle. Let us call it "Aristotle for lawyers."

All human rationality derives from, and is made possible by the common noun. But what is a common noun? By common noun we mean such as dog, horse, tree, sky, water, stone. "Dog" is a common noun. "Fido" is a proper noun. When we say "Fido" we mean a dog of that name. But Fido is identified as a dog before he is identified as Fido. "Dog" is the universal; "Fido" is a particular. It is the common noun, that is the foundation of all thinking, all rationality. It is a universal, abstracted from the particulars of sensible reality.[7] If I say, "This is a chair," I am saying, at the same time, and by necessary implication, that there are an infinite number of possible chairs,[8] each different from this one. We can, in ordinary conversation, speak of chairs, and understand each other when speaking of chairs, without pointing to a chair, only by virtue of sharing an idea of the chair. Since it refers to any possible chair, the common noun "chair" can itself have no color, form, or size. If we imagine a chair having any sensible attribute, we imagine a particular chair, itself recognizable only because the idea of the chair—or "chairness"—is already predicated of it. A common noun—from which all the parts of speech are compounded—can be perceived only by the eye of the mind. It can have no attribute accessible to sense perception. Yet this idea—this immaterial reality—is the necessary condition for sensible reality to become intelligible reality. Animals other than man, or many of them, have sense perception, memory, and imagination, and some employ these faculties in an extremely intelligent manner. But they do not have reason properly so called, because their thinking is tied to sensible images, from which their minds never escape. Their memories do not extend beyond the range of the experience provided by their own senses. Whereas human beings can, by virtue of language, have un-

---

[7] Or, we might add, of imagined sensible reality. Mythical creatures, like centaurs or gryphons, are compounded of experienced sensible reality, although not themselves perceived as such.

[8] If only because any finite magnitude is infinitely divisible.

bounded access to the experience of former generations. Subhuman animals can remember nothing that they have not experienced directly. They have neither written nor spoken language, and hence neither books nor verbal traditions.

Why is it that sensibles become intelligibles in the human mind, but not in the minds of horses or dogs or chimpanzees? According to Aristotle it is by virtue of the operation of the "agent intellect." But this is only giving a name to a question, it is not an answer. When the eye sees, it receives the form of the visible object, without its matter, in the same sense that a signet ring leaves its form upon the wax, without its matter. For an eye to see, however, three things are necessary: an eye that can see, an object that can be seen, and light. If the first two are present, but not the third, no seeing takes place. Someone or something had first to say, whether literally or metaphorically, "Let there be light."

For thinking to take place, there must also be three things. The first two are a mind that can think and something that can be thought. As with the eye of the body, the eye of the mind also requires an illumination that transforms potential thinking into actual thinking. Just as every one of us has experienced being in a dark room (or a dark night) before lights (or the sun) removed the darkness, we have all also experienced being in the dark about something we did not understand. Then suddenly (sometimes) we say that we see what we did not see before. Where did that "light" come from?

Animals other than man can witness the same parade of particulars, without abstracting the universals that classify the particulars into varieties, species, and genera. What is it in man—or in the universe—that transforms the sensible experience of particulars into the common nouns that are the building blocks from which all human understanding is compounded? What difference does it make whether we call it God or the agent intellect? It is still a mystery, but no less a reality for being so. It remains true that the freedom of the human mind—and of the human will—are grounded in fact that the mind, when it thinks, can comprehend the objects of sense perception because it is itself free of any material or sensible attributes.

Modern philosophy originated, in part, in the attempt to remove any need to find metaphysical or supernatural explanations of this phenomenon. Graglia is clearly a victim of the illusion that it succeeded. The greatest attempt to come to grips with this problem was that of Kant. Kant's "solution" was to posit two universes: the realm of necessity and the realm of freedom. As part of nature, human beings belonged to the realm of necessity. As part of nature human beings can have their behavior explained in the same way as that of any subhuman animals: as the wholly predetermined reaction to external stimuli and internal instincts. In short, as a natural phenomenon, man could be explained without any recourse to human rationality or human freedom. Yet Kant admitted that the experience of human freedom, was as much an indefeasible reality as the necessity of nature. The categorical imperative was the form of human reason when it obeyed the laws of freedom, which laws represented the complete emancipation of rationality from necessity. Yet, unlike Aristotle, Kant was compelled to posit two universes, and make man at once free and subject to inexorable necessity. Man as part of nature was no more free than the ant or the bee; man as rational being was altogether free. Yet how could man, at one and the same time, be both?

Contemporary behavioral psychology—which today dominates all the social sciences, including law and history—represents an inheritance from Kant. But it forgets Kant's realm of freedom, and treats only of the realm of necessity. It "solves" the problem of the thinking mind by treating all manifestations of thought as forms of non rational behavior, reducible to the same stimuli as determine the behavior of dogs, rats, or chimpanzees. That is to say, it "solves" the problem of human thinking by denying that there is human thinking. There is however one question that we must put to the behavioral psychologists: what is the behavioral explanation of behavioral psychology? Is behavioral psychology itself just a manifestation of, for example, behavioral psychologists' toilet training? The answer, of course, is that the behavioral psychologists recur to a shrunken version of Kant's dualism, by reserving to themselves—but to no one else—a privileged universe. In this universe they alone are not determined by material causes, and are free to pursue the truth as they discover it. But the universe that the behavioral psychologists reserve to themselves is the same one that is described by Aristotle. What then is the agent intellect that turns on the lights for them? And why would the agent intellect (or, God forbid, God!) turn on the lights for them, but not for anyone else? Has anyone, in the whole history of the world, made a greater demand upon human credulity than this? Is not human nature one and the same for all? Are not all men created equally free or equally unfree? Do we not have here a perfect demonstration of how the metaphysical and the supernatural, although expelled with a pitchfork, always return?

A skeptic, in the original meaning of the word, was one who inquires. To doubt was merely the prelude to inquiring. But Graglia's skepticism leads him to deny the metaphysical foundation of skepticism itself. He is another in that long line of descendants of the Cretan who said that all Cretans are liars.

The great proposition that all men are created equal rests upon the same metaphysical foundation as any common noun. For the same reason that the idea of the chair can have no color, the idea of man can have no color. Man is *homo sapien*, the rational animal. The thinking mind thinks only by virtue of language, which is human language only by virtue of the power of the mind to transform sensibles into intelligibles. It is because the common noun can have no color, that we say that the mind has no color, and therefore that man's humanity has no color. This is the ultimate source of the doctrine that the Constitution is, or of right ought to be, color blind.

Because the human species has reason, it has freedom, and with it power both of good and of evil, that no other species possesses. As Adam Smith observed, no one ever saw one dog deliberately exchange one bone for another bone with another dog. If there is an exchange between a big dog with a little bone, and a little dog with a big bone, it is probably because the big dog takes the big bone from the little dog! Yet we cannot say that the big dog is unjust. To call anyone unjust means to engage in a comparison of ideas which is possible only to *homo sapiens*.

Other creatures than man—such as bees and ants—live a communal life, in which there are complex divisions of labor, and elaborate relationships of ruling and being ruled. The queen bee is not elected, but is marked out by nature to perform the functions in the hive that she does perform. And the distinction between worker and drone is also marked by nature. There can be no justice or injustice in the allocation of work and food within the beehive.

It is the teaching of the Declaration of Independence—which Graglia thinks is a mere effusion of religious mysticism—that there is no such distinction between man and man, as there is between bees. Nature does not mark out who is to rule, and who is to be ruled. Nor does it decide, as in the beehive, how the burdens or the benefits are to be allocated. Every such allocation is therefore subject to deliberation and choice, and is therefore in some measure either just or unjust. Throughout human history, myths about human differences have persuaded, or have attempted to persuade human beings, that there are such natural or divinely appointed differences among them, and that some ought to rule, and others to be ruled, without the consent of the latter. And the rulers have invariably given to themselves the lion's share of the benefits, and to others the greatest share of the burdens, of the whole society. Under this dispensation, justice has indeed been nothing but the interest of the stronger.

Contrary to Graglia—and Thrasymachus—the American Revolution is rooted in the conviction that there is a non-arbitrary standard of just and unjust, right and wrong, rooted in man's nature as a rational being.

Shortly before his death, Jefferson wrote an address for a celebration of the fiftieth anniversary of the Glorious Fourth—which, as it turned out, was the day of his own and John Adams' apotheosis. In it Jefferson expressed the doctrine of the Declaration as the "palpable truth, that the mass of mankind has not been born with saddles on their backs, nor a favored few, booted and spurred, ready to ride them . . ." No more succinct summary is possible of how the American Revolution broke with the *ancien regime* of modern Europe, as well as of the ancient world. Or how the American Revolution represented natural right, more than any regime that had preceded it, ancient or modern. But the *novus ordo seclorum*, still proclaimed on the Great Seal (and the dollar bill) meant nothing less. Only in the American Revolution therefore was the conviction expressed that no man is marked out by nature to rule others, and that self-appointed or anointed ranks or privileges are contrary to natural justice. All ranks and privileges, the Americans held, must be justified by the services they render to the equal rights of all the citizens. And that such justification must be ratified by the citizens themselves, by the consent of the governed. It is not therefore mysticism, but the voice of reason itself that says the law of nature and of nature's God is on the side of equal rights, self-government, and the rule of law. It is the voice of reason that denounces tyranny, in whatever guise it may appear.

Let us listen to a passage from a sermon by the Reverend Doctor Samuel Chase, preached before the governor, John Hancock, and the Senate and House of Representatives of the Commonwealth of Massachusetts, on October 25, 1780:

> We want not, indeed, a special revelation from heaven to teach us that men are born equal and free; that no man has a natural claim to dominion over his neighbors, nor one nation any such claim upon another; and that as government is only the administration of the affairs of a number of men combined for their own security and happiness, such a society have a right

freely to determine by whom and in what manner their own af-
fairs shall be administered. These are the plain dictates of that
reason and common sense with which the common parent of
men has informed the human bosom. It is, however, a satisfaction to observe such everlasting maxims of equity confirmed,
and impressed upon the consciences of men, by the instruc-
tions, precepts, and examples given us in the sacred oracles;
one internal mark of their divine original, and that they come
from him "who hath made of one blood all nations to dwell
upon the face of he earth," whose authority sanctifies only
those governments that instead oppressing any part of his family, vindicate the oppressed, and restrain and punish the oppressor.

This lucid exposition of the principles of the Declaration of Independence, when the Revolution was in mid-course, served as prologue to the
inauguration of the government elected under the newly adopted Constitution of Massachusetts. There is not a word in it that could not be
applied equally to the Constitution of the United States of 1787.

According to the good parson, the dictates of right reason are the
dictates of God as much as those revealed in the "sacred oracles." The
first of those dictates is that "men are born equal and free." In the ver-
nacular of public discourse in the Founding, "born equal" and "created
equal" meant the same. Also, "equal" and "free" meant "equally free."
To say that men are born or created equal is to say that, within the human species, unlike bees or ants, who is to be ruler, and who is to be
ruled, is not decided by nature apart from reason. And this assertion is as
verifiable as any made in the name of the most certifiable Wittgen-
steinian positivist!

Because no man (or nation) has a natural right a priori to rule another,
legitimate government arises from the two-fold consent of the governed:
first the unanimous consent of each with all, and of all with each, to
form a political community; and the second, implied in the first, that
government shall be by the majority, as the surrogate for the whole. The
fact that the majority is understood to be the surrogate for the whole,
means that in principle, those who are elected to office represent those
who voted against them as much as those who voted for them. In Jefferson's words, "the minority has equal rights, which equal laws must protect, and to violate which would be oppression." Constitutional government, government by the consent of the governed, is a system of major-

ity rule and minority rights. There is no lawful power in the majority to do anything that would jeopardize the lawful rights of the minority, whether of speech, press, religion, or property. And this is neither more nor less than what is meant by the natural law foundation of the Constitution. Why should the understanding of these general principles, which guided the Framers and Ratifiers of our constitutions, not guide judges in construing those same constitutions? How can understanding the theory of limited government and the rule of law, incite judges to engage in judicial activism in disregard of the rule of law?

The Reverend Dr. Cooper says that the authority of God sanctifies only those governments that do not oppress, but that rather restrain and punish the oppressor. But the authority of God and the authority of right reason are, in the premises, one and the same. By identifying revelation with reason one denies authority to those who would attempt to supersede reason by spurious (or merely mystical!) appeals to the authority of God, as for example to the divine right of kings. Graglia says he is "unable to participate in discussions of such matters." Why?

* * * * *

Graglia writes that "[t]he Constitution makes no mention of the Declaration of Independence, and Jaffa has not produced a single statement by anyone at the constitutional convention or during the ratification debates indicating that it was intended to incorporate the Declaration." The Constitution of 1787, however, ends as follows:

> Done in convention, by the unanimous consent of the States present, the seventeenth day of September, in the year of our Lord one thousand seven hundred and eighty-seven and of the independence of the United States of America the twelfth.

Article V of the Constitution refers to "the year one thousand eight hundred and eight." The Framers clearly had the option of not referring to Christianity, yet "the year of our Lord" does so. And the dual dating links the origin of Christianity with the origin of the independence of the United States. What the Gospels were to Christianity, the Declaration of Independence was to the *novus ordo seclorum*.

Graglia simply ignores what I have written about the relationship of the Preamble of the Constitution to the Declaration. Suffice it that the "one people" that separated from Great Britain in 1776 is the same one "people" that ordained and established the Constitution in 1789. The same laws of nature that entitled them to their separate and equal station entitled them to institute new government. It would have been merely redundant to have repeated that justification. As Cooper's sermon demonstrates—and a thousand other documents could just as easily have been brought forward to prove the same thing—the principles of the Declaration were so universally regarded as "the common sense of the matter" (Jefferson) as not to need repetition.

Graglia writes:

> Jaffa offers only two items of evidence in support of his incredible theory. First, his theory or something like it was contained in the Republican Party platform of 1860 on which Lincoln ran for president. That platform was another document created in an attempt to justify an illegal or extra-legal act, the North's waging war on the South to prevent its withdrawal from the Union.

Now we come to the very head and front of our differences. What Graglia calls my "incredible theory" theory is embodied, by his own account, in two documents, the Declaration of Independence, and the Republican Party platform of 1860, and in two persons, Thomas Jefferson and Abraham Lincoln. Here are the key resolutions from the latter document that, according to Graglia, violate all canons of legal reason:

> 2. That the maintenance of the principles promulgated in the Declaration of Independence and embodied in the Federal Constitution,—"that all men are created equal; that they are endowed by their Creator with certain unalienable rights; that among these rights are life, liberty, and the pursuit of happiness; that, to secure these rights, governments are instituted among men, deriving their just powers from the consent of the governed," is essential to the preservation of our republican institutions; and that the Federal Constitution, the rights of the States, and the union of the States, must and shall be preserved.

> 7. That the new dogma [viz., of *Dred Scott*] that the Constitution, of its own force, carries slavery into any or all of the Territories of the United states, is a dangerous political heresy, at variance with the explicit provisions of that instrument itself, with contemporaneous exposition, and with legislative

and judicial precedent; is revolutionary in its tendency, and subversive of the peace and harmony of the country.

8. That the normal condition of all the territory of the United States is that of freedom; that as our Republican fathers, when they had abolished slavery in all our national territory [viz.. by the Northwest Ordinance] ordained [by the Fifth Amendment] that no person should be deprived of life, liberty, or property without due process of law, it becomes our duty, by legislation, whenever such legislation is necessary, to maintain this provision of the Constitution against all attempts to violate it; and we deny the authority of Congress, of a territorial legislature, or of any individual, to give legal existence to slavery in any Territory of the United States.

According to Graglia, Lincoln and the North waged war on the South "to prevent its withdrawal from the Union." In an earlier version of his paper, Graglia was less bashful in denouncing Lincoln for preventing what he called Southern self-determination. But his meaning has not changed. By calling the action of the elected government of the Union illegal, he assumes that the action of the secessionists was legal. But secession and self-determination are not only not the same, they are opposites. It was self-determination by the American people in 1776 to reject an attempt by the British Parliament, in which they were not represented, to tax them without their own consent. In 1861 the Southern states were however fully represented in the United States Congress, and there were no laws passed by that Congress, which even they had regarded as unconstitutional. The Southern states had freely ratified the Constitution of 1787. In so doing, they had ratified the lawfulness of elections conducted by the rules of that Constitution. What they called the right to secede meant nothing more nor less than setting aside a free and constitutional election because they did not like the results. In consenting to be a member of a free society, one consents to the rule of the majority, provided that that majority is formed in a free election, by free speech, free association, and with respect to the lawful rights of minorities. Self-determination means abiding by the outcome of the voting. It means allowing ballots, not bullets, to decide who shall occupy the offices of government. It means looking only to future elections to reverse the outcomes of elections one does not like. Here is a practical application of that natural law reasoning that Graglia denounces.

Secession would equally justify any State of the Confederacy from seceding from the Confederacy. It would justify any county in seceding from a state, or any township from a county, or any municipality from a township. In accordance with the idea of secession, the mayor of New York City in 1861 recommended that that city secede from the Union. In 1848 Henry David Thoreau had announced what was in effect his secession from Massachusetts, because Massachusetts would not secede in protest against the Mexican War. The idea of the right of secession is therefore, as Lincoln said, of the essence of anarchy.

Why then did the South secede? The heart of the sectional conflict of the 1850s concerned the status of slavery in the territories. This is a topic at once almost infinitely complicated and very simple. I have written at great length about it in *Crisis of the House Divided*, on the Lincoln-Douglas debates, and I am writing at still greater length about it in my work-in-progress on the Civil War. Here I will try to present it in its most simple aspects. In short, the South claimed, as a constitutional right, the right of citizens of the slave states to have the same (or equal) access to the territories, with their human property, as citizens of the free states had with their non-human property. With it, they claimed, also as a constitutional right, a federal guarantee of the security of that property. This opinion of what the Constitution required had long been held in radical proslavery circles. These people believed however that it had received absolute and final confirmation in 1857 in the opinion of Chief Justice Taney, in the case of *Dred Scott*. From the moment that that opinion was published, the proslavery South acted as if Taney's opinion was indistinguishable from the Constitution itself.

Taney had said that the only power possessed by Congress over slavery in the territories, was the power, coupled with the duty, of protecting the owner in his rights. That was interpreted to mean that Congress had a constitutional responsibility to pass laws protecting slave property in any territory that did not itself provide such protection. Such federal slave codes would have meant the greatest extension of federal police power before the New Deal, but in the name of state rights! If this federal guarantee of slavery in the territories had been put into effect, it would have meant that every territory would become a slave territory, and every state formed from a territory would become a slave state. This would have meant the indefinite extension and perpetuation of slavery. This commitment to slavery is the concrete meaning of that Southern right of self-determination that Graglia so earnestly endorses, and that he denounces Lincoln and the Republicans for opposing.

In April of 1860, the seven states of the deep South seceded from the Democratic National Convention in Charleston, when the majority—supporters of Senator Stephen A. Douglas—refused to endorse their demand for a slave code plank in the party platform. This was the original, and originating, act of secession, and it was directed against Douglas, not Lincoln. But the split in the Democratic Party elected Lincoln.

What was it in the *Dred Scott* decision that led to this demand for a slave code? It was, according to the chief justice, that the right to the ownership of slaves was "expressly affirmed" in the Constitution, an assertion manifestly untrue, since (before the Thirteenth Amendment) the words "slave" or "slavery" do not occur in the text of the Constitution. By Taney's dicta, any impairment of that right, in a United States territory, was a violation of the Constitution. The central idea in Taney's opinion—from which everything else radiated—was that, under the Constitution, Negroes, whether free or slaves, were "so far inferior that they had no rights which the white man was bound to respect." Because of this inferiority they did not, as chattel property, differ from horses or dogs or any farm animals. Constitutionally, they were not human beings at all.

Taney himself had recognized that Negroes did in fact belong to "the human family," But, he said, the Framers and Ratifiers of the Constitution did not, and he was bound by their opinions. But why was he bound by their opinions, if they were so wrong about what was a human being? Taney, like Graglia, was a legal positivist, who believed the judge was bound by the positive law, whatever it was. In a Nazi regime that would mean enforcing the laws against Jews or anyone else whose racial inferiority did not qualify them for membership in the same species as the master race.

In fact, everything that Taney said in proof of the assertion that Negroes were not regarded by the Framers and Ratifiers of the Constitution as belonging to the "human family" was false. The laws of the slave states themselves, never regarded slaves solely as chattel property. The state of the law in the slave states in 1787 is well expressed by that Southerner and slave owner, James Madison, in the *Federalist* No. 54. In justifying the compromise formula for federal numbers in Article I, Section 2, he writes:

> But we must deny the fact that slaves are considered merely as property, and in no respect whatever as persons. The true state of the case is, that they partake of both these qualities; being

considered by our laws, in some respects, as persons, and other respects, as property. In being compelled to labor not for himself, but for a master; in being vendible by one master to another master; and in being subject at all times to be restrained in his liberty, and chastised in his body, by the capricious will of another, the slave may appear to be degraded from the human rank, and classed with those irrational animals, which fall under the legal denomination of property. In being protected on the other hand in his life and in his limbs, against the violence of all others, even the master of his labor and his liberty; and in being punishable himself for all violence committed against others; the slave is no less evidently regarded by the law as a member of the society; not as a part of the irrational creation; as a moral person, not as a mere article of property.

And again:

[I]t is only under the pretext that the laws have transformed negroes into subjects of property, that a place is disputed them in the computation of numbers; and it is admitted that if the laws were to restore the rights which have been taken away, the negroes could no longer be refused an equal share of representation with the other inhabitants.

And again:

Might not some surprise also be expressed that those who reproach the southern States with the barbarous policy of considering as property a part of their human brethren, should themselves contend that the government to which all the States are to be parties, ought to consider this unfortunate race more completely in the unnatural light of property, than the very laws of which they complain.

No one not utterly and dogmatically blind can fail to see here the bearing of natural law upon constitutional law. The emancipation of the slaves would only be a restoration of "rights which have been taken away." Since these cannot be rights of positive law, they must be rights of natural law. The positive law, by which Negroes have been transformed into property, is called a "pretext."

Can anyone today, reading Madison's dry summary of the law of slavery—"being compelled to labor not for himself, but for a master . . . being vendible by one master to another master . . . being subject at all

times to be restrained in his liberty and chastised in his body by the capricious will of another"—not shudder in horror? Is this horror not even
greater when we realize that there was no legal marriage among slaves,
and that slave children owed obedience not to their parents but to their
masters? And, of course, that the children, like their parents, could be
sold just as if they had been dogs or horses. Is this not unnatural? Is it
not of the goodness of nature that we can recognize here why slavery is
morally wrong? Is not Graglia's denial that nature provides us with a
non-arbitrary moral standard rooted in will altogether divorced from reason?

That Negroes were not animals of another species was attested by
that supreme manifestation of a common nature: the presence in the
antebellum South of over four hundred thousands of mulattos—of persons in various degrees of mixed blood. These offspring were almost
invariably the result of intercourse between white male masters and
black female slaves, in which the latter had no power to deny their consent. Was this not legalized rape? And—contrary to our brute legal
positivists—is rape less morally offensive because legalized? As Lincoln
pointed out, the Southern obsession with miscegenation overlooked the
fact that slavery itself was the greatest cause of miscegenation. But nature does not permit miscegenation between different species.

Graglia thinks only of the secession of proslavery whites as self-
determination. What about the self-determination of nearly 4,000,000
slaves? Why does Graglia ignore them, although three-fifths of them
added to the representation of their owners, in Congress and in the electoral college. Their numbers therefore added to the power of their op-
pressors, which is exactly the opposite purpose for which the natural law
of representation is intended. According to Graglia, however, it is "an
expression of mystical feeling" to say that the slaves were human beings
with human feelings that accompanied their human nature.

* * * *

I return to Graglia's accusation against me of "a campaign of vilification" against Judge Bork and Chief Justice Rehnquist. In that alleged
campaign, I have repeatedly quoted Rehnquist's assertion that if a
democratic society adopts a constitution and incorporates in that constitution safeguards for individual liberty, these safeguards do indeed take
on a generalized moral rightness or goodness. They assume a general

social acceptance neither because of any intrinsic worth nor because of a unique origin in someone's idea of natural justice but instead simply because they have been incorporated in a constitution by the people. In *Original Intent and the Framers of the Constitution* I have subjected this astonishing oracle to extended analysis. Suffice it for now to notice that, on Rehnquist's own premises, such constitutional safeguards of individual liberty as the free exercise of religion, freedom of speech and of the press, and trial by jury, do not of themselves have "any intrinsic worth." That is to say, they are not chosen because they possess goodness, but possess goodness simply because they are chosen. Now I venture to say that 99.9% of the American people—outside the academy—do not believe this, nor should they. If the day comes when they do believe it, constitutional liberty will crumble into dust. Despotism is wrong because it treats some men as if they were beasts, and others as if they were gods. Hence despotism is condemned by the law of nature. A free constitution, with safeguards against despotism, is in conformity with nature, and possesses goodness from its nature, antecedent to its adoption. By Rehnquist's doctrine, the safeguards of slavery—in the Constitution of 1787—possess the same claim to goodness as the safeguards of individual liberty. By his doctrine neither slavery nor freedom has any standing in the court of reason. Their only standing is that of the positive law and nothing but the positive law. By this doctrine, if the law says that Negroes are chattels, then it is as morally good that they be bought and sold like animals, as that white men be secure in their persons and property. (If white men are slaves—as they were in the ancient world—their slavery would be equally justified.) To point out that this is the logical and necessary consequence of Rehnquist's and Graglia's legal positivism may indeed be shocking. It is also shocking to realize that this in essence was the constitutional doctrine of John C. Calhoun, the philosopher-king of the proslavery South, and the father of the doctrine by which secession was justified. But it is not vilification to tell the truth, however unpleasant that truth may be.

* * * * *

Appendix

Graglia writes:

It is in my view both foolish and false to assert, as Jaffa does, following Salmon P. Chase, that slavery "had never lawfully existed in any territory of the United States" after the states' ratification of the Fifth Amendment in 1791. The Constitution could not have been ratified in 1789, of course, without accepting slavery, and the ratification of the Fifth Amendment was plainly not intended to do what could not be done two years earlier. To think that the Fifth Amendment made slavery illegal is simply to succumb to the temptation to understand words not as tools of communication between human beings but as bearers of inherent power, able to work grand effects regardless of human intent.

The foregoing is an astonishing example of both arrogance and incompetence. What Graglia calls "foolish and false" was in the Republican platform. It was therefore not only Chase's opinion, but Lincoln's, the Republican Party's, and presumably that of everyone who voted Republican in 1860, and who then formed the constitutional majority of the American people.

Graglia writes that the Constitution could not have been ratified in 1789 without accepting slavery. What Graglia should have said—if he had only known it—was that the Constitution could not have been ratified *without accepting slavery in the states in which it already existed.* Like Judge Bork, Graglia is confused about the legal distinction between state and territory in the antebellum Constitution.[9] The fugitive slave clause (Article IV, section 2) says that "no person held to service or labor in one State, under the laws thereof, escaping into *another*, shall . . . be discharged from such service or labor, but shall be delivered up on claim of the party to whom such service or labor may be due" (emphasis added). Fugitive slaves escaping from one state to another state is all that the Constitution here contemplates. Nothing whatever is said about slavery in the territories. However, at the same time that the Convention was meeting, the Congress of the Confederation was passing (July 13, 1787) the Northwest Ordinance, in which it was provided (Article 6) that

---

[9] See, Bork, *The Tempting of America,* p. 30. Judge Bork writes of Taney's opinion in *Dred Scott,* that "When he was done he had denied the power of the federal government to prevent slavery in any state or territory and the power of the federal government to permit a state to bar slavery within its territory." In the antebellum Constitution, each state's "domestic institutions: were exclusively within its own power, and the Republican Platform of 1860 affirmed this without qualification. By common consent, before the Thirteenth Amendment, the federal government *never* had the constitutional power to prevent slavery in a state, and it *never* had the constitutional power to prevent a state from abolishing slavery.

There shall be neither slavery nor involuntary servitude in the said territory, otherwise than in the punishment of crimes whereof the party shall have been duly convicted: *Provided always*, That any person escaping into the same, from whom labor or service is lawfully claimed *in any one of the original states*, such fugitive may be lawfully reclaimed and conveyed to the person claiming his or her labor or service as aforesaid [emphasis added].[10]

Here the rendition of fugitive slaves is limited to the original states. As Lincoln would point out in his great speech at Cooper Union (New York, February 27, 1860):

In 1789, by the first Congress which sat under the Constitution, an act was passed to enforce the Ordinance of '87, including the prohibition of slavery in the Northwestern Territory. . . . In this Congress there were sixteen of the thirty-nine fathers who framed [i.e. signed] the original Constitution. . . . This shows that, in their understanding, no law dividing local from federal authority, nor anything in the Constitution, properly forbade Congress to prohibit slavery in federal territory.

There is therefore no evidence whatever that the ratification of the Constitution of 1787 depended in any way upon the acceptance of slavery in the territories. When Congress gave the Northwest Ordinance full legal status under the new Constitution, it abolished slavery in all the territory then owned by the United States. It was fully consistent with this that, as Chase maintained, the Fifth Amendment should have contemplated that in all future territories—and in the states to be formed from them—the natural law of liberty should prevail.

---

[10] Article VI of the Constitution provides that "The migration or importation of such persons as any of the States *now existing* shall think proper to admit shall not be prohibited prior to the year one thousand eight hundred and eight . . ." (emphasis added). This too repels any idea that the compromises with slavery in the original Constitution extended beyond the original states.

Slaying the Dragon of Bad Originalism: Jaffa Answers Cooper

Robert Bork and Lino Graglia having broken their lances and retired from the field, a new champion has entered the lists. Charles (Don Carlos) Cooper has now saddled his Rosinåte, charging to the rescue of the Dulcinea of Good Originalism, from the Jaffa dragon of Bad Originalism. We must see whether he has fared better than his predecessors. Of course, we must also suspend judgment as to which originalism is the bad, and which is the good—who is the knight and who is the dragon.

For uninstructed readers, this controversy centers upon my book, *Original Intent and the Framers of the Constitution: A Disputed Question.* In it I agreed with the campaign by attorney general Meese, and his Department of Justice, that liberal judicial activism was a great evil, and that a necessary (if not sufficient) antidote to it was a jurisprudence of original intent. My differences with the attorney general, and those to whom he looked for guidance, centered upon the fact that, by and large, they were legal positivists, who denied the relevance, for original intent, of the principles of "the laws of nature and of nature's God"—principles largely but not exclusively enshrined in the Declaration of Independence—which had guided the Framers and Ratifiers of the Constitution.

Nothing better illustrates the distance of legal positivism from the original intent of the Framers and Ratifiers, than the pronouncements of Mr. Justice Rehnquist. He is the Philosopher-King of the legal positivist version of original intent jurisprudence (otherwise called "originalism"). In his landmark essay, "The Notion of a Living Constitution,"[1] Rehnquist admonishes those who

> Ignore . . . the nature of political value judgments in a democratic society. If such a society adopts a constitution and incorporates in that constitution safeguards for individual liberty, these safeguards do indeed take on a generalized moral rightness or goodness. They assume a general social acceptance neither because of any intrinsic worth nor because of any unique origins in someone's idea of natural justice but instead simply because they have been incorporated in a constitution by a people.

---

[1] 54 *Texas Law Review* 693 (1976) [reprinted in Gary L. McDowell, ed., *Taking the Constitution Seriously: Essays on the Constitution and Constitutional Law* (1981)].

To say that "safeguards of individual liberty" are not incorporated in a constitution because of "any intrinsic worth" is as much as to say that individual liberty does not possess any intrinsic worth, which in turn implies that human life does not possess any intrinsic worth. Now this is more than legal positivism, it is moral relativism and nihilism in their most naked form. Whatever its merits—and there are none—it cannot by any stretch of the imagination have anything in common with the political philosophy of the generation that framed and ratified the Constitution. Yet Bork's and Cooper's "good originalism" subsists wholly within the parameters defined by Rehnquist. Any appeal to antecedent principles defining what is intrinsically—or by nature—good or bad, right or wrong, just or unjust, which the law is meant to implement or uphold, is not recognized.

The Constitution of 1787, together with the Bill of Rights, included many safeguards of individual liberty. But it also included a number of safeguards of slavery, most notably the fugitive slave clause of Article IV. By Rehnquist's "originalism" the safeguards of slavery and the safeguards of individual liberty have exactly the same moral standing. Both were incorporated into the same constitution by the same people, and both—according to Rehnquist—must have acquired the same "moral goodness and rightness" by virtue of that incorporation. From this perspective there can be no more intrinsic rightness or goodness in the safeguards of liberty than in the safeguards of slavery. Accordingly, there can be no more intrinsic rightness or goodness in the Civil Rights Act of 1964 than in the Fugitive Slave Act of 1850! Can it be merely coincidental that this neutrality of constitutional morality as between freedom and slavery is in the tradition of John C. Calhoun, the Philosopher-King of the antebellum South? And that it formed the principal justification for secession in 1860 and 1861? This is the position being upheld by my opponents in this controversy. They are very angry at me for exposing it, and are doing all they can to discredit me while evading the argument itself.

Judge Bork's *The Tempting of America: The Political Seduction of the Law*[2] has as its central theme that liberal activist judges have invented rights which are nowhere in the Constitution, and have then invented remedies for violations of the rights they have invented. This, he says, is judicial legislation. It is an assumption of authority that violates the constitutional separation of powers, and that usurps the legislative authority that the Constitution has placed in Congress. Bork calls this "substantive due process." If and when this occurs, and to the extent that it does occur, I am in full agreement with Bork.

---

[2] Robert H. Bork, *The Tempting of America: The Political Seduction of the Law* (1990).

Bork, however, asserts erroneously that substantive due process entered American constitutional law in the case of *Dred Scott v. Sandford* (1857). What Bork says about Taney's opinion in *Dred Scott* is however riddled with error and Cooper attempts to defend Bork mainly by repeating (and compounding) those errors.

Speaking of Taney's opinion in *Dred Scott*, in *Tempting*, Bork writes:

> There is no need to examine all of its dubious arguments; it was quite evident not only that Scott was to remain a slave but that Taney intended to read into the Constitution the legality of slavery forever. When he had done he was done he had denied the power of the federal government to prevent slavery in any state or territory and the power of the federal government to permit a state to bar slavery within its territory.[3]

However, Taney did not read the legality of slavery into the antebellum Constitution. It is Bork who has attempted to read it out of the Constitution. In the foregoing statement Bork is in error in saying that Taney denied the power of the Congress to "prevent slavery in any state or territory." *Dred Scott* applied to territories, not to states. Bork is also in error in saying that Taney had denied the power of the federal government "to permit a state to bar slavery." In the antebellum Constitution, the right of each state to the exclusive control of its own "domestic institutions" was regarded as an essential element of state sovereignty.[4] In 1857, neither the proslavery nor antislavery parties challenged it. It is true that Lincoln, in the joint debates with Douglas in 1858, asserted that Taney's opinion supplied the premises by which the Court in a *future* decision might declare that no state had the power to exclude slavery. If the *Dred Scott* decision was ratified by public opinion in future elections, Lincoln said, that is what would happen. But not even he asserted that it had already done so. Prior to the Thirteenth Amendment, the federal government never had the power either to permit or to bar slavery within any state. To repeat, Taney's opinion, as far as it went, did not affect the power of the states, whether free or slave, either to include or exclude slavery from among their domestic institutions.

---

[3] *Id.*, p. 30.

[4] The Fourth Resolution in the Republican Party platform of 1860 declared

> That the maintenance inviolate of the rights of the states, and especially the right of each state to order and control its own domestic institutions [especially slavery] according to its own judgment exclusively, is essential to that balance of power on which the perfection and endurance of our political fabric depends.

Lincoln incorporated this resolution into his inaugural address and, in addition, offered to support an amendment making it part of the Constitution.

Bork again:

> Taney was determined to prove that the right of property in
> slaves was guaranteed by the Constitution. He led up to his
> crucial point by noting, unexceptionably, that when the federal
> government entered into possession of a territory, "It has no
> power of any kind beyond [the Constitution]; and it cannot . . .
> assume discretionary or despotic powers which the Constitu-
> tion has denied to it." He illustrated his point: "No one, we pre-
> sume, will contend that Congress can make any law in a Terri-
> tory respecting the establishment of religion, or the free exer-
> cise thereof, or abridging the freedom of speech or of the press,
> or the right of the people of a Territory peaceably to assemble,
> and to petition the government for the redress of grievances."

> All well and good. But there is no similar constitutional provi-
> sion that can be read with any semblance of plausibility to con-
> fer a right to own slaves. It may well have been the case that
> the federal government could not then have freed slaves in
> states where the law allowed slavery without committing a
> taking of property for which the fifth amendment of the Con-
> stitution would have required compensation.[5]

Turning to Bork's last point: here he again displays his ignorance of the
law of the antebellum Constitution. The federal government possessed no
constitutional power to free slaves in the slave states, with or without
compensation to their owners.[6] In a passage to which we shall return,
Bork asserts categorically that a right of slave ownership "is nowhere to
be found in the Constitution." Cooper quotes me as rejoining that "the
Constitution most assuredly recognizes such a right" in three places.
Cooper then observes that

> Jaffa is certainly correct that the original Constitution recog-
> nized a right to slave ownership. But Bork did not deny that the
> Constitution recognized such a right to slave ownership; he
> said instead that the Constitution does not "*confer* a right" to
> slave ownership. While the distinction is, I trust, obvious, let
> me illustrate. The Fugitive Slave Clause recognizes both that
> the laws of some states permit the ownership of slaves and that
> the laws of other states prohibit the ownership of slaves. In
> other words the Constitution recognizes the right of freedom in
> all men guaranteed by some states no less than it recognizes the

---

[5] Bork, *Tempting*, p. 30.
[6] See the Fourth Resolution of the Republican Party platform of 1860 cited in note 4.

right of property in slaves guaranteed in other states. But the key point is that in either case the right being recognized in the Constitution is a right under *state* law. It is not a federal constitutional right. In contrast, the Second Amendment confers a federal constitutional right to keep (and thus presumably own) arms. The federal government lacks power to legislate in a manner that infringes on this right. There is no similar constitutional provision conferring a right to keep slaves. Bork, in his critique of Taney's analysis, said no more, and no less, than this, as Jaffa well understands.

Contrary to Cooper, however, Bork in his book did *not* draw a distinction between rights conferred and rights recognized. When Bork denounces Taney for inventing a right of slave ownership, he does so by assuming that Taney had discovered that right in the due process clause of the Fifth Amendment alone. But Taney did nothing of the kind. Taney had found a right of slave ownership recognized in both the importation clause of Article I, section 9, and the fugitive slave clause of Article IV, section 2. Whether those recognitions of the right of slave ownership justified Taney's conclusions concerning slavery in the territories is altogether a separate question from whether or not he had merely invented the right he recognized.

Let us however pause to examine Cooper's assertion that "the Second Amendment confers a federal constitutional right to keep (and thus presumably to own) arms." This is a remarkable assertion for a former assistant attorney general who was once the head of the Office of Legal Counsel, the elite corps of legal eagles within the Meese Justice Department. The Ninth Amendment says that "The enumeration in the Constitution of certain rights shall not be construed to deny or disparage others retained by the people." The Constitution, whether of 1787, or as amended in 1791, *enumerates* rights, it does not *confer* them. Contrary to Cooper, "the right of the people to keep and bear arms" is *not* conferred. It is a right already possessed by the people, a right which the amendment says "shall not be infringed." This right, like all other such rights—e.g., the free exercise of religion, freedom of speech and of the press, freedom of peaceable assembly—may not be denied or disparaged. These enumerated rights, and others not enumerated, but (according to the Ninth Amendment) nonetheless possessed (because retained), must have their origin and existence independently of the Constitution. As they are prior to the Constitution, they are prior to positive law. Madison, in his speech in the House of Representatives June 8, 1789, introducing what became the first ten amendments, invited the House "expressly [to] declare the great rights of mankind secured under the Constitution."[7] The "great rights of mankind" can refer to nothing less than what the Declaration of Independence meant in proclaiming that all men are equally endowed by their Creator with certain unalienable rights. The Declaration, moreover, anticipates the Ninth Amendment, when it says that the rights mentioned are only "among" the rights possessed. The enumeration of rights, whether in the Declaration, or in the Constitution, is not exhaustive. Accordingly, we have Madison's authority that the right to keep and bear arms, like all the rights in the first eight amendments, are among the *great rights of mankind*, that they are, in short, natural rights prior to becoming constitutional rights. And they have become constitutional rights because they are natural rights. Neither Bork nor Cooper nor Rehnquist understands what is in dispute in *Dred Scott* because they do not understand the tension—in the antebellum Constitution—between property rights in accordance with the "laws of nature" and property rights contrary to "the laws of nature," albeit sanctioned by the positive law of the slave states.

Unlike the enumerated rights to which Madison referred, the right of slave ownership, so far from arising from a natural right, is against nature. In the documents of the Revolution and the Founding, life, liberty, and property, are mentioned over and over again as among the natural rights of mankind. The ground in nature—prior to all positive law—of all property rights, is to be found in the *natural right of every human being to own himself.* It is because a man owns himself that he owns the fruit of his own labor, and that he owns the things he acquires by exchanging the fruit of his labor for the fruit of another man's labor. The right to own slaves did indeed originate in the positive laws of the slave states, because it could have originated nowhere else. To anyone who, like Bork or Cooper or Rehnquist, thinks that "the great rights of mankind" are (as Rehnquist explicitly says) mere "value judgments" with no foundation in reason, that they are "conferred" rather than recognized, the positive law of slavery is not in principle different—or less moral than—the positive law of freedom.[8] Here is James Madison again, in the 54th *Federalist*:

> In being compelled to labor not for himself, but for a master; in being vendible by one master to another master; and in being subject at all times to be restrained in his liberty, and chastised in his body, by the capricious will of another, the slave may

---

[7] 1 *Annals of Congress* 449 (Gales and Seaton ed. 1834).

[8] In Calhoun's theory, *state rights* are severed from *natural rights.* All legal rights, whether of freedom or of slavery, are thereby "conferred" by government. There can therefore be no rights against government as such. This is the kernel of all totalitarian constitutions of the twentieth century.

appear to be degraded from the human rank, and classed with those irrational animals which fall under the denomination of property. In being protected on the other hand in his life & in his limbs, against the violence of all others, even the master of his labor and his liberty; and in being punishable himself for all violence committed against others; the slave is no less evidently regarded by the law as a member of the society; not as a part of the irrational creation; as a moral person, not a mere article of property.

Taney, in *Dred Scott*, declared that the slave was regarded by the Constitution solely as property, and therefore in law as merely part of the irrational creation. This was his error of errors, and the basis of everything wrong in his opinion. Yet neither Bork nor Cooper (nor Rehnquist) even alludes to it. Although there may have been little practical benefit to the slave himself in the reservation of his rights against his master, the fact remains that he was recognized as a human person even by the terrible laws of slavery. Madison adds that

it is only under the pretext that the laws have transformed the negroes into subjects of property, that a place is disputed to them in the computation of numbers; and it is admitted that if the laws were to restore the rights which have been taken away, the negroes could no longer be refused an equal share of representation with the other inhabitants.

The positive law of slavery is called a "pretext" by Madison, and he speaks of restoring "the rights which have been taken away." That part of the law of slavery which recognized the slave as a human person, endowed with a rational will, reflected the truth. That part of the law of slavery that regarded him as part of the irrational creation was a "pretext" or, in plainer language, a lie. In nature, a chattel cannot be a person, and in nature, a person cannot be a chattel. One cannot, at one and the same time, belong to the irrational creation and have a rational will. Yet this contradiction is enshrined in the antebellum Constitution, which acknowledges the laws of the slave states by which persons are chattel property. The legal definition of a slave was a legal fiction, but it was a fiction *contra naturam*. Contrary to Rehnquist, Bork, and Cooper, to understand the antebellum Constitution, and the debates that raged around *Dred Scott*, the distinction between positive law and natural is indispensable. In maintaining that there is no natural law, and only positive law, they cannot make the distinction that Madison makes between the slave as human person and the slave as part of the irrational creation.

Let us turn to the central text in Bork's attack on Taney's opinion in *Dred Scott*. Bork asks:

> How then can there be constitutional right to own slaves where a statute forbids it? Taney created such a right by changing the plain meaning of the due process clause of the fifth amendment. He wrote: "[T]he rights of property are united with the rights of the person, and placed on the same ground by the fifth amendment to the Constitution, which provides that no person shall be deprived of life, liberty, or property, without due process of law. And an act of Congress which deprives a citizen of the United States of his liberty or property, merely because he came himself or brought his property into a particular Territory of the United States and who had committed no offense against the laws, could hardly be dignified with the name of due process of law."

Bork then comments:

> The first sentence quotes the guarantee of due process, which is simply a requirement that the substance of any law be applied to a person through fair procedures by any tribunal hearing a case. The clause says nothing whatever about what the substance of the law must be. But Taney's second sentence transforms this requirement of fair procedure into a rule about the allowable substance of a statute. The substance Taney poured into the clause was that Congress cannot prevent slavery in a territory because a man must be allowed to bring slaves there. The second sentence is additionally dishonest because it postulates a man who had "committed no offense against the laws," but a man who brings slaves and keeps them in a jurisdiction where slavery is prohibited does commit an offense against the laws. Taney was saying that there can be no valid law against slavery anywhere in the United States.

> How did Taney know that slave ownership was a constitutional right? Such a right is nowhere to be found in the Constitution. He knew it because he was passionately convinced that it *must* be a constitutional right. Though his transformation of the due process clause from a procedural to a substantive requirement was an obvious sham, it was a momentous sham, for this was the first appearance in American constitutional law of the concept of "substantive due process," and that concept has been used countless times since by judges who want to write

their personal beliefs into a document that, most inconveniently, does not contain those beliefs.[9]

We begin here by repeating that Bork shows utter confusion, in thinking that the decision in *Dred Scott* applied to states no less than to territories. Moreover, before the Civil War the Fifth Amendment, like the rest of the bill of rights, was understood to apply only to the federal government.[10] Where it had no jurisdiction—and it had none over slavery in the states—the Fifth Amendment had no application. Bork here assumes that the Missouri Compromise restriction of slavery was constitutional. I agree that it was constitutional but its constitutionality cannot be assumed. To assume that Taney was wrong is to beg the question.

It is Bork's thesis—endorsed by Cooper—that "the guarantee of due process [in the Fifth Amendment] is simply a requirement that the substance of the law be applied to a person through fair procedures. . . . The clause says nothing whatever about what the substance of the law must be." Applied to the question of the constitutionality of the Missouri law of 1820 (which excluded slavery in the remaining Louisiana Territory north of 36 degrees 30 minutes), Bork's and Cooper's interpretation of the due process clause would mean not only that Congress had a perfect right to pass that law, but that it also had an equal right to enact a law protecting slavery in the same territory. The due process clause, according to Bork and Cooper, is perfectly neutral between freedom and slavery in the territories. As we shall see, this is an opinion that was shared by neither side in the antebellum slavery dispute.

This view of the neutrality of the due process clause towards the substantive ends of legislation is repeated like a mantra by Bork and his followers (including Cooper). It is however contradicted by Douglas Kmiec, Cooper's successor as head of the Office of Legal Counsel. In *The Attorney General's Lawyer: Inside the Meese Justice Department*, Kmiec writes of Bork's conception of the due process clause that

> It is analytically silly not to recognize that at some point, procedure is substance and that appropriate procedures must include a check against arbitrary governmental actions. To posit that the framers were willing to allow life, liberty, and property to not be safeguarded against arbitrary decision making is almost to refute the argument by its mere statement.[11]

---

[9] Bork, *supra* note 2, at 31.
[10] See Chief Justice John Marshall's opinion in *Barron v. Baltimore*, 32 U.S. (7 Pet.) 243 (1833).
[11] *The Attorney General's Lawyer* (1992), p. 42.

We observe again that in *Tempting*, Bork asserts without *any* qualification that a right of slave ownership "is nowhere to be found in the Constitution." Contrary to what Cooper has argued, Bork does not say that slave ownership is recognized but not conferred. However, four years after the publication of *Tempting*, and after I had exposed his egregious error, Bork in his diatribe against *Original Intent* pretended that he had all along recognized the right of slave ownership in the antebellum Constitution. The following is Bork, not in *Tempting*, but in *National Review*, February 7, 1994:

> The Constitution certainly recognized that slaves were held pursuant to the laws of some states, but the Constitution most emphatically did not guarantee such a right.

However, what the Constitution certainly recognized, Bork himself had certainly *not* recognized before I had pointed it out to him! I have quoted at such length from Bork's book to prove that he and Cooper have attempted to create the false impression that I had misrepresented what Bork wrote in *Tempting*. Cooper has attempted to give Bork credit *ex post facto* for having written in his book, what in fact he had only written years later.[12]

There is however little advantage to Bork in his graceless refusal to admit his mistake. In saying that the Constitution recognized but "emphatically did not guarantee" a right of slave ownership, he only jumps from the frying pan into the fire. What in the world is the fugitive slave clause if it is not a guarantee? What is the pledge that runaway slaves "shall be delivered up" to their owners? Consider that by the positive law of slavery a runaway slave is stolen property, and the runaway is a thief. What the thief is stealing is himself, but by positive law he is no less a thief for that.[13] In promising to return the stolen property to its owner, the

---

[12] Both Bork and Cooper wax indignant (as Groucho Marx might have said) because I had said that Bork had bowdlerized the text of the Constitution, by declaring that the right of slave ownership "is nowhere to be found" in it. My Oxford English Dictionary defines "bowdlerizing" as expurgating a book or altering words or passages in it. I have used "bowdlerizing" only to avoid a less polite term.

[13] And anyone helping a slave escape is, as an accessory to theft, also a thief. Considered the tortured conscience of Huckleberry Finn, as he attempts to help the runaway Jim escape to freedom:

> And at last, when it hit me all of a sudden that here was the plain hand of Providence slapping me in the face and letting me know my wickedness was being watched all the time from up there in heaven, whilst I was stealing a poor old woman's nigger that hadn't ever done me no harm . . . (Mark Twain, *Huckleberry Finn*, ch. 31).

Constitution pledges to add its police power to that of the slave states, when the stolen property is outside the jurisdiction of the police power of the aforesaid slave states. If this does not constitute a guarantee of the security of slave property, what would?

We return once more to Bork's assertion, in *Tempting*, that a right of slave ownership "is nowhere to be found in the Constitution." We have quoted at such length because we want the reader to see the entire context of Bork's assertion, so that there can be no doubt as to the reality of Bork's monumental mistake. Cooper may be a clever lawyer,[14] but there are limits even to the best advocate's ability to deny the reality of the evidence against his client.

We turn next to Bork's charge that Taney had transformed the due process clause from a merely procedural to a substantive requirement. Bork calls this "a momentous sham." As we shall see, however, the "sham" is Bork's. Bork has a habit of denouncing others for doing exactly what he himself is doing! Taney's conception of the due process clause of the Fifth Amendment was however anything but original. Consider the following from Don E. Fehrenbacher's *Slavery, Law, and Politics: The Dred Scott Case in Historical Perspective*:

> The principal antislavery arguments were proslavery arguments turned upside down. Thus the due process clause of the Fifth Amendment, to which Southerners occasionally appealed, with emphasis on the word *property*, could be invoked by northern radicals, with emphasis on the word *liberty*. "Slavery," wrote Salmon P. Chase in 1844, "never has lawfully existed in any territory of the United States since the adoption of that amendment which declares that no person shall be deprived of liberty without due process of law." This argument was incorporated

---

It takes a present day reader some time to realize that it is the "poor old woman" and not the runaway slave who "hadn't done me no harm." Huck however accepts slavery as part of the moral order over which God presides, and believes that he will go to Hell for that lowest of crimes in the Old South, "nigger stealing." We ourselves however understand, what Huck himself (like Bork, Rehnquist, and Cooper) does not understand, namely, that Huck's nature (or natural goodness) rejects the conventional order, represented by proslavery theology as well as by the positive law of slavery. We, like Mark Twain, Jefferson, and Lincoln—but unlike Bork, Rehnquist, and Cooper—know that God is the God of freedom, not of slavery.

[14] In our debate sponsored by the Goldwater Institute at Phoenix, in November, 1995, I called him Robert Bork's Johnnie Cochran!

into the platforms of the Liberty Party in 1844, the Freesoil Party in 1848, and the Republican Party in 1856 and 1860.[15]

I do not know whether incorporation in a party platform may be said to constitute an "appearance in constitutional law." It certainly appeared in the very center of the political process, by which constitutional law was to be determined. In that process, what Bork calls "substantive due process," so far from being a radical innovation, was a commonplace. In 1857, the only question was whether the substantive due process of the Fifth Amendment favored slavery or freedom in the territories. Here is what the Republican Party platform of 1856 said:

> Resolved, That the maintenance of the principles promulgated in the Declaration of Independence and embodied in the Federal Constitution, is essential to the preservation of our Republican institutions, and that the Federal constitution, the rights of the states, and the union of the states shall be preserved.

> Resolved, That with our Republican fathers we hold it to be a self-evident truth, that all men are endowed with the unalienable rights to life, liberty, and the pursuit of happiness, and that the primary object and ulterior designs of our federal government were to secure these rights to all persons within its exclusive jurisdiction; that, as our republican fathers, when they had abolished slavery in all our national territory[16] ordained that no persons should be deprived of life, liberty, or property without due process of law, it becomes our duty to maintain this provision of the Constitution against all attempts to violate it for the purpose of establishing slavery in any Territory of the United States, by positive legislation, prohibiting its existence or extension therein. That we deny the authority of Congress, or a Territorial legislature, of any individual or association of individuals, to give legal existence to slavery in any Territory of the United States, while the present Constitution shall be maintained.[17]

With only minor differences, the identical language appears in the Republican Party platform of 1860, upon which Abraham Lincoln was

---

[15] Don Fehrenbacher, *Slavery, Law, and Politics: The Dred Scott Case in Historical Perspective* (1981), pp. 67-68.

[16] This has reference to the Northwest Ordinance, adopted by the Confederation Congress, but reenacted by the first Congress under the Constitution in 1789. The Ordinance forbade slavery in all the Northwest Territory, from which the states of Ohio, Indiana, Michigan, and Illinois were later formed.

[17] Edward Stanwood, *A History of Presidential Elections*, 2nd ed. rev. (1888), pp. 205-6.

elected to the presidency. The 1856 platform is more material to our purpose, because that platform was a burning presence to Taney when he wrote his opinion in *Dred Scott*. In all probability, Taney's use of the due process clause in the interest of slavery was unusual, and was a direct reaction to its use in the opposite sense by the Republicans. At that time it was more characteristic of proslavery speeches, whether in or out of Congress, to rely upon Calhoun's theory of state rights: namely, that the Constitution was a compact among the states, that the territories were the common property of the states, and that Congress as the collective trustee of all the states had no lawful power to discriminate against any form of the property lawful in any of them. When Taney composed his opinion in *Dred Scott*, he had before him not only the Republican platform of 1856, but the election return of that year. They showed that only the division of the antislavery vote had allowed Buchanan's election. The slave power saw itself being overwhelmed in the political process by the growing ranks of the antislavery forces in the free states. They saw in the judicial process the last alternative to secession as a means of preserving slavery. Taney, and his court, were anything but independent players in the drama that culminated in *Dred Scott*.

Lincoln's House Divided speech of June 16, 1858—a speech which may have changed the course of events more than any in the history of free government—charged a conspiracy to extend slavery, encompassing two presidents, a United States senator, and the chief justice. Lincoln pointed to the fact that after the 1856 election, the outgoing president, Pierce, and the incoming president, Buchanan, endorsed the *Dred Scott* decision before it was announced, and called upon the public to accept it sight unseen as a final resolution of the slavery question.[18] So also did Senator Douglas, and some Southern leaders, all of whom—at least in a general way—knew very well what that decision would be.[19] In the ter-

---

[18] Here is Buchanan in his inaugural address, three days before *Dred Scott* was announced. Concerning the question of the constitutional status of slavery in the territories, he said:

> . . . it is a judicial question, which legitimately belongs to the Supreme Court of the United States, before whom it is now pending, and will, it is *understood*, be speedily and finally settled. To their decision, in common with all good citizens, I shall cheerfully submit, whatever this may be . . . (italics added). John Basset Moore, ed., 10 *Works of James Buchanan* p.106

This was cosmic hypocrisy, and it gives the lie to those—like Rehnquist, Bork, and Cooper—who think that *Dred Scott* was mere judicial usurpation.

[19] Fehrenbacher writes that

> Alexander H. Stephens informed his brother on December 15 [1856] that he was urging the Court to a prompt decision, with the full expectation that it

ritorial laws of Utah and New Mexico that formed part of the Compromise of 1850, it was provided that any dispute as to the right of property in slaves could be appealed from the supreme court of the territory to the Supreme Court of the United States. Thus Congress itself had given the direction for a judicial resolution of the territorial question. It is historical ignorance to suppose that Taney's opinion represented a merely gratuitous judicial intrusion into the political process.

Cooper makes much of a "hypothetical case" in *Original Intent*, in which I imagine that a proslavery antebellum Congress has enacted a slave code for the territories. Dred Scott, having been held as a slave in a territory under this law, sues for his freedom on the ground that the law was unconstitutional. I imagined a Republican Supreme Court, with Abraham Lincoln as chief justice. I said I believed that such a court would have agreed with Dred Scott and set him free. Cooper crows like a rooster:

> Thus, Taney's illegitimate invention—substantive due process—is no less central to Jaffa's constitutionalism than it was to Taney's. Jaffa has no problem with Taney's methodology, just with his moral values, and, hence his result.

Let us repeat—and keep repeating—the Republican platforms of 1856 and 1860. They assert without equivocation

> That we deny the authority of Congress, of a Territorial legislature, of any individual or association of individuals, to give legal existence to slavery in any Territory of the United States, while the present Constitution shall last.

Can Cooper—can anyone—imagine a justice appointed to the Court by a president elected on that platform, hesitating to pronounce unconstitutional a law giving "legal existence to slavery in any Territory of the United States"? Yet that is neither more nor less than what was at issue in my "hypothetical case."

Cooper says I agree with Taney's "methodology" and disagree only with his "moral values and, hence, his result." But it is not *my* agreement with what Cooper calls Taney's methodology that counts. The names

---

would settle the territorial issue in the South's favor. A likely object of Stephens's influence was his fellow Georgian, Justice Wayne, and Wayne proved to be the pivotal figure in an abrupt reversal of the strategy first adopted by the Court's majority (Fehrenbacher, pp. 306-7).

Alexander Stephens, the leading "intellectual" of the antebellum South, and soon to become vice president of the Confederacy, was a cousin of Justice Daniel, with whom he had a correspondence about the decision before it was announced.

that count are those of Chase, Seward, Sumner, and Lincoln. If Cooper wants to hold me guilty by association, I could wish no better company!

Cooper holds in contempt the fact that I, in common with Chase, Seward, Sumner, and Lincoln, appear to disagree with Taney only on the basis of "his moral values." Cooper—like Bork and Rehnquist—thinks that what they call "moral values" should play no part in the business of rendering judgment under the law of the Constitution. But what if the Constitution itself embodies, not "moral values," but moral truths. Let us look once again at the Republican platform of 1856, which says that "the principles promulgated in the Declaration of Independence [are] embodied in the Federal Constitution." It goes on to say that it is "a self-evident truth that all men are endowed with the unalienable rights to life, liberty and the pursuit of happiness." It ways that *because* this truth is *embodied* in the Constitution, no person may be deprived of life, liberty, or property without due process of law. It says that *because* this truth is *embodied* in the Constitution, Congress has no authority to give legal existence to slavery in any territory. It is not *my* morality that is here being imposed upon constitutional interpretation. It is the morality of the Constitution itself, as propounded by Abraham Lincoln and the Republican Party, and endorsed by the American people in electing Lincoln to the presidency in 1860.

Cooper, following Bork, however, makes much of what is said to be "Justice Curtis's originalist response to Taney's substantive due process analysis." According to Bork and Cooper, Curtis's dissent is a very model of "good originalism." Unfortunately for Cooper and Bork, however, the facts concerning Curtis's "originalism" are the very opposite of what the suppose. Curtis's dissenting opinion in *Dred Scott* is fully consistent with the Republican Party platform of 1856. Taney, we recall, maintained that the due process clause of the Fifth Amendment meant that an owner of slaves could not be lawfully deprived of those slaves in any United States territory. To reach this conclusion he had first to establish that they were property, and not persons, under the meaning of the Constitution. To establish this, he made his infamous assertion that under the Constitution Negroes, whether free or slave, were so far inferior that they had no rights which white men were bound to respect. In proof whereof, Taney alleged that the proposition that all men are created equal—which he also took to be embodied in the Constitution—had not been understood (either in 1776 or 1787 or 1791) to include Negroes. It would have been inconsistent with the dignity of the Founding Fathers, Taney had said, to have included Negroes in that assertion and yet to have continued to hold them as slaves. Here is how Curtis dealt with that contention:

My own opinion [concerning the meaning of those who asserted, in the Declaration of Independence, that all men are
created equal . . .] is, that a calm comparison of these assertions
of universal abstract truths, and of their own individual opinions and acts, would not leave these men under any reproach of
inconsistency; that the great truths they asserted on that solemn
occasion, they were ready and anxious to make effectual wherever a necessary regard to circumstances, which no statesman
can disregard without producing more evil than good, would
allow; and that it would not be just to them, nor true in itself, to
allege that they intended to say that the Creator of all man had
endowed the white race, exclusively, with the great natural
rights which the Declaration of Independence asserts.[20]

Lincoln followed the same reasoning as Curtis in his speech on *Dred
Scott* some six months later. The authors of the Declaration of Independence, said Lincoln

did not mean to assert the obvious untruth, that all were then
actually enjoying that equality, nor yet, that they were about to
confer it immediately upon them. In fact they had no power to
confer such a boon. They meant simply to declare the right, so
that enforcement of it might follow as fast as circumstances
should permit.[21]

When Curtis comes to the question of what provision of the Constitution could inhibit the power of Congress to outlaw slavery in a territory
(as in the Missouri law of 1820) he writes:

The only one suggested [by Justice Taney] is that clause in the
5th article of the Amendments of the Constitution which declares that no person shall be deprived of his life, liberty, or
property, without due process of law. I will now proceed to examine the question, whether this clause is entitled to the effect
thus contributed [attributed?] to it. It is necessary, first, to have
a clear view of the nature and incidents of that particular species of property now in question.

---

[20] *Dred Scott v. Sandford,* 60 U.S. (19 How.) 574-5 (1857).
[21] 2 *Collected Works* 406 (1953). Earlier in this speech, Lincoln had observed that the
Founding Fathers "did not at once *or ever afterwards*, actually place all white people on
an equality with one another" (italics original). Lincoln's use of the word "people"
means that he almost certainly had in mind the rights of women. At that time, a married
white woman had less control over her own property than a free black man. Lincoln
endorsed the principle of women's suffrage in one of his early speeches.

Slavery being contrary to natural right, is created only by municipal law. This is not only plain in itself, and agreed by all writers on the subject, but is inferable from the Constitution, and has been explicitly declared by this court. . . . In *Rankin v. Lydia* . . . the Supreme Court of Appeals of Kentucky said: "Slavery is sanctioned by the laws of this state. . . . But we view this as a right existing by positive law of a municipal character, without foundation in the law of nature or the unwritten common law."[22]

Nothing could be clearer than that Curtis rejected Taney's interpretation of the due process clause of the Fifth Amendment, not because it represented substantive due process, but because slavery was "contrary to natural right" and "without foundation in the law of nature . . . " Curtis rejected the idea that the positive law of the slave states extended to the territories, and Curtis held—as did the Republican Party—that the "normal" condition of the territories was freedom. At every point, Curtis's opinion is governed by the assumption that, in the absence of the positive law of slavery, the status of Negroes is governed by the natural law or natural right. Curtis's opinion does indeed represent genuine "originalism," but it is an originalism that relies entirely upon that relationship between the principles of the Declaration of Independence, and of the Constitution, expressed in the Republican Party platforms of 1856 and 1860.

To summarize: the heart of Taney's opinion was, first and foremost, the denial that Negroes were included in the Declaration of Independence; second, that because of this denial, they were property and not persons within the meaning of the Fifth Amendment; and third, that the ownership of this property in the territories was protected by the due process clause. *Every one of these points was the negation of identical propositions in the Republican platforms.* The initiative in the "substantive" use of the due process clause came from the Republicans. Taney's use of it was essentially reactive. Bork's and Cooper's condemnation of the use of the due process clause for purposes other than procedural applies first and foremost not to Taney, but to the Republicans, and to the American people who endorsed it in the election of 1860. Bork's and Cooper's idea of the merely procedural character of the due process clause has no foundation in constitutional history and is entirely anachronistic. They might as well have faulted the underground railroad for not using helicopters.[23]

---

[22] *Scott v. Sandford,* at 575.
[23] The depths of absurdity into which Cooper's notion of due process leads him is illustrated by the following:

* * * * *

In my bicentennial book, *How to Think about the American Revolu-*
tion (1978), I commented at some length on the correspondence of Jefferson and Madison, concerning the *norma docendi* (in Jefferson's
words) to be prescribed for the law faculty of the newly founded University of Virginia. This correspondence culminated in a resolution of the
Board of Visitors, embodying what the two former presidents had agreed
upon. Cooper has reprinted the text of that resolution as an appendix to
his article. I had cited, as the opinion of Madison and Jefferson,

> that on the distinctive principles of the government of our
> State, and of that of the United States, the best guides are to be
> found in 1. The Declaration of Independence, as the funda-
> mental act of union of these States. 2. The book known by the
> title "The Federalist" . . .

I have repeated many times since, that according to the Author of the
Declaration, and the Father of the Constitution, the *first* of the *best*
guides to the principles of the Constitution was the Declaration of Independence. Cooper has expended unbelievable ingenuity to deny that

---

Jaffa thinks that Taney got it right, as a matter of Borkian originalism, in
concluding that a slaveholder was entitled under the Due Process Clause to
take his slaves with him into a United States Territory. This raises some difficult questions for Jaffa. Is Congress's plenary legislative authority over the
territories similarly limited with respect to other substances or activities that
are permitted in at least some of the states? Would Congress, for example, be
barred by the Fifth Amendment from outlawing the possession and use of cocaine in the territories simply because some of the states had not outlawed it?
If citizens of Utah, for example, enjoyed the freedom to practice polygamy,
would Congress be prohibited under the Due Process Clause from outlawing
the practice? Would a prostitute from Nevada be constitutionally entitled to
engage in her profession in the territories? I think the answer to these questions is plainly no.

I answer, not as a Borkian, but as a Lincolnian originalist. Moreover, Cooper's quests are
not as hypothetical as he seems to suppose. The Republican Platform of 1856, also resolved that "it is both the right and duty of Congress to prohibit in the Territories those
twin relics of barbarism, polygamy and slavery." It was the *Republican* understanding
that polygamy should be outlawed for the same reason as slavery. It degrades women
and is inconsistent with the principles of human equality. Drug use and prostitution are,
or certainly may be, judged to be inconsistent with that "transcendent law of nature and
of nature's God which declares that the safety and happiness of society are the objects at
which all political institutions aim, and to which all such institutions must be sacrificed"
(*The Federalist*, No. 43). The legislative power, either of Congress, or of a territorial
legislature, flowing from the law of nature, should be competent to deal with these issues.

these assertions of Jefferson and Madison actually mean what they obviously do mean.

Cooper says (erroneously) that in *How to Think* I had interpreted Madison and Jefferson to mean that the Declaration was a "fine guide on the principles of American government, but a poor one on the meaning of the American Constitution." He finds it "startling" that, in *Original Intent*, I had "equat[ed] the principles of the Declaration with the principles of the Constitution . . ." But in its preamble, the Resolution of the Visitors required the law faculty of the University of Virginia

> to pay especial attention to the principles of government which shall be inculcated therein, and to provide that none shall be inculcated which are incompatible with those on which the Constitutions of this State, and of the United States were genuinely based.

Where is the distinction between the genuine principles of government and the genuine principles of the constitutions of Virginia and the United States?

Cooper thinks it absurd that I (or Madison or Jefferson or Lincoln) should look to the Declaration, and not to the Constitution itself, for the principles of the Constitution. But where in the Constitution is there any statement of its principles? The United States is obligated by Article IV, section 4, of the Constitution to guarantee a "Republican form of government" to every state of the Union. But where in the Constitution are we provided with a definition of a republican form of government? Is slavery, which is guaranteed by Article IV, section 2, an acceptable element in a republican form of government? Or is it to be explained, as Justice Curtis explained it, as arising from

> a necessary regard to circumstances, which no statesman can disregard without producing more evil than good . . .

According to Cooper, the language of the Constitution is "meticulously crafted" and therefore we have no right to ask whether the fugitive slave clause is there as a necessary evil or as a positive good. Calhoun would have loved Cooper!

Cooper complains that (apart from Madison and Jefferson!) I have no citations from the Founders—as I do from the Republican party of 1856—characterizing the Declaration of Independence as an authoritative source of the principles of the Constitution. It is true that we do not find such citations in the abundance that we find them once the struggle over slavery began in earnest in 1833. The most general reason for this is that those principles were so generally accepted, and so seldom called into question, that no authority for them was necessary. It was only when the positive good theory of slavery arose, and the "great rights of mankind" were denied, that the Declaration became the banner of freedom that we see in the Republican platforms.

Consider, however, Jefferson's explanation of the Declaration in his famous letter to Henry Lee in 1825. Jefferson had been told that Timothy Pickering and John Adams had said that the Declaration

> contained no new ideas, that it was a common-place compilation [and that] its sentiments [had been] hackneyed in Congress for two years before . . .[24]

That its ideas had been hackneyed in Congress—that they were commonplaces of public opinion[25]—was one of its great virtues. The object of the Declaration of Independence, Jefferson wrote in 1825, was

> Not to find out new principles, or new arguments never before thought of, nor merely to say things which had never been said before; but to place before mankind the common sense of the subject, in terms so plain and firm as to command their assent, and to justify ourselves in the independent stand we were compelled to take. Neither aiming at originality of principle or sentiment, nor yet copied from any particular and previous writing, it was intended to be an expression of the American mind, and to give to that expression the proper tone and spirit called for by the occasion. All its authority rests, then, on the harmonizing sentiments of the day, whether expressed in conversation, in letters, printed essays, or in the elementary books of public right, as Aristotle, Cicero, Locke, Sidney, etc.[26]

The Declaration of Independence was indeed an expression of the American mind at the time of the Revolution and of the framing and ratifying of the Constitution. Contemporaries did not need to cite it because it expressed what they already believed, and what others accepted without question. Cooper quotes the following from Washington's Farewell Address:

> Respect for its authority [viz., the Constitution], compliance with its laws, are enjoined by the fundamental maxims of true liberty. The basis of our political systems is *the right of the people to make and alter their constitutions of government.* But the constitution which at any time exists till changed by an explicit and authentic act of the whole people is sacredly obliga-

---

[24] 10 *Writings of Thomas Jefferson* 267 (Ford ed., 1892-99).
[25] Especially in Tom Paine's *Common Sense*, which had an enormous distribution.
[26] 10 *Writings of Thomas Jefferson* 343.

tory upon all. *The very idea of the power and the right of the people to establish government* presupposes the duty of every individual to obey the established government. (emphasis added)

Cooper comments "Washington made no reference to the Declaration of Independence." What in the world did Cooper think Washington meant by "the fundamental maxims of true liberty?" Washington may not have referred to the Declaration by name, but in the passages italicized above, he was doing no more than paraphrasing passages. When Washington speaks of the right of the people to make, alter, and establish governments, he implies all of the principles of the Declaration of Independence, beginning with the assertion that all men are created equal. The doctrines of the Declaration form a seamless web, like the definitions, axioms, and propositions in Euclid, and were so understood.

Cooper grants an authority to the *Federalist* that he denies to the Declaration. But how does the *Federalist* itself conceive of the relationship of the Constitution to the principles of the Declaration? We have already seen that Madison, in *Federalist* No. 54—like Curtis in his dissenting opinion in *Dred Scott*—could not discuss the constitutional status of slavery without declaring that it was against natural right. Consider the following from *Federalist* No. 39:

The first question that offers itself is, whether the general form and aspect of the government [under the Constitution] be strictly republican? It is evident that no other form would be reconcilable with the genius of the people of America; with the fundamental principles of the revolution; or with the honorable determination, which animates every votary of freedom, to rest all our political experiments on the capacity of mankind for self-government. If the plan of the Convention therefore be found to depart from the republican character, its advocates must abandon it as no longer defensible.

The Constitution, says Madison, must be reconcilable "with the fundamental principles of the revolution." Can anyone doubt that the fundamental principles of the Revolution are to be found—not only but preeminently—in the Declaration of Independence? Madison says that the Constitution must pass the test of these principles. According to Madison, but contrary to Cooper, the standards by which the Constitution is to be justified and defended, are prior both logically and chronologically to the Constitution itself.

In *Federalist* No. 40, Madison justifies the departure of the Convention from its commission by the Congress of the Confederation:

[I]n all great changes of established governments, forms ought
to give way to substance . . . a rigid adherence in such cases to
the former, would render nominal and nugatory the transcendent and precious right of the people to "abolish or alter their
governments as to them, shall seem most likely to effect their
safety and happiness."

After the word "happiness" in the text of the *Federalist* there is an aster-
isk, and a footnote, by Madison (or Publius) which says "Declaration of
Independence." The quotation combines parts of a sentence that are separated in the Declaration itself, and omits a part. Obviously Madison was
quoting from memory, but what he attributed to the Declaration is
authentic and authoritative.

In *Federalist* No. 78, Hamilton writes:

I trust the friends of the Constitution will never concur with its
enemies in questioning that fundamental principle of republican government, which admits the right of the people to alter or
abolish the established Constitution, whenever they find it inconsistent with their happiness.

Here we find Hamilton, partly quoting and partly paraphrasing the
same passage in the Declaration of Independence as Madison had done.

In *Federalist* No. 43, Madison asks,

On what principle the Confederation, which stands in the form
of a solemn compact among the states, can be superseded without the unanimous consent of the part to it?

He replies:

by recurring to the absolute necessity of the case; to the great
principle of self-preservation; to the transcendent law of nature
and of nature's God which declares that the safety and happiness of society are the objects at which all political institutions
aim, and to which all such institutions must be sacrificed.

Once again we find not only the ideas but the words of the Declaration
interwoven into the text of the *Federalist.* Can there be any doubt that the
fundamental principles of the Revolution, by which the Constitution is
tested at every point, are the same as those set forth in the Declaration of
Independence? And can there by any doubt that the presence of slavery,
within the constitutional order, is intrinsically inconsistent with those
principles? It is a departure to be justified only by the political necessities
of the time. It is a departure to be justified only as a lesser evil than the
continuance of the weak government of the Articles, a government

tending to dissolution and disunion. It is a departure to be justified because only the stronger government established by the Constitution could circumscribe the boundaries of slavery and place it, as Lincoln said, "in course of ultimate extinction." To repeat, slavery was no less an evil for being the lesser evil, and was recognized generally at the Founding as being intrinsically incompatible with the principles of natural justice and republican government.

* * * * *

Cooper, like his fellow legal positivists, would detach the Constitution from its anchor in the principles of the Declaration of Independence. To do so, however, is to detach it from its history, no less than from its philosophy. It is to see the Constitution as a mere legal abstraction, torn from the political culture which gave it birth, and by which it was nurtured. In the Revolution, all thirteen states adopted constitutions for themselves individually, as well as jointly adopting the Articles of Confederation. Is there any reason to doubt that, whether severally or individually, in ratifying their state constitutions, they did so "to secure these rights," rights possessed by nature, rights which all men have been endowed by their Creator? Is there any reason to doubt Jefferson when he said that the Declaration had expressed "the American mind," the consensus upon which the American people not only fought the Revolution but, by adopting constitutions, acted to provide "new guards for their future security?" Is there any reason to doubt that the people of the several states, when they ratified the Constitution of 1787, did so for any reasons other than the "safety and happiness" for the sake of which they had ratified their state constitutions?

John Hancock, President of the Continental Congress, in his official letter transmitting the Declaration to the States remarked that since it would serve as the "Ground and Foundation" of any future government, the people should "be universally informed of it."[27] Eight of the original thirteen state constitutions were prefaced by "bills of rights," each in its own way articulating the principles of the Declaration as the ground and foundation of government. For example, the Virginia Constitution of 1776, which actually preceded the Declaration of Independence by nearly a month,[28] was prefaced by

---

[27] *See* Edward Erler, "Introduction," This volume, xxx.

[28] This only proves that both the Declaration and the state constitutions drew upon that common stock of ideas Jefferson called "the American mind." There is no reason whatever to think that the Framers and Ratifiers of the Constitution of 1787 had purposes different in any respect from those for which they had ratified their state constitutions.

A declaration of rights made by the representatives of the good people of Virginia . . . which . . . do pertain to them and their posterity as the basis and foundation of government.

The first article of the aforesaid, asserts

That all men are by nature equally free and independent, and have certain inherent rights, of which when they enter into a state of society, they cannot by any compact deprive or divest posterity; namely, the enjoyment of life and liberty, with the means of acquiring and possessing property, and pursuing and obtaining happiness and safety.

A dictum of James Madison, repeated many times in his writings, is that "Of all free government, compact is the basis and the essence."[29] The ground or basis of this pronouncement is the proposition of human equality, given the place of honor in the Article above, as it is in the Declaration of Independence, and as it one day would be in the Gettysburg Address. By this proposition, no human person has, by nature, or in the state of nature, more authority over another than another has over him. Hence lawful authority—the authority of free government—arises only by "compact" when free and equal individuals agree, one with another, to form a civil society with a government to which they have all freely consented.

Four years after Virginia, Massachusetts adopted a new constitution, which was also prefaced by a bill of rights, which was itself preceded by a preamble which was neither more nor less than a dissertation on the political philosophy of free government. It will be seen that the doctrines of this preamble, being philosophical, are not in any sense particular to Massachusetts, but are universally applicable. Here is the first paragraph of the aforesaid preamble:

The end of the institution, maintenance, and administration of government, is to secure the existence of the body politic, to protect it, and to furnish the individuals who compose it with the power of enjoying in safety and tranquillity their natural rights, and the blessings of life; and whenever these great objects are not obtained, the people have the right to alter the government, and to take measures necessary for their safety, prosperity, and happiness.

---

[29] 9 *Writings of James Madison* 573 (Hunt ed. 1900-10). Consider also: "It must not be forgotten, that compact, express or implied is the vital principle of free governments as contradistinguished from governments not free." *Id.* at 605.

The author of these words was John Adams, a member of the committee of the Continental Congress that had chosen Jefferson to be its draftsman for the Declaration of Independence. The "end of . . . government" referred to above, is the end of *any* government. Hence the people of Massachusetts, in ratifying the Constitution of 1787, could not possibly have had any different purposes than when, in 1780, they had ratified the constitution of their state. It is notable that the president[30] of Massachusetts ratifying convention was the same John Hancock who in 1776 had recommended the Declaration of Independence as expressing the "ground and foundation" of any future government.

What follows is the beginning of the second paragraph of the preamble to the Massachusetts Bill of Rights of 1780:

> The body politic is formed by a voluntary association of individuals; it is a social compact by which the whole people covenants with each citizen and each citizen with the whole people that all shall be governed by certain laws of the common good.

When Massachusetts turns to its declaration of rights proper, under Article I asserts that:

> All men are born free and equal, and have certain natural, essential, and unalienable rights; among which may be reckoned the right of enjoying and defending their lives and properties; that of acquiring and protecting property; and in fine, that of seeking and obtaining their safety and happiness.

It is, to repeat, because all men are by nature (or *originally*) equal in authority that civil society arises from consent. The body politic is a voluntary association, constituted in its foundation by a unanimous agreement, of each with all, and of all with each. After the unanimous agreement *constituting* civil society, rule by the majority legitimates both the establishing and the operating of government. But the boundaries within which majorities may rule are set by the original unanimous agreement, which is to secure, without invidious discrimination, the equal natural rights of all. Within civil society, majority and minority may differ as to the best means to protect the aforesaid rights. They may not, however, differ as to whether they ought to be protected. For example, no majority may, because it is a majority, confiscate the property of a minority. Nor can it forbid or abridge the rights enumerated in the First Amendment. To do so would contradict the reason for the existence of the government, and invite its overthrow. The rights of majorities and minorities are the rights of individuals, and have their origin in the state of nature, and

---

[30] Hancock was also the first governor of Massachusetts under the 1780 constitution.

in the unanimous agreement by which civil society is brought into being. They do not originate in any act of the majority itself.

That the principles governing the ratification of the Constitution of 1787 do not differ from those that governed the ratification of any of the state constitutions, is shown by Washington's letter of September 17, 1787, transmitting the Constitution to the Congress. He commented on the fact that the new Constitution would require the states to give up some of the independence they had possessed under the Articles of Confederation.

> It is obviously impracticable in the federal government of these states, to secure all the rights of independent sovereignty to each, and yet provide for the interest and safety of all: Individuals entering into society, must give up a share of liberty to preserve the rest.

"Individuals entering into society" means what Madison meant by saying that "compact is the basis and essence of free government." These are commonplaces of the Revolution and the Founding, repeated or implied in nearly all its documents. Washington compares the individual states, entering into the compact of the Constitution, to individual persons entering into the compact of civil society. In each case, so much of the antecedent liberty must be surrendered as will result in the safety that is sought. The safety sought from the state governments was not adequate, as is shown by the fact that independence could never have been achieved by the states separately. But union under the Articles of Confederation was also inadequate, so the greater and stronger Union of the Constitution was necessary. The powers that must be surrendered to government depend in each case upon the nature of the dangers and opportunities for which government is asked to provide.

The text of the Constitution does not contain the text of the Declaration of Independence, or any part of it. Therefore, according to Cooper, the assertion in the Republican party platforms of 1856 and 1860, that the principles of the Declaration of Independence are embodied in the Constitution, is merely gratuitous. But the Constitution became law only by virtue of its ratification by the people of the states. Before it was ratified, the Constitution and the intentions of its framers, had no more standing in law than the private papers of any members of the Convention. Even Cooper must concede that what the Constitution became, when it became a law, must be understood by reference to the state of mind of the ratifiers. It so happens that three of the states placed in their instruments of ratification, prologues that correspond to the bills of rights that formed prologues to eight of the original state constitutions. We have just seen excerpts from those of Virginia and Massachusetts. The following is quoted from the ratification by New York, July 26:

> We the delegates of the people of the state of New York . . . do declare and make known
>
> That all power is originally vested in and consequently derived from the people, and that government is instituted by them for their common interest, protection, and security.
>
> That the enjoyment of life, liberty and the pursuit of happiness are essential rights which every government ought to respect and preserve.
>
> That the powers of government may be reassumed by the people, whensoever it shall be necessary to happiness . . .
>
> That the people have an equal, natural and unalienable right, freely and peaceably to exercise their religion according to the dictates of conscience . . .

Similarly, North Carolina, in Convention, August 1, 1788, resolved, "*previous* to the ratification of the Constitution" that there should be

> a declaration of rights, asserting and securing from encroachment, the great principles of civil and religious liberty . . .

The first of these is:

> That there are certain natural rights of which men, when they form a social compact, cannot deprive or divest their posterity, among which are the enjoyment of life, and liberty, with the means of acquiring, possessing, and protecting property, and pursuing and obtaining happiness and safety.

The State of Rhode Island also prefaced its instrument of ratification, May 29, 1790, with an assertion of principles, the first of which was

> That there are certain natural rights, of which men when they form a social compact, cannot deprive or divest their posterity, among which are the enjoyment of life and liberty, with the means of acquiring, possessing and protecting property, and pursing and obtaining happiness and safety.[31]

---

[31] The texts of the ratifications of the Constitution, from which these quotations are taken, are to be found in *Documents Illustrative of the Formation of the Union of the American States* 1010-1059 (1927).

Is it not beyond dispute that the three states aforesaid, understood their ratifications as incorporating into the Constitution the principles of the Declaration of Independence, exactly as the Republican platforms of 1856 and 1860 would assert? Nor is there even the slightest evidence that the omission of such declarations of principles, from the other ratifications, meant anything except that they regarded them as redundant.

*   *   *   *   *

We ask the reader to return for a moment to the words of Chief Justice Rehnquist's quote above, in which he asserts that constitutional safeguards for individual liberty do not have "any intrinsic worth," nor an origin in "any . . . idea of natural justice." However, he says, they may take on a "generalized moral rightness or goodness" (whatever that means) if they are incorporated into a constitution by a people. Whatever "moral rightness or goodness" is attributed to them depends solely upon the aforesaid incorporation. Noting again that the safeguards for liberty and the safeguards for slavery were incorporated into the same constitution by the same people, we conclude that—on Rehnquist's premises—they possess equally the same "moral rightness or goodness." On such premises it is not permitted to say that the safeguards for liberty are consistent with the principles of the Constitution, while the safeguards for slavery represent compromises with those principles.

The controversy over the legal status of slavery in the United States territories, in the period from 1848 to 1860, led directly to secession and civil war. The opposing sides saw in the due process clause of the Fifth Amendment two absolutely contradictory commands: one, that of the Republican platforms outlawing slavery in every territory; the other, that of Chief Justice Taney, not only declaring slavery lawful in every territory, but requiring its protection, if necessary, by the federal government.[32] These two interpretations of the due process clause of the Fifth Amendment were paralleled by equally contradictory interpretations of Article IV, section 4, of the Constitution: "The United States shall guarantee to every State in this Union a Republican form of government . . ." We are told by the *Federalist* No. 39 that a republican government is one that "derives all its powers, directly or indirectly, from the great body of the people . . ." It is government, in short, that derives its just powers from the consent of the government. In 1860, there were, however, four million slaves, who were held under forcible restraint by governments in which they were not represented, and to which they had given no con-

---

[32] This demand was incorporated in the Southern Democratic platform of 1860.

sent. Were the government of the states republican by which these human beings were held by force against their will?

If we look not to Madison, but to Rehnquist for an answer, we again see that the same people at the same time incorporated into the same constitution both the republican guarantee and the slavery guarantee. Certainly there is nothing on the face of the Constitution—or in its text—that compels us to choose Madison over Rehnquist or Rehnquist over Madison. Madison, of course, assumed that the republican guarantee had to be interpreted in the light of the principles of the Declaration of Independence, and that the presence of slavery was an anomaly, a compromise that had to be tolerated as a matter of political necessity, if the Constitution was to be ratified. The proslavery Southerners, however, insisted—like Rehnquist, Bork, Graglia, and Cooper—that the Declaration of Independence was not part of the Constitution, and had no standing in constitutional law. They said not only that slavery existed by positive law, but that it was a positive good, and could not be condemned by any "higher law" principle. By 1860, they had been instructed in this doctrine by Calhoun for a period of thirty years. Hence they demanded that slavery be extended to all the United States territories, and thereby to all the new states to be formed from them.

Even before the Union victory in the Civil War, the Republican Congress prohibited slavery in all United States territories. That meant that, if the Union prevailed, there would be no more slave states. However, in the enabling acts by which Congress has prepared territories for statehood, from Nebraska in 1864, until Hawaii and Alaska in 1959, it has been laid down as a requirement of the new state constitutions, that they be "republican in form," and that there by nothing in them "repugnant to the Constitution of the United States and the principles of the Declaration of Independence." Here the identification of the republican guarantee with the principles of the Declaration, in the public law of the United States, is explicit and unambiguous. This is as much a vindication of the Republican platform of 1860 as the Thirteenth, Fourteenth and Fifteenth amendments. It is not only a repudiation of Calhoun's and Taney's interpretation of the republican guarantee clause, but of Rehnquist's and Bork's and Graglia's and Cooper's.

* * * * *

Both Bork, in *Tempting*, and Cooper,[33] quote the following passage from Justice Iredell's opinion in *Calder v. Bull* (1798)[34] as evidence of the uselessness of natural law for constitutional adjudication.

---

[33] *Tempting*, p. 20; Cooper, supra, p. 149.

The ideas of natural justice are regulated by no fixed standard; the best and the purest men have differed upon the subject; and all that the court could properly say, in such an event, would be that the legislature (possessed of an equal right of opinion) had passed an act which, in the opinion of the judges, was inconsistent with the abstract principles of natural justice.

Both Bork and Cooper take this to be proof positive that any appeal to natural justice or natural law is nothing more than a method of disguising the judge's "personal moral vision." As in Curtis's dissenting opinion in *Dred Scott*, they have completely misrepresented the opinion they have cited.

The case of *Calder v. Bull* arose from the fact that the legislature of the State of Connecticut had set aside a decree of a probate court with respect to an inheritance of real estate. The important point before the Supreme Court was whether the State had violated the constitutional prohibition against *ex post facto* laws. It decided that it had not, that the prohibition of *ex post facto* laws extended only to criminal, and not to civil cases, and that the State had acted within its constitutional jurisdiction.

Here is how Iredell expounded the "general principles" which, he said, influenced his opinion:

If then a government composed of Legislative, Executive, and Judicial departments, were established, by a Constitution, which imposed no limits on legislative power [as in the constitution of Great Britain], the consequence would inevitably be, that whatever the legislative power chose to enact, would be lawfully enacted, and the judicial power cold never interpose to pronounce it void. It is true that some speculative jurists have held, that a legislative act against natural justice must, in itself, be void; but I cannot think that, under such a government, any court of justice would possess a power to declare it so.

What Iredell is saying is that in a government, like that of Great Britain, where there was no constitutional separation of powers, and where the crown in parliament may pass any law "not naturally impossible," judicial review is legally impossible. He dismisses the "speculative jurists," not because he disagrees with their ideas of natural justice, but because in such a case those ideas would have no legal basis for enforcement. What Iredell has in mind, as an example of natural justice, is the prohibition against *ex post facto* laws. As we shall see, it never occurs to Iredell,

---

[34] All citations to Iredell's opinion are in 3 U.S. (1 Dall.) 386, 398-9.

that such laws (like bills of attainder) do not violate natural justice. Iredell continues:

> In order therefore to avoid so great an evil it has been the policy of all the American states which have individually framed their state constitutions since the Revolution, and of the people of the United States, when they framed the Federal Constitution, to define with precision the objects of legislative power, and to restrain its exercise within marked and settled boundaries. If any act of Congress, or of the legislature of a state violates those constitutional provisions, it is unquestionably void. . . . If on the other hand, the Legislature of the Union, or the legislature of any member of the Union, shall pass a law, within the general scope of their legislative power, the Court cannot pronounce it to be void, merely because it is, in their judgment, contrary to the principles of natural justice.

It is at this point in Iredell's opinion that the passage occurs which Bork and Cooper quote. But how different the sense of that passage now appears!

What is that "great evil" that the American constitutions have been framed to avoid? It is one in which there is no legal power to void a legislative act that is "against natural justice." It is precisely because the wisdom of "speculative jurists" has been brought to bear in the framing of our constitutions, that *ex post facto* laws and bills of attainder (but not only *ex post facto* laws and bills of attainder) can now be pronounced void in our courts.

In *Federalist* No. 47, Madison writes that

> [t]he accumulation of all powers, legislative, executive, and judiciary in the same hands, whether of one, a few, or many, and whether hereditary, self-appointed, or elective, may justly be pronounced the very definition of tyranny. Were the federal Constitution therefore really chargeable with the accumulation of power, or with a mixture of powers, having a dangerous tendency to such an accumulation, no further arguments would be necessary to inspire a universal reprobation of the system.

Separation of powers, which is implied throughout the Declaration of Independence, is a maxim of the natural law. It is another example of how, in the *Federalist*, the Constitution is tested by the fundamental principles of the Revolution. Perhaps most revealing, because so taken for granted, is the use of the word "tyranny." This is identical with the "great evil" which, according to Iredell, the American constitutions were framed to avoid. Iredell, like Madison, assumes the moral order of the natural law, which defines the distinction between tyranny and freedom, good and evil, as the basis of American constitutionalism.

Iredell says that if an act of Congress, or of the legislature of a state, violates the constitutionally "marked and settled boundaries" of legislative power, then "it is unquestionably void." There can be no question then as to the power of the Court in such an event to declare acts of Congress unconstitutional;[35] although Iredell says it is a power that ought to be exercised only in a "clear and urgent case." Iredell's stricture against justices invoking "ideas of natural justice" applies only to cases in which the legislature is acting within the boundaries marked out for it by the Constitution. In such cases, the legislators "exercise the discretion vested in them by the people, to whom alone they are responsible . . ." This division of responsibility, between judiciary and legislature, is itself a dictate of the natural law, by which we avoid so great an evil as the tyranny inherent in unseparated powers.

At the end of his opinion Iredell remarks:

> Upon the whole . . . there cannot be a case in which an *ex post facto* law in criminal matters is requisite or justifiable . . . for Providence never can intend to promote the prosperity of any country by bad means.

The Declaration of Independence ends with an appeal to "the supreme Judge of the world" for the rectitude of the intentions of the American people. Confident of that rectitude, they place a firm reliance upon the protection of divine Providence. Iredell assumes as the foundation of constitutional jurisprudence the identical natural and divine moral order that is invoked by the Declaration of Independence.

* * * * *

A penetrating insight into the mind of Cooper's (and Bork's) "originalism" is the following:

> For Jaffa, the Declaration defines "the legal . . . and moral personality" of the American people . . . once and for all. The American people are thus enslaved to the "moral and political philosophy" of the founders, powerless to redefine their "legal and . . . moral personality." Any attempt by the American people to "compromise" the natural law principles of the Declaration—for example, by amending their Constitution—would

---

[35] Here, although somewhat less dramatic in presentation, is Marshall's doctrine, some five years before *Marbury v. Madison*.

conflict with the "genuine principles" of the Constitution and thus be void.

Jaffa illustrates his point vividly by arguing that the American people lack the "inherent authority" to repeal the Thirteenth Amendment . . . for which there is no support among decent people.[36]

According to Cooper, I would "enslave" the American people to the moral and political philosophy of the Founding Fathers, that is to say, I would enslave them to the principles of freedom! This is, to say the least, a curious way of thinking for someone who is committed to a jurisprudence of original intent. I had thought that the right to redefine ourselves legally and morally—a refusal to be "enslaved" to obsolete eighteenth century doctrines—was the heart of the liberal jurisprudence to which Cooper (and Bork) profess to be opposed. Why, indeed, should the justices (or the American people) be "enslaved" to the Constitution at all?

Among the fundamental rights of the Declaration of Independence—cited repeatedly in the *Federalist* (and by Washington in his Farewell Address)—is the right of the people to alter or abolish their government, and to change such governments in any way that to them shall seem most likely to effect their safety and happiness. It is difficult to see how this doctrine can enslave anyone.

But Cooper finds slavishness is my assertion that the American people lack the inherent authority to repeal the Thirteenth Amendment. To Cooper, that is a limitation upon their freedom. So, of course would be prohibition on suicide. Let us then suppose instead an amendment to change the Constitution from republican to monarchical, an amendment designating some family, e.g., the Kennedy's, as the royal family. As in the Roman Empire, all authority would be a delegation or devolution from the king or emperor. Do the people have the right to annihilate their own authority? They may, of course, have the power to do so. But power and right are two different things—a distinction which however is lost upon legal positivists.

As to repealing the Thirteenth Amendment, Cooper says that this is something "for which there is no support among decent people." But what, to a legal positivist, does "decency" have to do with constitutionalism? According to Rehnquist, constitutions derive whatever moral goodness—or decency—that may be attributed to them from the mere fact of being adopted, and from nothing else. As we know from *Huckleberry Finn*, in the antebellum South, the most despised character of all was the "nigger stealer." No one was lower in the scale of decency. After

---

[36] Cooper, This volume, p. 146.

the end of Reconstruction, the worst of epithets in the postbellum South was "nigger lover."[37] Today decency is defined differently, although not everywhere. Legal positivism and moral relativism go hand in hand: what is called "decency" is nothing but the prevailing moral fashion. For Cooper—who would not be enslaved to any permanent standards—true freedom would allow one to be proslavery at one time and antislavery at another. Let us then have no squeamishness about decency. Let us not masquerade personal preferences behind the moral and political philosophy of the Declaration of Independence!

Epilogue

> *How art thou fallen from Heaven,*
> *O Lucifer son of the morning!*

When *National Review* published "Jaffa v. Bork: An Exchange" (March 21, 1984), the editors, in their wisdom, decided to give Bork the last word. My rebuttal to his reply was not published. In the light of the subsequent "exchanges" between Lino Graglia, Charles Cooper, and myself, Bork's aforesaid "last word" deserves to be noticed. It seems to me that this is a proper place to notice it.

Bork wrote:

> The odd notion, which Jaffa shares with Taney, that the Constitution contained a right, good against the federal government, to own slaves rests entirely upon a few provisions that attempt to cope with the brute fact that slaves were held in the Southern states and the North could do nothing about that if a nation was to be created.

From "nowhere in the Constitution" to "a few provisions" of the Constitution! Has there ever, since Lucifer, been such a Fall? How many provisions of the Constitution are there, protecting the right of free speech, or the free exercise of religion, or the right to petition the government for redress of grievances?

Bork cannot admit to being wrong. Like a bear with a paw in a trap, he (and his disciples) strike out at me, but they cannot free the trapped paw: Bork can no longer say that a right to won slaves is to be found "nowhere in the Constitution."

---

[37] Not long ago, I received a Christmas card from the John Wilkes Booth Society, addressing me by this very epithet—of which I am very proud.

What then is the "odd notion" that I am said to share with Taney? It is "that the Constitution contained a right good against the federal government to own slaves." Here is what Abraham Lincoln said about the fugitive slave clause, in the last of his seven joint debates with Douglas, October 15, 1858:

> I suppose most of us (I know it of myself) believe that the people of the Southern States are entitled to a Congressional fugitive slave law—*that it is a right fixed in the Constitution.* . . . And as *the right is constitutional* I agree that legislation shall be granted to it. . . . Why then do I yield support to a fugitive slave law? Because I do not understand that the Constitution, *which guarantees that right*, can be supported without it.[38]

I will plead guilty then to sharing, with Abraham Lincoln, the "odd notion" that there are rights of slave owners "fixed in the [antebellum] Constitution."

Bork now grudgingly admits that the right to own slaves was indeed recognized in the Constitution. But he tries to dismiss it as a matter of no importance. (One wonders why, if it was so unimportant, he denied it in the first place!) They were entirely due, he says, to the necessity

> to cope with the brute fact that slaves were held in the Southern states and that the North could do nothing about that if a nation was to be created.

What Bork says here, however ungraciously, is neither more nor less than what Lincoln (and Jaffa) have all along maintained. Bork calls the presence of slavery a "brute fact." But the Constitution itself says nothing to distinguish its brute from its non-brute provisions. By the principles of Borkian originalism the judge has no right to intrude his personal moral judgments into the interpretation of the Constitution, by calling one part of it—but not another—"brute."

Bork attempt to use Robert Goldwin as a witness for his expurgated (or non-brute) version of the Constitution. He quotes from *Why Blacks, Woman, and Jews Are Not Mentioned in the Constitution.*[39] According to Goldwin, says Bork, there is no

> evidence [in the original Constitution] of the kind of thinking ascribed to the founders by Chief Justice Taney in the *Dred Scott* case . . . there is no such racism to be found in the Constitution, then or now, not a word of it.

---

[38] 3 *Collected Works* 317 (italics added).
[39] Robert Goldwin, *Why Blacks, Women, and Jews Are Not Mentioned in the Constitution* 15 (1990).

We now repeat the above quotation, with the words that Bork has left out inserted in italics in their proper place. According to Goldwin, there is no

> evidence [in the original Constitution] of the kind of thinking ascribed to the founders by Chief Justice Taney in the *Dred Scott* case. *Taney said that the founders thought that blacks were jot included in the declaration that "all men are created equal," and that blacks were "so far inferior that they had no rights which the white man was bound to respect." But Taney was wrong*, there is no such racism to be found in the Constitution, then or now, not a word of it.

Taney was wrong, according to Goldwin, not because of substantive due process, or of anything of the kind, but because he left blacks out of the Declaration of Independence. According to Goldwin, they are included as human persons in the Constitution *because* they are included as human persons in the Declaration. The Declaration is accordingly the key to the interpretation of the Constitution. Goldwin's position is identical with that of the Republican Party of Abraham Lincoln. Goldwin is my witness, not Bork's. Bork, however, is true to form in shamelessly expurgating Goldwin's text, twisting it to mean something that Goldwin never intended, just as he had done with the text of the Constitution, and with Curtis's and Iredell's opinions.

* * * * *

In a letter in the May, 1995 issue of *Commentary*, Judge Bork replied to a critic of an article of his on the First Amendment.[40] The critic commended to Bork words of the Declaration of Independence that seemed to him to justify a broader conception of freedom of speech than Bork's. Bork responded as follows:

> It is particularly nonsensical to quote the Declaration of Independence's enunciation of a right to alter or abolish government. That right was asserted against an English government in which Americans had no say and which they regarded as tyrannical. Having established a representative government here, the Founders proceeded to enact laws that denied any right of revolution on these shores.

It is fitting to conclude our discourse with this evidence of the complete alienation of Judge Bork from the political thought of the Founders. The right of revolution is a manifestation of the right of self-preservation,

---

[40] I had no part whatever in this dispute.

which is a right of nature, and cannot be denied. The laws that Judge Bork said the Founders enacted, never existed, never could exist, and so far as I know, were never thought to exist by anyone except Judge Bork.

In the *Federalist* No. 43, James Madison justified the action of the Convention in scrapping the Articles of Confederation for an entirely new Constitution, an action as revolutionary, in its own right, as the separation from Great Britain. He did so by appealing to

> the great principle of self-preservation; to the transcendent law of nature and of nature's God, which declares that the safety and happiness of society are the objects at which all political institutions aim, and to which all political institutions must be sacrificed.

It frequently happens that a new government cannot be instituted unless an older one is abolished. That is what happened in 1787. Hence, it was an exercise of the right of revolution, that the Constitution itself came into being. The right of revolution cannot be denied, without denying the ground of the authority of the Constitution itself.

In the Kentucky Resolutions of 1798, Jefferson denounced the Congress and president "of our choice" in terms scarcely distinguishable from those in which he had denounced the king and Parliament of Great Britain in 1776. By the Alien and Sedition Act, he said, they may "drive these States into revolution and blood." The Founding Fathers feared the tyranny of the majority no less than the tyranny of autocratic government. They never for a moment supposed that by establishing representative government they had rendered the right of revolution superfluous or extraneous. In his first inaugural address, Abraham Lincoln (as usual) gives us the last word:

> This country, with its institutions, belongs to the people who inhabit it. Whenever they shall grow weary of the existing government, they can exercise their *constitutional* right of amending it, or their *revolutionary* right to dismember or overthrow it. (emphasis original)

"The Whole Theory of Democracy":
Antonin Scalia, Meet James Madison and Friends

Recently Mr. Justice Antonin Scalia addressed the Gregorian University in Rome. Following the address, there was a question and answer period in which the justice delivered himself of a number of opinions, among them the following:

> It just seems to me incompatible with democratic theory that it's good and right for the state to do something that the majority of the people do not want done. Once you adopt democratic theory, it seems to me, you accept that proposition. If the people, for example, want abortion the state should permit abortion. If the people do not want it, the state should be able to prohibit it.

And again:

> The whole theory of democracy . . . Is that the majority rules; that is the whole theory of it. You protect minorities only because the majority determines, that there are certain minority positions that deserve protection.

And again:

> You either agree with democratic theory or you do not. But you cannot have democratic theory and then say, but what about the minority? The minority loses, except to the extent that the majority, in its document of government, has agreed to accord the minority rights.[1]

It is difficult to say which is the greater, the confidence, or the simplicity, with which Justice Scalia tells us what is "the whole theory of democracy." He says that "once you accept democratic theory" then the state "should" do whatever a majority of the people want. If a majority of the people want abortion to be lawful, he says, it should be lawful. If they do not, it should not. Does he accept that same standard with respect to slavery, the confiscation of property, or the waging of a war of aggression to plunder and enslave another nation? What of the prohibition of *ex post facto* laws, and bills of attainder? If the majority "wanted" them re-

---

[1] "Justice Scalia/Rome Address." *Origins, CNS Documentary Service,* Vol. 26, No. 6 (June 27, 1996).

moved from the Constitution, then should they be? What about *habeas corpus*? If "once you adopt democratic theory" (as Scalia says) the will of the majority ought always to prevail, then democracy can vote itself into tyranny, as when the majority of the German people scrapped the Weimar Constitution and declared that henceforth Hitler would be the voice of the people.

I have been teaching political philosophy for more than half a century, and I do not recall any protagonist of democracy among the ranks of political philosophers—beginning with Spinoza—who subscribes to the democratic canon laid down by Scalia. While the majority of the American people certainly subscribe to majority rule, they have never done so in the sense espoused by Scalia. Few, even today, would disagree with Jefferson, in the *Notes on the State of Virginia*, when he said "It was not an elective despotism that we fought for." In the Kentucky Resolutions of 1798, denouncing the Alien and Sedition Acts, Jefferson used language closely resembling that with which in 1776 he had denounced the tyranny of the king and Parliament of Great Britain:

> it would be a dangerous delusion were a confidence in the men of our choice to silence our fears for the safety of our rights . . . let the honest advocate of confidence read the alien and sedition acts . . . and say what the government is if it be not a tyranny which the men of our choice have conferred on the President, and the President of our choice has assented to.

After the electoral sweep of the Republicans in 1800 had calmed the storm of 1798, Jefferson in his inaugural pronounced these magisterial words:

> All, too, will bear in mind this sacred principle, that though the will of the majority is in all cases to prevail, that will to be rightful must be reasonable; that the minority possess their equal rights, which equal law must protect, and to violate would be oppression.

According to Jefferson, but contrary to Scalia, "the minority possess their equal rights" altogether independently of the majority. In all the pronouncements of the Founding Fathers it is assumed that the right which minorities possess are antecedent to majority rule, and that majority rule is circumscribed by these rights.

Notwithstanding the foregoing, the "theory" of which Scalia speaks is very old. In Plato's *Republic* Thrasymachus declares that justice is the interest of the stronger. This means that in a democracy in which a majority of mere numbers may enforce its will—justice means obeying the laws that the people have laid down as in their interest. Thrasymachus's doctrine has been repeated endless times, often in recent centuries on the supposed authority of Machiavelli. But Socrates demolished it with a simple question: do the rulers, e.g. the majority, always decree what is really in their interest? Or are they sometimes mistaken, and do they not sometimes decree what is against their interest? Thrasymachus must concede that they are sometimes mistaken. Only insofar as rulers know what is in their true interest, as distinct from what they may think in the passion of the moment is their interest, can there be an unqualified duty of obedience. In a democracy, no less than in any other form of government, the will of the people to be defensible must be a rational will.

In American history, the most notable exponent of the Scalia theory was Stephen A. Douglas, Lincoln's redoubtable opponent in the great debates of 1858. Douglas said he didn't care whether slavery was voted up or voted down in the territories. He cared only for the sacred right of the people to decide that question for themselves. But Lincoln thought that slavery in the territories should be prohibited by Congress, and that the people of the territories should be denied such a right. Here in essence, is Douglas's idea of majority rule:

> We in Illinois . . . tried slavery, kept it up for twelve years, and finding that it was not profitable we abolished it for that reason.

Here is Lincoln's answer:

> [Judge Douglas] says he "don't care whether [slavery] is voted up or voted down in the Territories. . . . Any man can say that who does not see anything wrong in slavery, but no man can logically say it who does see a wrong in it; because no man can logically say he don't care whether a wrong is voted up or voted down.

Lincoln did not think that right and wrong could be put to a vote. In this he faithfully reflected those who framed and those who ratified the Constitution. In their minds, the foundation of all our free institutions is the doctrine that, under the laws of nature and of nature's God, all human beings are endowed with certain unalienable rights, and that it is for the sake of these rights that governments are instituted. As these rights belong a priori to every human person, they are of necessity the rights of every minority. Here is what the Massachusetts Constitution of 1780, drafted by John Adams, says:

> The end of the institution, maintenance, and administration of government is to secure the existence of the body politic, to protect it, and to furnish the individuals who compose it with the power of enjoying in safety and tranquillity their natural

rights, and the blessings of life. . . .The body politic is formed
by a voluntary association of individuals; it is a social compact
by which the whole people covenants with each citizen and
each citizen with the whole people that all shall be governed by
certain laws or the common good.

In the foregoing we note the logical (and ontological) priority of individuals (and the rights of individuals) to the political community which
they form. The body politic is formed by a "social compact," an agreement among human beings no one of whom, prior to the formation of the
body politic, has more authority over another, than the other has over
him. Accordingly there must be unanimous consent—each agreeing with
all and all with each—that the government they are establishing will furnish each individual with the power of enjoying their natural rights. According to Article I of the same Massachusetts Constitution:

All men are born free and equal, and have certain natural, essential, and unalienable rights; among which may be reckoned
the right of enjoying and defending their lives and liberties;
that of acquiring, possessing, and protecting property; and in
fine of seeking and obtaining their safety and happiness.

Majority rule can arise only among those who have previously reached
such an agreement to honor and respect each other's natural rights. The
majority cannot be authorized to do anything inconsistent with this
agreement. This is, if not the whole theory of democracy, its true and
necessary foundation. Rationality—mutual respect for each other's natural rights—must characterize the community that agrees to abide by the
rule of the majority. Without such rationality governing the majority, the
majority itself has no right to govern. The legitimacy of majority rule
depends at every point upon the enlightenment of the community to be
governed by it. Hence George Washington, in one of his magisterial de-
liverances:

The foundation of our empire was not laid in the gloomy age of
ignorance and superstition, but at an epoch when the rights of
mankind were better understood and more clearly defined, than
at any former period.

In the 1830s, near the end of his life, James Madison was engaged in
a bitter battle with John C. Calhoun and the South Carolina doctrine of
the right of a state to nullify an act of Congress. At bottom was the question of what was the ultimate source of sovereignty, of legitimate authority under the Constitution. Calhoun did not, like Jefferson and Adams
and Madison, recognize authority arising from individuals. According to

Calhoun, it was communities, not individuals—the states as collective entities—that were the source of authority. Here is a passage from an essay by Madison entitled "Sovereignty," in which he articulates with great precision the origin and limits of majority rule:

> To go to the bottom of this subject let us consult the Theory which contemplates a certain number of individuals as meeting and agreeing to form one political society, in order that the rights the safety & the interest of each may be under the safeguard of the whole.
>
> The first supposition is that each individual being previously independent of the others, the compact which is to make them one society must result from the free consent of every individual.
>
> But as the objects in view could not be attained, if every measure conducive to them required the consent of every member of society, the theory further supposes, either that it was part of the original compact, that the will of the majority was to be deemed the will of the whole, or that this was a law of nature, resulting from the nature of political society itself, the offspring of the natural wants of man.
>
> Whatever be the hypothesis of the origin of the *lex majoris partis*, it is evident that it operates as a plenary substitute of the will of the majority of the society for the will of the whole society; and that the sovereignty of the society as vested in & exercisable by the majority, may do anything that could be rightfully done by the unanimous concurrence of the members; the reserved rights of individuals (of conscience for example) in becoming parties to the original compact being beyond the legitimate reach of sovereignty, wherever vested or however viewed. [Emphasis original]

It is an oft-repeated maxim of the Father of the Constitution that "Of all free government compact is the basis and essence." The underlying reason is that all men being created equal, or being born free and equal, legitimate authority must arise from a voluntary agreement. Before 1776, few if any governments rested upon such an assumption. At most they were based upon force or fraud, or some combination thereof. What Madison says is true of *free* government, government based upon reason and the nature of man. This is certainly what, in the mind of the Father of the Constitution, is the basis and essence of the Constitution.

The original compact, which is to make them members of one society, requires, Madison says, "the free consent of every individual." The importance of this assertion is indicated by Madison's own emphasis. Unanimous consent is the necessary foundation of majority rule, and circumscribes majority rule. It means that the majority may do only those things that have been agreed to by everyone, prior to the formation of the government. That every individual must consent as aforesaid, means that those who do not consent are not part of the body politic: they have no right to share in making the laws, and they are not obligated to obey the laws—except as resident aliens—that they do not share in making.

This rule of unanimity as a feature of the law of nature is reflected in Article VII of the Constitution. Considering the states as moral persons, their joining to form the United States under the Constitution is governed by the same rules that govern individuals in the state of nature forming a body politic. Once nine states have ratified, the Constitution begins to operate, but only as between those who have so ratified. The majority of nine states has no authority over the four, until the four have joined the nine. Today all fifty states in the Union have ratified the Constitution, so that today as in Madison's day, the Constitution stands adopted by the unanimous consent of every state. Amending the Constitution does not require unanimity, because the amending procedures have been previously authorized by the original unanimity. But the amending process, the outcome of prior unanimity, is itself far from majoritarian. Ratification by three-fourths of the states, preceded by two-thirds of both houses of Congress, means that a minority may veto a decision of the majority. The Bill of Rights is not then, as Scalia supposes, an act of condescension by the majority, nor do the rights in question originate, in any sense, with the majority. But, it may be objected, when each of the states ratifies the Constitution, it does so by the action of a majority within each state. We are reminded however by the Massachusetts Constitution of 1780 (and John Adams), that each state was itself formed originally by unanimous consent, by which majority rule in that state came into being.

The majority, Madison says, may do anything that might rightfully be done by unanimous concurrence. It is notable that unanimity is a necessary, but not a sufficient condition, for the exercise of legitimate authority. Jonestown, we may recall, committed communal suicide, apparently by unanimous consent. A war to conquer, plunder, or enslave another nation, cannot be justified by any majority, not even one that is unanimous. Rightfulness is not what the majority decides, nor is it what the minority decides. In a letter to Spenser Roane, Jefferson said that the ultimate authority for the principles of the Constitution, was "the people en masse." They, he said, are independent of everything "but moral law." Contrary to Scalia, the people do not make the moral law, the moral law makes the people. No matter what honor there may be among thieves, a band of robbers is not a people. The Declaration of Independence, be it noted, was not issued on the authority of the people, but of "the good people of these colonies." Their goodness is attested by their appeal "to the Supreme Judge of the world for the rectitude of [their] intentions." It is because of their conscientious belief in this rectitude that they are able to place "a firm reliance on the protection of Divine Providence." At every point, the authority of the majority depends upon its operating within the moral boundaries of "the laws of nature and of nature's God."

According to Madison, the government of the body politic that originates in unanimous consent is limited government. Not even unanimous concurrence can justify invading the reserved rights of individuals. The free exercise of religion—the rights of conscience—are beyond the reach of any majority because they are "beyond the legitimate reach of sovereignty, wherever vested or however viewed." Madison and the other Founders knew that unless sectarian religious dogmas or doctrines were beyond the reach of political majorities, government by majority rule would be impossible. No Protestant, Catholic, or Jew would submit voluntarily to a government which undertook to tell him what he must believe in such matters. But it was also the case that no majority could possess legitimacy that was not formed by a political process in which there were guarantees of freedom of speech, press, and association. These rights are natural rights, because they are inherent in free government, and no majority can rightfully govern without them. Personal liberty, and private property, are grounded in our rights under the laws of nature, and the majority exists to protect them, not to decide whether they shall be protected. It is simply not true then, as Scalia says, that "the majority determines that there are certain minorities or minority positions that deserve protection." What positions deserve protection is determined by reason and nature, not by the majority.

In 1786 Madison wrote a letter to James Monroe, with thoughts that might as well have been addressed to Justice Scalia:

> There is no maxim in my opinion which is more liable to be misapplied, and which therefore more needs elucidation than the current one that the interest of the majority is the political standard of right and wrong. Taking the word "interest" as synonymous with "ultimate happiness," in which sense it is qualified with every necessary moral ingredient, the proposition is no doubt true. But taking it in the popular sense, as referring to the immediate augmentation of property and wealth, nothing can be more false. In the latter sense it would be in the interest of the majority in every community to despoil & enslave the

> minority of individuals . . . In fact, it is only establishing under
> another name and a more specious form, force as a measure of
> right.

The foregoing was written in the year before the Constitutional Convention, nearly a half century before the essay on sovereignty. It expresses Madison's fears of the tyranny of the majority, so rampant in the states, constituted as they were under the Articles of Confederation. The prohibitions laid upon the states in the Constitution (e.g. coining money, and impairing the obligation of contracts) were among the means for preventing such tyranny. But the overall design of the Constitution, as we know from the 10th and 51st *Federalist*, was relied upon more profoundly to prevent the formation of a tyrannical majority. Unlike Scalia, Madison never thought that the unqualified interest of the majority should be taken as the political standard of right and wrong. Like Socrates, Madison does however distinguish the popular from the philosophic meaning of the interest of the majority in "ultimate happiness." Madison is also Socratic in asserting that "ultimate happiness" is consistent only with "every moral ingredient." Whenever the majority despoils and enslaves the minority, it is acting against its own true interests. It is therefore of the essence of constitutional government that, so far as possible, the majority be formed in such a manner as to prevent this from happening. But Madison did not rule out the possibility that, even under the best of circumstances, majorities might fail in their respect for the rights of individuals. In his great speech commending the Bill of Rights to the Congress in 1789, he said that:

> If [these rights] are incorporated into the Constitution, independent tribunals of justice will consider themselves in a peculiar manner the guardians of these rights; they will be an impenetrable bulwark against every assumption of power in the Legislative or Executive; they will be naturally led to resist ever encroachment upon rights expressly stipulated for in the Constitution by the declaration of rights.

Certainly the Father of the Constitution envisaged judicial review as a means of safeguarding the rights of minorities against depredations by the elected branches of government. This was once recognized by Judge Bork, when he was younger and wiser than he is today. In a 1968 article, he wrote:

> A desire for some legitimate form of judicial activism is inherent in a tradition that runs strong and deep in our culture, a tradition that can be called "Madisonian." We continue to believe there are some things no majority should be allowed to do to

us, no matter how democratically it may decide to do them. A Madisonian system assumes that in wide areas of life a legislative majority is entitled to rule for no better reason than that it is a majority. But it also assumes there are some aspects of life a majority should not control, that coercion in such matters is tyranny, a violation of the individual's natural rights. Clearly, the definition of natural rights cannot be left to either the majority or the minority. In the popular understanding upon which the power of the Supreme Court rests, it is precisely the function of the Court to resolve this dilemma by giving content to the concept of natural rights in case by case interpretations of the Constitution.[2]

Judge Bork was mistaken in saying that there are areas in which a legislative majority is entitled to rule for no better reason than that it is a majority. As we have seen, by the theory of natural rights, which Bork here invokes, there is no governmental power which is not a delegation from the governed to the government. However, when Bork says that "we" believe that there are some things no majority should be allowed to do, no matter how democratically it may decide to do them, he is in exact agreement with the original intentions of "We the people" who ordained the Constitution. And, we might add, in exact disagreement with the "whole theory of democracy" propounded by Scalia.

What Bork here calls the "popular understanding" upon which the power of the Supreme Court rests, is one shared by both majority and minority. It assumes moreover that the Supreme Court has access to the reason underlying majority rule and minority rights, and that it will not be afflicted with the passions of partisanship in articulating the aforesaid reason. In 1968 Bork saw clearly that natural rights were an integral element of a constitutional jurisprudence of original intent, and not (as he thinks today) a vehicle for inventing rights not sanctioned by the Constitution.

In response to a question of the relationship of the Constitution to the Declaration of Independence—and to "the laws of nature and of nature's God"—Scalia responded as follows:

Well unfortunately, or to my mind fortunately, the Supreme Court of the United States, no federal court to my knowledge, in 220 years has ever decided a case on the basis of the Declaration of Independence. It is not part of our law.

---

[2] Quoted in *Original Intent and the Framers of the Constitution*, p. 278.

Unfortunately, the most important (and disastrous) case ever decided by the Supreme Court—that of *Dred Scott*—turned upon the assertion by the chief justice in the opinion of the Court, that the proposition in the Declaration of Independence, that all men are created equal, did not include the Negro. It was upon this basis that Taney said that Negroes, whether free or slave, could not become citizens. Taney also said that slaves, as property, could be taken to any United States territory, and that such property had a constitutional right to protection there. Taney's opinion in 1857 was a direct response to the Republican Party platform of 1856, which had declared that slavery was unlawful in any United States territory. The question of the constitutional status of slavery in the territories was the direct and immediate cause of the breakup of the Union and the Civil War. The answer that the contending parties gave to this question turned entirely upon how they read the Declaration, and how they viewed its relationship to the Constitution.

According to the Republicans, the Declaration of Independence, had declared that all men of all colors are created equal. Hence when the Fifth Amendment was incorporated into the Constitution, it became unlawful to deprive any person of any color of his liberty in any United States territory, without due process of law. This latter qualification meant without having been convicted of any crime. The Republicans held that slavery existed legally in the United States, only by the positive law of the slave states. Outside their jurisdiction—as in federal territories—the natural law of freedom took precedence. Taney attempted to undercut this position by denying that the Negro was included in the Declaration, and therefore by denying that there was any such natural law of freedom as the Republicans had asserted.

Taney's denial of the inclusion of the Negro in the Declaration was notoriously false, and he knew it. But the election returns of 1856 clearly presaged a Republican victory in 1860. He sought desperately to find a constitutional argument that would divide the Free Soil coalition and prevent their impending victory. In this he failed, thanks largely to the efforts of Abraham Lincoln, who argued relentlessly not only that the Declaration did include the Negro, but that the rights of white men, no less than of Negroes, turned upon the recognition of this truth.

But the story of *Dred Scott*, and the importance of the Declaration in constitutional jurisprudence did not end with Lincoln's election, or with the Union victory in the Civil War. The Thirteenth Amendment reversed one part of Taney's opinion, by ending slavery. But another part of that same opinion, that Negroes, whether free or slave, could not become citizens of the United States, required still another amendment. Hence the first sentence of Section 1 of the Fourteenth Amendment, declares that

All persons born or naturalized in the United States and subject to the jurisdiction thereof, are citizens the United States and of the State wherein they reside.

The second sentence adds to this:

No State shall make or enforce any law which shall abridge the privileges and immunities of citizens of the United States, nor shall any State deprive any person of life, liberty, or property, without due process of law; nor deny to any person within its jurisdiction the equal protection of the laws.

In the last half century the greatest constitutional controversies have swirled around the "due process" and "equal protection" clauses. Liberals, by and large, have argued that these clauses were intended to protect the rights of Negro citizens. And so they assuredly were. But do they protect the rights of Negroes because they are Negro, or because they are human persons? If the former, then non-Negro citizens are not protected by the Fourteenth Amendment, and "reverse discrimination" or "benign discrimination" are constitutional. If the latter, then there can be no such thing as constitutional discrimination on the basis of race or color.

The answer to the question of whether the equal protection clause protects Negroes as a class, or as individuals, must be looked upon in the light of the original intent of the Fourteenth Amendment. That intent included reversing Taney's decision that Negroes could not be citizens by reversing the opinion upon which Taney's decision was based. And that opinion, to repeat, was that Negroes were not included in the proposition of equality in the Declaration of Independence. If then the Fourteenth Amendment assumes the inclusion of Negroes in the Declaration, it assumes that the rights protected by the Fourteenth Amendment are the rights of "all men," and hence are individual rights, not group rights. This goes to the heart of every equal protection case that the Supreme Court might hear.

Scalia is simply mistaken when he says that the Declaration of Independence is "no part of our law." Every enabling act for the admission of new states into the union, beginning with Nebraska in 1864 and ending with Hawaii and Alaska in 1959, has had a provision that the constitution of the new state shall be "republican in form" and that there shall be in it, nothing "repugnant to the Constitution of the United States and to the principles of the Declaration of Independence." It may be true that no case has yet been decided on the basis of these enabling acts, but they are laws nonetheless. These acts settled once and for all the question of whether slavery is consistent with the republican form of government guaranteed to every state of the Union in the Constitution of 1787. They not only represent the Union victory in the Civil War but the victory of the constitutional doctrine of the Republican platform of 1860. The Constitution of 1787, while guaranteeing to every state of the Union a republican form of government, nowhere defines what that form is. Since this republican guarantee left the slavery of the slave states undisturbed, it could plausibly be maintained that slavery was not repugnant to the republican form of government. Now however the public law of the United States contradicts that position. The republican guarantee is now explicitly and indissolubly linked to the principles of the Declaration of Independence. The republican guarantee now reinforces the position that the equal protection clause of the Fourteenth Amendment must be understood in the light of the principles of the Declaration of Independence.

Afterword

Jaffa's Quarrel with Bork: Religious Belief Masquerading as Constitutional Argument

Lino A. Graglia

Harry Jaffa has long engaged in a campaign of vilification against Robert Bork and Chief Justice William Rehnquist, a campaign I consider both sad and shabby. It is sad because he is attacking people who are on my and, he says, his side of the basic issue of constitutional law—the issue of the proper role of the Supreme Court in our system of government. One must expect attacks on Bork and Rehnquist from Ronald Dworkin, Bruce Ackerman, and Larry Tribe, and one can derive satisfaction from refuting them. But Jaffa is a hard-core political conservative; he was an advisor to Senator Barry Goldwater at a time when the name Goldwater was a liberal epithet. Indeed, he claims to be responsible for the famous slogan about extremism in defense of liberty being no vice, a stroke of genius that surely cost Goldwater whatever slim chance he ever had of winning the election. More important for present purposes, he is also, he tells us, a judicial conservative, a staunch foe of the judicial activism of the last forty years that has served to make the Supreme Court the enacting arm of the ACLU's political agenda. There is no pleasure for me in disagreeing with a man who opposes government by judges.

But if Jaffa is opposed to judicial activism, why does he devote his time and energy to reviling its two most prominent and effective opponents in the past half-century—joined now by justices Scalia and Thomas—excepting possibly only Learned Hand? How is the public interest served by that? And reviled them he has. His campaign against them has been shabby because he has attacked them not as a friendly critic or a disinterested scholar, but personally, bitterly, and arrogantly. Jaffa tells us that Bork "no doubt in his own mind. . . has taken on something of the status of a martyred saint of conservatism," a statement for which he has not the slightest basis.

Senator Hatch's support of Bork, Jaffa says, has "the tone of triumphant martyrology." "Surely hyperbole can go no further," he sneers, than for Senator Hatch to "compare Bork's prose to Churchill's," something that Senator Hatch has not done.[1] Judge Bork's critics, Jaffa tells us, had reason to persuade the public that he "really has no principles." Bork, Jaffa says, engages in "the most shameless expurgating and bowdlerizing of the Constitution's text" and his "mental confusion . . . is boundless." Jaffa substitutes arrogance for argument, as when he says "It is embarrassing to have to instruct Judge Bork in . . . the simplest elements of the political philosophy of the American Founding." Chief Justice Rehnquist is not the subject of these pieces, but Jaffa cannot resist a passing contemptuous reference to him as "that fountain of authority."

What sins can Bork and Rehnquist have possibly committed in Jaffa's eyes to deserve such contempt? Which of Bork's many decisions as a court of appeals judge or of Rehnquist's many more on the Supreme Court does Jaffa consider acts of judicial misbehavior or does he even disagree with? As far as I can tell, there are none. I could fault Bork and Rehnquist—as well as Scalia, Thomas, and even Hand—as rather too activist for my taste, too ready to hold laws unconstitutional, but that is not Jaffa's complaint. How, then, have Bork and Rehnquist offended him? It happens that Harry Jaffa's principal contribution to constitutional scholarship and political theory is his peculiar notion, following Abraham Lincoln, that the Constitution incorporates the Declaration of Independence. He considers this the most crucial and incisive insight in the history of American constitutional theory and political science, and he is enraged that Bork and Rehnquist have failed to appreciate his insight.

I. JAFFA'S "NATURAL LAW POSITIVISM"

Jaffa agrees with Bork. He says, that,

> the notion that the justices of the Supreme Court may in any way alter or amend the law of the Constitution by importing into it ideas or principles drawn from outside the Constitution itself is utterly abhorrent to sound jurisprudence. Like Judge Bork, I am devoted to the principle that the justices of the Su-

---

[1] Senator Hatch's statement was that Bork, like Churchill, was one of the rare "great scholars or writers of a talent sufficient to explain momentous events."

preme Court are bound unqualifiedly by the positive law of the Constitution, and that the positive law of the Constitution is to be understood in terms of the original intent of those who framed it and those who ratified it.

Jaffa is as opposed as Bork, he claims, to "liberal judicial activism," and differs from Bork only in his "answer to the question, What was the original intent of those who framed and those who ratified the Constitution?" What Bork fails to understand, according to Jaffa, is that "natural law principles are present *within* the Constitution, as elements of the *positive law* of the Constitution." Thus, Jaffa is able to insist that he is, like Bork, a positivist—a proponent of the view that the only function of judges is to enforce enacted law—despite also being a believer in natural law. In fact, however, he is chasing an oxymoron, "positive natural law" or "natural law positivism."

It is very important, Jaffa agrees with Bork, that judges stick to enforcing positive law in order to avoid the danger of having unelected government officials substitute their policy views for the views of the elected representatives of the people. This danger is avoided, however, Jaffa apparently thinks, when the positive law (here, the Constitution) simply enacts the natural law. Natural law then becomes positive law, and a judge who decides cases on the basis of his understanding of the principles of natural law is simply performing the ordinary judicial function of interpreting and applying law. It would be abhorrent for a judge to import ideas and principles into the Constitution from the outside, Jaffa says, but for a judge to decide constitutional cases on the basis of natural law presents no problem, because natural law is a part of the Constitution. All of which, of course, is utter confusion.

It seems incredible that Jaffa can think that his theory of the incorporation of natural law into the Constitution avoids the danger of rule by judges, that a judge authorized to enforce his view of natural law is or can be something other than the ultimate policy maker. Jaffa is angry with Bork because Bork does not believe this. Bork believes, on the contrary, that to give such authority to the justices of the Supreme Court would be, as a practical matter, to make the Court our supreme lawmaker, and that such authority would be in violation of the principles of separation of powers, representative self-government, and federalism that are the essence of the Constitution.

II. DOES THE CONSTITUTION INCORPORATE THE DECLARATION OF INDEPENDENCE?

The Constitution incorporates natural law because, according to Jaffa, it incorporates the Declaration of Independence. The Declaration, he thinks, constitutes "a compressed summary" of natural law and is the "perfection" "of a natural law tradition that goes back at least to Aristotle, and that embodies the ethical core of the Judaeo Christian tradition as well." The Declaration, however, consists largely of a lengthy indictment of King George III for a series of alleged misdeeds. It is hardly the sort of thing you would expect to find in a nation's constitution. What it is, of course, is a document meant to justify revolution, that is, illegal action. Having no real law to rely on—being in defiance of law-revolutionaries necessarily come to rely on the law of God, God being so marvelously unprotesting.

The Constitution, however, a framework of government constructed by sober and law-abiding men, has no need for such rhetoric or supernatural support. The Constitution makes no mention of the Declaration of Independence, and Jaffa has not produced a single statement by anyone at the constitutional convention or during the ratification debates indicating that it was intended to incorporate the Declaration. Jaffa offers only two items of evidence in support of his incredible theory. First, his theory or something like it was contained in the Republican Party platform of 1860 on which Lincoln ran for president. That platform, however, was another document created in an attempt to justify a nonlegal or extra-legal violent action, the North's waging war on the South to prevent its withdrawal from the Union.

The only evidence, if such it may be called, offered by Jaffa from near the founding era is a suggestion made by Madison in 1825 in response to a request by Jefferson for recommended materials for the law faculty at the newly established University of Virginia. Jaffa states: Madison recommended, and Jefferson agreed, "that, of the 'best guides' to the principles of the Constitutions of Virginia, and of the United States, the *first* was 'the Declaration of Independence as the fundamental act of Union of these States.'"[2] This is, to say the least, a far cry from a

---

[2] "To speak of the Declaration as the 'act of Union,'" Jaffa continues,

> means of course that it is the first law of the United States, the law which is constitutive of the American people as a legal person among the nations. . . . The principles enunciated in the Declaration are therefore not only those justifying separation, but also those by which the union of the states will be

statement that the Declaration is incorporated in the Constitution.[3] There is no evidence that the people of the ratifying states had any such notion.

Imagine, however, if you can, that the Declaration was meant to be incorporated and is now a part of the Constitution; what effect would that have on constitutional interpretation? As noted above, the Declaration, according to Jaffa, contains a compressed summary and perfection of natural law as well as an embodiment of the core of the Judeo-Christian tradition. Where exactly in the Declaration is this perfected statement of natural law to be found? Jaffa refers, apparently, to the statement of truths held to be self-evident in the Declaration's first sentence after the introductory sentence, namely, "that all men are created equal; that they are endowed by their Creator with certain unalienable rights; that among these are life, liberty and the pursuit of happiness; that to secure these rights, governments are instituted among men, deriving their just powers from the consent of the governed." This is the part of the Declaration quoted in the 1860 Republican Party presidential platform on which Jaffa strongly relies.

Although he refers constantly to the principles of natural law, Jaffa never undertakes to list these principles, or even define or describe them, except by reference to the few phrases quoted above from the Declaration. To a lawyer, at least, this is highly unsatisfactory. If by law Jaffa means lawyers' law, as he seems to, law enforceable against individuals by the power of the state, his principles must meet the minimum requirements of such law. To constitute effective judicially enforceable law, statements must provide meaningful guidance to those to whom they apply, and they must limit the discretion of those who apply them. Nothing could be clearer, it seems to me, than that the quoted phrases from the Declaration do not do this; they may be useful as exhortations or aspirations, they may embody the core of a religious tradition, but they are not useful as rules of law.

---

governed. The more perfect union under the Constitution will therefore be one more perfectly embodying these principles.

It would seem more likely to mean, however, only that the Declaration was the act by which the colonies combined to assert their independence from Great Britain. See Jaffa, *Original Intent and the Framers of the Constitution, pp.* 11, 22 (1994).

[3] In fact, Madison stated that the Declaration provided "no aid" in interpreting the Constitution, *i.e.*, in "guarding our Republican Charter against constructive violations." See Charles Cooper, *Harry Jaffa's Bad Originalism*, this volume p. 137 According to Madison, it was not the Declaration but *The Federalist* which provides "the most authentic explanation of the text of the federal Constitution." *Id.*

III. JAFFA'S ARGUMENT IS BASED ENTIRELY ON A MISUSE OF LANGUAGE

That the Declaration of Independence does not provide a useful guide to constitutional interpretation seems so clear to me that I have trouble understanding how it can be less than clear to anyone else. And this leads me to conclude that what we have here is a failure of communication. Nowhere more than in discussions of natural law does dispute seem to turn purely on semantics, on different understandings of the meaning of terms. The core of the problem, it seems to me, is the insistence of proponents of "natural law" on stating prescriptions as descriptions, on elevating their beliefs as to what ought to be into assertions as to what is. They appear to be confused about the nature of language, succumbing to the belief that because they can control words they can control reality, that saying something makes it so. Wittgenstein said that the function of philosophy was to cure the diseases—the intellectual puzzles—that result from the misuse of language. Among proponents of natural law the intellectual disease caused by language misuse is an epidemic; they are in need of at least an entire wing in Wittgenstein's philosophical hospital.

Jaffa's abuse of language fills his writings with statements that are either silly or untrue when language is used in its ordinary sense and with regard to its limits. He asks, for example, "where did the people [of the American colonies] get the authority . . . to separate themselves from Great Britain and then to institute new governments for themselves?" It is a meaningless question because no issue of authority was involved. The American colonists separated from Great Britain not because they had the "authority" to do so—they were acting in defiance of authority—but simply because they had the power to do so, the capability of resisting British arms.

Justice Holmes said that nothing is the source of more confusion in law than misuse of the word "right"; proponents of natural law maximize and exploit this confusion. For example, Jaffa says that people have the right to overthrow their government, but only if it is a government of a certain kind. But if what is meant is a legal right—that is, a legally protected interest—and it is only this connotation that gives the statement its apparent force—the statement is obviously self-contradictory: you cannot have a legal right to act illegally. On the other hand, if Jaffa means only a "moral right"—that is, an interest that he thinks should be protected—he is merely asserting his opinion that it is good that certain governments be overthrown. The statement, like other statements of natural law, is simply an attempt to present a statement of opinion as if it were a statement of fact.

Similarly, Jaffa states that a society cannot "enact ex post facto laws." But society does so all the time; recently, for example, Congress passed an ex post facto tax law (Revenue Reconciliation Act of 1993). When Jaffa says "cannot," he merely means "should not," as he shows by quickly adding that if a society does enact such a law—admitting that it can—it would be acting "inconsistently with the doctrine of unalienable rights." But by actually enacting and enforcing such laws, a society effectively demonstrates that there is no such right in that society. If human history shows anything, it shows that what we could wish were unalienable rights are in reality all too alienable. In other words, Jaffa is merely asserting, again, his opinion that a society ought not to enact such laws.

It is in my view both foolish and false to assert, as Jaffa does, following Salmon P. Chase, that slavery "had never lawfully existed in any territory of the United States" after the states' ratification of the Fifth Amendment in 1791. The Constitution could not have been ratified in 1789, of course, without accepting slavery, and the ratification of the Fifth Amendment was plainly not intended to do what could not be done two years earlier. To think that the Fifth Amendment made slavery illegal is simply to succumb to the temptation to understand words not as tools of communication between human beings but as bearers of inherent power, able to work grand effects regardless of human intent.

Another example of a sweeping and seemingly impressive statement that cannot be taken as literally true is Jaffa's statement that "no distinction among human persons can be drawn on the basis of race or color that is not morally and constitutionally irrelevant." In fact, many valuable and unobjectionable such distinctions can be drawn: for example, by the FBI in selecting agents to infiltrate the Black Panthers or the Ku Klux Klan, or by the leader of a racially mixed Boy Scout troop deciding how to distribute a limited supply of suntan lotion before a day on the beach.

IV. IT'S NOT LAW, IT'S THEOLOGY

I must admit to a feeling, however, that although my refutations of Jaffa seem to me logical, rational, and unanswerable, they are nonetheless somehow beside the point. One thing I am certain of is that their unanswerability will have absolutely no effect on Jaffa; he has been doing his thing professionally for much too long to be stopped now by logic. If his treatment of Bork and Rehnquist (and others) is any indication, he will consider it a sufficient and appropriate response to issue a slanderous ad hominem attack.[4] The problem is that I am futilely formulating rational responses to arguments to which rationality does not apply. Jaffa does not so much engage, or even purport to engage, in rational discourse as in religious and moral exhortation. His call to acceptance of "the laws of nature and of nature's God" is obviously an invitation to participate, not in policy analysis or constitutional interpretation, but in a religious exercise. The source of his displeasure with Bork and Rehnquist is that they do not share his religious beliefs; that, claiming knowledge, professionally at least, only of human law, they must decline Jaffa's invitation to adjudicate upon the basis of any other.

Similarly, Jaffa's statement that "the goodness of the Constitution is rooted in the goodness of the created universe" is not a statement of fact, testable and falsifiable, but an expression of mystical feeling to which only another mystic can respond. It is meant not to communicate thought, but to impart religious conviction. If taken as meant to convey meaning, one would have to ask whether "goodness" or even "created" are words that can properly be applied to the universe. I think Wittgenstein would see the need for some drastic philosophical therapy, probably shock treatment.

Along this same line, Jaffa uses as an epigraph for one of his writings a quotation from Thomas Aquinas, "Good and being are convertible terms." Perhaps nothing better or more concisely illustrates the difference between believers and skeptics regarding natural law than their reactions to such a pronouncement: believers get a thrill of profound insight, and skeptics hear only meaningless noise. Believers think some deep thinker has announced an important discovery; skeptics realize that another pedant has become so fascinated by the magic of language that he has forgotten its function and limits.

My difficulty with Jaffa, as well as other proponents of natural law, is not that he is interested in discussing such things as "the goodness of the

---

[4] Cooper notes that Jaffa's

references . . . to contemporary thinkers, including former friends such as fellow Straussians Martin Diamond and Walter Berns, are laced with derision and personal insult. Thomas Pangle, political science professor at the University of Torn onto and a target of Jaffa's vitriol, has remarked on the phenomenon. Noting Jaffa's "wounded sense of self-importance," Pangle lamented that Jaffa now "seems incapable of arguing issues in moral and political theory without labeling his opponents and their views immoral."

Cooper, p. 141 this volume.

created universe" or that "good and being are convertible terms," but that he wants to make it sound as if he is discussing law. While theological discussion is beyond my ken, law is my field of professional expertise. The only useful contribution I can hope to make in a discussion on natural law is to point out that it is not "real" or "legal" law—law created by a government and properly enforceable by government officials—that is being discussed.

Harry Jaffa's Bad Originalism

Charles J. Cooper

ORIGINAL INTENT AND THE FRAMERS OF THE CONSTITUTION: A DISPUTED QUESTION by Harry Jaffa. Washington, D. C.: Regnery Gateway, 1994, 386 pp., $24.00

I

"We should, of course, distinguish between good originalism and bad originalism." [1]

The author of this statement, Judge Richard A. Posner of the United States Court of Appeals for the Seventh Circuit, was selected for his judgeship because the judicial selection team of the Reagan Justice Department believed that he was a "good originalist." He was in the freshman class of President Reagan's judicial appointments, which also included Antonin Scalia, Ralph Winter, and Robert Bork. He was selected, like his classmates, because he believed, or at least was thought to believe, that federal judges are bound to interpret the Constitution's provisions to mean what they were intended to mean.

That's all. Contrary to the Reagan administration's liberal critics, the only "litmus test" applied by the Justice Department to candidates for judicial appointment was, to borrow Posner's definition of originalism, a firm belief in "interpretative fidelity to a text's understanding by its authors." [2]

Not long after his appointment to the federal bench, Posner began to learn the language of the activist. In 1984 he said: "I am sympathetic to functional analysis and to flexible, nonliteral constitutional interpretations, especially of a provision such as Article III that belongs to the original Constitution, which means it was written 197 years ago." [3] By 1990 Posner's fulfillment of the Actonian postulate was complete. Now he advocates the use of his awesome judicial power—the power to void

---

[1] Richard A. Posner, "Bork and Beethoven," 42 *Stanford Law Review* 1365, 1378 (1990).
[2] *Id.*, at 1365.
[3] *Geras v. Lafayette Display Fixtures, Inc.,* 742 F.2d 1037, 1051 (7th Cir. 1984).

the work of legislatures—to achieve socially desirable (in his view) results. He calls himself a legal "pragmatist" in the tradition of Justice Benjamin Cardozo, from whom he takes his "pragmatist creed": "The final cause of law is the welfare of society. The rule that misses its aim cannot permanently justify its existence."[4] For Posner, constitutional interpretation is controlled by the result to be achieved, not by the understanding of those who framed and ratified the provision at issue. This is how he puts it: "In the capacious, forward-looking account that I am calling pragmatic, the social consequences of alternative interpretations are decisive; to the consistent originalist they are irrelevant."[5]

Posner anticipates and denies the charge that his prescription for "pragmatist constitutional adjudication" is "lawless." After all, the pragmatist judge "does not, in order to do short-sighted justice between the parties, violate the Constitution and his oath, for he is mindful of the systemic consequences of judicial lawlessness."[6] Thus, for Posner's pragmatist judge, even the question whether to "violate the Constitution and his oath" is determined by weighing its consequences and, it appears, can be ruled out only when the benefits of doing so are limited to "short-sighted justice between the parties."

Posner rejects originalism—"good originalism," that is—for the same reason that all activists reject originalism: interpreting the Constitution to mean only what it was intended to mean would permit legislative bodies to enact measures at odds with the activist's conception of the "welfare of society." But not all activists reject originalism, for there are "bad originalists," who use the rhetoric of originalism to support any result they want to reach. As Posner correctly points out: "Some of the most activist judges, whether of the right or of the left, whether named Taney or Black, have been among the judges most drawn to the rhetoric of originalism. For it is a magnificent disguise. The judge can do the wildest things, all the while presenting himself as the passive agent of the sainted Founders. . . ."[7]

To give this point contemporary illustration, Posner asserts: "The conservative libertarians whom Bork criticizes (Richard Epstein and Bernard Siegan) are originalists; his disagreement with them is not over

---

[4] *Supra* note 1, at 1380 quoting Benjamin N. Cardozo, *The Nature of the Judicial Process* 66 (1921).

[5] *Supra* note 1, at 1380. See also Richard A. Posner, *The Problems of Jurisprudence* (1990).

[6] *Supra* note 1, at 1380.

[7] *Id.* at 1378-79.

method but over result."[8] But here Posner gets it exactly backward. It is true that Bork disagrees with Epstein and Siegan "over result" in the sense that he does not believe that the results they seek—judicial invalidation of rent control ordinances, minimum wage requirements, and other restrictions on economic rights—can be reached through an originalist interpretation of the Constitution. But Bork agrees with Epstein and Siegan "over result" in the sense that he is largely in "sympathy with their political ends."[9] In other words, Bork agrees generally that reducing government restriction on economic rights and the free market would promote the "welfare of society," but does not believe that this result is ordained by the Constitution. And that is the real difference between good originalism and bad originalism.[10] A good originalist yields to the intended meaning of a constitutional provision even when it hurts.

A bad originalist is just another judicial activist. And all judicial activists, whether of the right or of the left, have one thing in common: they all come to results that harmonize with their own personal policy views. The exclusive purpose of departing, whether openly or through deceit, from originalist constitutional interpretation—from the intended meaning of a constitutional provision—is to free the judge to resolve the dispute in a manner congenial to his personal policy views. No proponent of judicial activism has ever disavowed the binding effect of the framers' intentions in order to reach a judicial result that he loathed. The bad originalist cannot bring himself to deny that the judge is bound by the intentions of the framers and ratifiers of a constitutional provision, but also cannot abide the result yielded by an intellectually honest originalist interpretation. Faced with this dilemma, the bad originalist—that is, the activist originalist—can force the desired result out of the Constitution's text, structure, and history only by violating what Professor William Van Alstyne has called the "first obligation" of constitutional interpretation: "The first obligation of a judge is merely not to lie in administering the Constitution."[11]

---

[8] *Id.* at 1378.

[9] Robert H. Bork, *The Tempting of America* 223 (1990).

[10] For more on Posner and Bork, *see* Lino A. Graglia, "Interpreting" the Constitution: Posner on Bork," 44 *Stanford Law Review* 1019 (1992).

[11] William Van Alstyne, "Notes on a Bicentennial Constitution: Part II, Antinomial Choices and the Role of the Supreme Court," 72 *Iowa Law Review* 1281, 1292 (1987).

I do not mean to suggest that any disagreement between self-described originalists means that one of them does not actually believe that his interpretation is consonant with the intended meaning of the constitutional provision at issue. To the contrary, on most serious constitutional questions there is wide latitude for honest disagreement among those searching in good faith for the intended meaning of the provision at issue. But the work of some self-described originalists is so analytically flawed, so logically strained, so biased in the assessment of evidence, and so transparently result-oriented that the candid mind is compelled to doubt the good faith of the interpreter.

II

Which brings me to the specific subject of this essay: Professor Harry Jaffa, bad originalist extraordinaire. Jaffa, Professor Emeritus of Political Science at Claremont McKenna College, turned his enormous energy and learning, and even larger passion, to the subject of originalism in the late 1980s. His latest book, *Original Intent and the Framers of the Constitution: A Disputed Question*, is a collection of his articles, essays, and even letters on the subject, along with polite responses by professors Bruce Ledewitz, Robert L. Stone, and George Anastaplo.

The great bulk of Jaffa's labor is devoted to analyzing conservative thought on interpreting the Constitution, particularly as reflected in the work of Robert Bork, Chief Justice William H. Rehnquist, and former Attorney General Edwin Meese. Although he shares with them, he says, "a priori a commitment to the idea of 'original intent' jurisprudence," his purpose is to prove that "their jurisprudence does not, in the most important respect, correspond with the intent of those who framed and those who ratified the Constitution" (p. 238). The defect in the thinking of conservative (henceforth "Borkian") originalists, as well as that of liberal activists, lies in its failure to accept natural law principles, especially as reflected in the Declaration of Independence, as the governing constitutional intention of the founders: "The political philosophy of natural rights and natural law, expressed in virtually all the great documents of the revolution and Founding period—but quintessentially in the Declaration of Independence—was the common ground for both Framers and Ratifiers. It is in the rejection of this common ground that we see the common ground of both Left and Right today" (p. 239).

Those familiar with Jaffa's work know that he does not suffer fools gladly, and that very nearly everyone he encounters in his research, at least among the living, is a fool. He speaks with respect only of the dead, such as Madison, Jefferson, and his teacher Leo Strauss. Of Lincoln, his idol, he speaks with reverence. His references, however, to contemporary thinkers, including former friends such as fellow Straussians Martin Diamond and Walter Berns, are laced with derision and personal insult. Thomas Pangle, political science professor at the University of Toronto and a target of Jaffa's vitriol, has remarked on the phenomenon. Noting Jaffa's "wounded sense of self-importance," Pangle lamented that Jaffa now "seems incapable of arguing issues in moral and political theory without labeling his opponents and their views immoral."[12]

In *Original Intent*, Jaffa preserves and strengthens his well-earned reputation as master of the cheap shot. Herewith a few examples:

"One wonders whether Judge Bork has ever read a single document of our Founding" (p. 31).

"Comparing Bork's prose to Churchill's is approximately on a level with comparing Andy Warhol's Campbell's Soup can to Leonardo da Vinci's *Last Supper*" (p. 293).

"[I]t would take at least 50 pages to explain . . . all of Bork's innumerable errors in dealing with [the Dred Scott] case" (p. 298).

"What then was the fundamental question in *Dred Scott*? Although I have written often on this subject, what I have written seems not to have penetrated the emanations or penumbrae that surround. . . Mr. Justice Rehnquist" (p. 101).

"Because [Meese] followed [Bork and] Rehnquist, [he] utterly misinterpreted the significance of the Dred Scott decision, as I believe I have shown beyond a reasonable doubt (or beyond a possible doubt by a reasonable person!)" (p. 391).

"The attempt by Bork no less than Rehnquist (or Meese) to treat Dred Scott as primarily a matter of judicial usurpation, shows as profound an ignorance of constitutional history as

---

[12] Dinesh D'Souza, "The Legacy of Leo Strauss," *Policy Review*, Spring 1987, at 36, 41.

Taney himself displayed in his opinion for the Court in that case" (p. 275).

These lines are revealing not just for what they tell us about their author, but also for what they tell us about the central importance of the *Dred Scott* case in his attack on Borkian originalism. As Professor Lino Graglia has noted, "The most common and effective argument against originalism is simply a recitation of the parade of horribles that supposedly would emerge in a world without activist judicial review."[13] *Dred Scott* is a one-case parade of horribles in Jaffa's indictment of Borkian originalism. For according to Jaffa, Taney's opinion, far from representing a departure from orthodox Borkian originalism, is in truth the perfect exemplar of it. As Professor Ledewitz puts it in his reply essay, Jaffa believes that "Taney was in fact interpreting the Constitution precisely in accordance with original intent as [Bork,] Meese and the others understand that concept" (p. 110). To Jaffa, the significance for the original intent debate of the *Dred Scott* decision is that Taney's (and thus the Court's) error lay not in any departure from Borkian originalism, but rather in Taney's failure to interpret the Constitution in accord with the Constitution's own principles, which Jaffa says are the natural rights principles of the Declaration of Independence. (I shall return to Jaffa's analysis of *Dred Scott* in the last part of this essay.)

All of Jaffa's thinking on the subject of constitutional interpretation is grounded upon and flows from the premise that "the principles of the Declaration of Independence are the principles of the Constitution" (pp. 18, 55, 64, 239, 394). Most originalists agree that in some cases the principles expressed in the Declaration can inform and illuminate our understanding of the intended meaning of the principles of the Constitution. But Jaffa says that "the principles of the Declaration of Independence are indeed the principles of the Constitution" (p. 394). And because "the principles of the Declaration are the principles of the Constitution . . . we do not look outside the Constitution but rather within it for the natural law basis of constitutional interpretation" (p. 60). He acknowledges that his view is unorthodox, confessing that he is "probably the only living soul who has written on original intent who agrees with [this] central thesis" (p. 395). When one follows Jaffa's thesis where it leads—indeed,

---

[13] Graglia, *supra* note 10, at 1033.

where he takes it himself, as we shall see—it is not surprising that it has attracted so few adherents.[14]

Jaffa's thesis would be remarkable enough even if understood to mean no more than that the principles of the Declaration are positive law of equal dignity with the principles of the Constitution, as though the Declaration was somehow incorporated into the Constitution itself. But Jaffa goes even further than this, arguing that the principles of the Declaration—specifically, the "central idea . . . 'that all men are created equal'" (p. 239)—are truer to the principles of the Constitution than is the Constitution itself. On its face this proposition is, to say no more, counterintuitive, so Jaffa fortunately provides an explanation.

He begins by dismissing those who "regard the question of the Constitution's principles as something that one discovers merely by looking at the Constitution" (p. 21). The extraordinary care devoted by the framers and ratifiers of the Constitution to its every word and phrase suggests that they too were under the delusion that the language of the document, read in light of its historical context and purposes, reflected the principles that they intended to "ordain and establish." Madison, who was both a framer and a ratifier, was among the misinformed, for he

> entirely concur[red] in the propriety of resorting to the sense in which the Constitution was accepted and ratified by the nation. In that sense alone it is the legitimate Constitution. And if they be not the guide in expounding it, there can be no security for a consistent and stable, more than for a faithful exercise of its powers.[15]

But the language meticulously crafted and ratified by the founders, Jaffa argues, reflected in many instances only the Constitution's "compromises," not its "genuine principles." For example, the provisions of the Constitution protecting slavery were "compromises" necessary to persuade the slave states to agree to the establishment of a stronger central government, which in turn would lead inevitably to the extinction of slavery. But, says Jaffa, since "[t]here is nothing in the Constitution it-

---

[14] Jaffa, however, is no longer alone. In a foreword to Jaffa's book, Lewis E. Lehrman adopts a view closely similar to Jaffa's—that the "original intent of the Founders and the United States Code incorporated the Declaration of Independence into the Constitution of the United States" (p. 5).

[15] Letter from James Madison to Henry Lee, in 9 *The Writings of James Madison* 191 (Gaillard Hunt ed., 1910).

self by which . . . one can distinguish the compromises of the Constitution from the principles of the Constitution," one must look to the Declaration (p. 21). Its principle of the natural equality of all men "tells us why slavery must be regarded as an anomaly, a necessary evil entailed upon the Constitution, but not flowing from—or consistent with—its genuine principles" (p. 23).

Having thus discarded the inconvenient language of the Constitution's "compromises" and replaced it with a much more serviceable transplant from the Declaration, Jaffa makes short work of *Dred Scott*. The question in *Dred Scott* under Jaffa's Constitution—one might call it his "Declartution"—was "whether slavery was right or wrong, under 'the laws of nature and of nature's God'" (p. 68).

Jaffa's originalism does indeed make constitutional adjudication easy, at least for those who know the difference between right and wrong. Make no mistake, I know what I think is right, and what I think is wrong. But there are those who disagree with me, and I cannot demonstrate that my views on right and wrong harmonize unerringly with the constitutional rules of law by which the American people have consented to be governed. Jaffa thinks he can. He is certain that natural justice is objectively determinable through reason, and his writing drips with the moral conceit that he is possessed of the ability, "supplied by right reason," to discern the "philosophic truth concerning the just and the unjust, the right and the wrong, the good and the bad" (p. 35). For those who share his conservative moral values, Jaffa's natural justice prescription for constitutional adjudication would yield consistently satisfactory results—so long as Jaffa is doing the adjudicating. But natural justice also can be invoked by, say, Justice Brennan, who is no less certain than Jaffa of his ability to discern his own liberal version of natural justice—"the constitutional vision of human dignity"[16]—through "a personal confrontation with the well-springs of our society."[17] Justice Brennan's vision of human dignity tells him, among other things, that the Constitution forbids capital punishment in all cases, notwithstanding express recognition of the practice in the Fifth Amendment. Jaffa, in contrast, believes that the death penalty is entirely consistent with natural justice, and thus within the Constitution. Neither Brennan nor Jaffa

---

[16] Justice William J. Brennan, Jr., "Remarks to the Text and Teaching Symposium," Georgetown University, Washington, D.C. (Oct. 12, 1985), in *The Great Debate: Interpreting Our Written Constitution* 22 (1986) (Federalist Society Occasional Paper No. 2).
[17] *Id*. at 20.

makes a serious effort to discern the genuine meaning of the Constitution on the issue; for both, the issue is determined by what is right and what is wrong. That Jaffa's conclusion harmonizes with the genuine meaning of the Constitution is just a happy coincidence.

The point is that natural justice is regularly invoked by both liberal and conservative activists as a dispute-resolving principle for constitutional issues, but with precisely opposite results. For every "conservative libertarian," such as Richard Epstein or Bernard Siegan, invoking natural justice in the service of property rights, there is a liberal egalitarian, such as Ronald Dworkin or William Brennan, invoking natural justice in pursuit of a contrary result. But this is not surprising. Locke himself recognized that "the law of nature [is] unwritten, and so no where to be found but in the minds of men." Justice Iredell, in his famous 1798 opinion in *Calder v. Bull*, recognized this fact in rejecting the legitimacy of natural law as a decisional basis for reviewing the work of legislatures:

> The ideas of natural justice are regulated by no fixed standard; the ablest and the purest men have differed upon the subject; and all that the court could properly say, in such an event, would be that the legislature (possessed of an equal right of opinion) had passed an act which, in the pinion of the judges, was inconsistent with the abstract principles of natural justice.[18]

Justice Iredell's objection to natural law as a constitutional principle, however, is its virtue to judicial activists, including bad originalists. For, again, while activists often come to polar-opposite results, they all come to results that harmonize with their personal policy preferences. In other words, when a judge invokes "natural justice," or "the constitutional vision of human dignity," or "philosophic truth" concerning right and wrong, or "the welfare of society" as the constitutional principle for resolving a judicial dispute, you can be certain that the dispute will be resolved in a manner congenial to the judge's personal moral vision.

III

Lumping Jaffa, however, with garden-variety activists does not do him justice. The judicially liberating effect of most activist theories of constitutional interpretation is generally confined to cases in which dis-

---

[18] 3 U.S. (3 Dall.) 386, 399.

cerning the governing constitutional rule of law actually requires some *interpretation*. Under Jaffa's originalism, however, the natural law principles of the Declaration trump even the plain language of the Constitution. In other words, for Jaffa, specific provisions of the Constitution—that is, the "compromises" of the Constitution—must fall when in conflict with the natural law principles of the Declaration, just as federal statutes must fall when in conflict with the Constitution. Jaffa premises this conclusion on the proposition that the Declaration "authorized" the Constitution and thus "remains the most fundamental dimension of the law of the Constitution." As he explains (p. 23):

> [The Declaration] defines at once the legal and moral personality of that "one People". . . who separated themselves from Great Britain and became free and independent. It thereby also defines the source and nature of that authority which is invoked when "We the People of the United States" ordained and established the Constitution. For the same principle of authority—that of the people—that made the independence of the states lawful, made lawful all the acts and things done subsequently in their name.

Accordingly, "[i]n asking what were the original intentions of the Founding Fathers, we are asking what principles of moral and political philosophy guided them" (pp. 41-42).

For Jaffa, the Declaration defines "the legal . . . and moral personality" of the American people, not only "at once," but once and for all. The American people are thus enslaved to the "moral and political philosophy" of the founders, powerless to redefine their "legal and . . . moral personality." Any attempt by the American people to "compromise" the natural law principles of the Declaration—for example, by amending their Constitution—would conflict with the "genuine principles" of the Constitution and thus be void.

Jaffa illustrates this point vividly by arguing that the American people lack the "inherent authority" to repeal the Thirteenth Amendment, for "there can be no rightful and lawful exercise of sovereignty ultimately inconsistent with" natural law (pp. 58-59).[19] Nor is this feature of

---

[19] Jaffa couches this point in the form of an inquiry: "it is an interesting question whether 'We the people. . .' have the same inherent authority to repeal the Thirteenth as to repeal the Eighteenth Amendment" (p. 58). His discussion of this issue, however, leaves no doubt whatsoever how he would answer it (pp. 58-59):

Jaffa's originalism confined to propositions—like repealing the Thirteenth Amendment—for which there is no support among decent people. For example, Ledewitz argues that under Jaffa's reasoning the unalienable right to "life" proclaimed in the Declaration brings capital punishment into conflict with the "genuine principles" of the Constitution, notwithstanding the language of the Fifth Amendment. Jaffa, as mentioned earlier, rejects the claim, not because the Constitution cannot at once both permit capital punishment and forbid it, but rather because the natural law principle proclaimed in the Declaration is a "right of innocent life" (p. 247). Thus, an "attempt to ground an objection to capital punishment in the 'original intent' of the Constitution—seen as an expression of the principles of the Declaration of Independence—is without foundation" (p. 248). On the other hand, he makes clear that "the right of innocent human life to the protection of law—the first of the rights proclaimed in the Declaration—" extends to the unborn child and thus presumably renders the doctrine of *Roe v. Wade* unconstitutional even if added to the Constitution by amendment in the manner prescribed under Article V (p. 249). Similarly, Jaffa leaves little doubt concerning his view on the "inherent authority" of the people to enact a constitutional amendment outlawing official discrimination on the basis of sexual orientation: "[S]odomy and lesbianism . . . are unnatural acts and, being unnatural, the very negation of anything that could be called a right according to nature" (p. 263).[20]

Jaffa's natural justice theory of constitutional interpretation is thus the very negation of the idea of self-government. As a self-described originalist, Jaffa understands that he must bear the burden of proving that his theory "correspond[s] with the intent of those who framed and those who ratified the Constitution." And in light of the paradoxical nature of his theory (a provision of the Constitution can be unconstitutional), only the most compelling evidence will suffice.

If however the sovereignty of the American people means supreme power, without any qualification, then the American people have the same constitutional right to institute or adopt slavery as to abolish it. If the sovereignty of the American people—or of any people—can be rightfully exercised only in the service of the inherent and unalienable rights with which all human beings have been equally endowed, by the laws of a moral and rational nature, then there can be no rightful and lawful exercise of sovereignty ultimately inconsistent with such ends.

[20] *See also* Harry V. Jaffa, *Homosexuality and the Natural Law* 28-30 (1990).

IV

Jaffa says that we have nothing less than "Madison's and Jefferson's word that the principles of the Constitution . . . nowhere defined in the Constitution, are those of the Declaration of Independence" (p. 43). As proof for this assertion, he cites an 1825 exchange of correspondence between the two men concerning the books and other documents that the Board of Visitors of the University of Virginia, of which both men were members, ought to recommend (Madison) or prescribe (Jefferson) to the law faculty as authoritative sources on the principles of government. This correspondence led to a resolution by the Board of Visitors prescribing for use by the faculty of the law school "the text and documents" in which the principles of the Virginia and federal governments "are to be found legitimately developed." Throughout his writing on constitutional interpretation, Jaffa resorts to this resolution as the dispositive and singular evidence of the Declaration's "authoritative role" in constitutional interpretation.

Despite the enormous load that Jaffa heaps upon the Board of Visitors resolution, he quotes it only in his initial reference to the document, and then he quotes only a single phrase. In describing the list of documents specified in the resolution, Jaffa says: "[O]f the 'best guides' to the principles of the Constitutions, of Virginia and of the United States, the first was 'the Declaration of Independence as the fundamental act of Union of these States'" (p. 22). The Declaration does not remain a mere "guide" to the Constitution's principles for long, however, for a few pages later Jaffa reads the resolution to elevate the Declaration over the Constitution itself in revealing the Constitution's own principles: "Madison and Jefferson turned first to the Declaration of Independence—and not to the Constitution (or *The Federalist*)—to instruct the young law students at the University of Virginia in the principles of the Constitution" (pp. 33- 34). But Jaffa is still not satisfied; a few more pages and the Declaration actually becomes the Constitution: "Jefferson and Madison believed that the principles of the Declaration of Independence ought to be . . . taught to the law students at the University of Virginia as the principles of the Constitution" (p. 44).

Thus, in short order Jaffa transforms the principles of the Declaration into the principles of the Constitution and gives Madison and Jefferson all the credit. Indeed, he is puzzled that the significance of the resolution has thus far been ignored by all but him: "[I]n all the discussion of 'original intent' it has apparently not occurred to any of the luminaries of present-day conservative (or of course liberal) jurisprudence even to consider it" (p. 23). A reading of the resolution and the correspondence that forms its backdrop solves the mystery, and tells us why Jaffa quotes so little of it.[21]

The idea of a resolution prescribing texts for the law school on the principles of government originated with Jefferson, who feared that "heresies may be taught," such as principles of "quondam federalism, now consolidation."[22] He thought it the Board's "duty to guard against such principles being disseminated among our youth" by "prescribing the texts to be followed in their discourses." Although the draft resolution enclosed by Jefferson apparently cannot be found, much about its content is known from Madison's reply.

Madison's response warrants extended examination. He opens by agreeing generally with the purpose of Jefferson's "proposal of a text book for the Law School," but laments that it is "not easy to find standard books that will be both guides & guards for the purpose." He then addresses five specific documents, all of which were apparently included in Jefferson's draft resolution: the writings on government by Algerian Sidney and John Locke, the Declaration of Independence, *The Federalist*, and the Virginia Resolutions of 1799.

Of the writings of Sidney and Locke, Madison says that they are "admirably calculated to impress on young minds the right of Nations to establish their own Governments, and to inspire a love of free ones; but afford no aid in guarding our Republican Charters against constructive violations." And the Declaration of Independence, said Madison, "falls nearly under a like observation." That is, it too affords "no aid in guarding our Republican Charters against constructive violations." Thus, the Declaration, according to Madison, provides little if any protection against misconstructions of the Constitution. This is, to put it charitably,

---

[21] As will be seen, I do not believe that the resolution and background correspondence can reasonably be read to support the propositions that Jaffa derives from them. So that the reader may be his own judge, all three documents are set out, in relevant part, in the appendix to this essay.

[22] According to Jaffa, Jefferson's letter to Madison has not been identified with certainty, but Jefferson's biographers have concluded that he wrote a similar letter at the same time to Joseph Cabell, who was also a member of the Virginia Board of Visitors. The quoted passages are from a letter by Jefferson apparently to Cabell. *See* Harry V. Jaffa, *How to Think About the American Revolution* 94 (1978).

a very odd way of saying that the Declaration embodies constitutional principles even more authoritatively than does the Constitution itself. Indeed, Madison's summary dismissal of the Declaration as an aid in understanding the meaning of the Constitution contrasts sharply with his treatment of the interpretive significance of *The Federalist*:

> The "Federalist" may fairly enough be regarded as the most authentic exposition of the text of the federal Constitution, as understood by the Body which prepared & the Authority which accepted it. Yet it did not foresee all the misconstructions which have occurred; nor prevent some that it did foresee.

Madison cautioned against "requiring an unqualified conformity" to any of the listed documents in the law school—again, seemingly odd advice if he viewed the Declaration as the authority *ne plus ultra*.

Madison concluded his response to Jefferson by suggesting the addition of Washington's Inaugural Speech and Farewell Address, and enclosed a revised draft of the operative passage of the resolution. Because it is identical in all material respects with the resolution as ultimately adopted by the Board of Visitors, I set out Madison's revised resolution in full:

> And on the distinctive principles of the Government of our own State, and of that of the United States, the best guides are to be found in—1. The Declaration of Independence, as the fundamental act of Union of these States. 2. the book known by the title of the "Federalist," being an Authority to which appeal is habitually made by all & rarely declined or denied by any, as evidence of the general opinion of those who framed & those who accepted the Constitution of the U. States on questions as to its genuine meaning. 3. the Resolutions of the General Assembly of Virginia in 1799, on the subject of the Alien & Sedition laws, which appeared to accord with the predominant sense of the people of the U.S. 4. The Inaugural Speech & Farewell Address of President Washington, as conveying political lessons of peculiar value; and that in the branch of the School of law which is to treat on the subject of Government, these shall be used as the text & documents of the School.

On reading the relevant text of the resolution, one is struck by the distance between what it says and what Jaffa tells us it says. Even his most modest reading of the resolution—that the Declaration is listed as first among the "best guides" to the principles of the Constitution—is wrong. The language of the resolution actually says something quite different. It says that the Declaration, as well as *The Federalist*, the Virginia Resolutions of 1799, and Washington's Inaugural and Farewell Addresses,[23] are "the best guides" on "the distinctive *principles of the Government* of our own State, and that of the United States."

The authors of the resolution plainly did not use the term "government . . . of the United States" as a synonym for "Constitution of the United States." Rather, they clearly used the term "government" in its larger sense, of which the Constitution is a part but not the whole. The preamble to the resolution says as much, noting that "it is the duty of this Board . . . to pay especial attention to the principles of government which shall be inculcated therein, and to provide that none shall be inculcated which are incompatible with those on which the Constitutions of this State and of the United States are genuinely based, in the common opinion . . . ." Obviously, the resolution's authors understood that "the principles of government" are not confined to those on which the Constitution was based, and indeed include some which are quite incompatible with the Constitution.

That Madison and Jefferson meant what they said in the resolution is further demonstrated by the simple fact that what they said makes sense, while what Jaffa attributes to them does not. All four of the documents listed in the resolution are excellent guides to the "principles of government." Only one item listed in the resolution—*The Federalist*—is an excellent guide on "the principles of the Constitution." And it is specifically characterized in the resolution as a familiar and commonly accepted "authority" on "the general opinion of those who framed & those who accepted the Constitution of the United States on questions as to its genuine meaning." This accords with the view expressed by Madison in his letter to Jefferson, in which he described *The Federalist* "as the most authentic exposition of the text of the federal Constitution, as understood by the Body which prepared & the Authority which accepted it." Again, this view of *The Federalist*'s relationship to the "genuine meaning" of the Constitution follows on the heels of Madison's dismissal of the Declaration as being of little if any aid "in guarding our Republican Charters against constructive violations." And while the Declaration was described in the resolution as "the fundamental act of Union of these

---

[23] Washington's inaugural speech was deleted from the final version of the resolution adopted by the Board of Visitors.

States," which it plainly was, neither Madison nor Jefferson suggested that the Declaration embodied or prescribed the terms of that continued union, which it plainly did not.

In sum, Madison told Jefferson both that *The Federalist* is the "most authentic" guide to the genuine meaning of the Constitution, and that the Declaration, in contrast, offers little aid in construing the Constitution. And Madison's view was reflected in the resolution adopted by the Virginia Board of Visitors. Yet Jaffa says that Madison and Jefferson turned to the Declaration before *The Federalist* for guidance on the "principles of the Constitution"![24]

---

[24] In a 1978 book entitled *How To Think about the American Revolution*, Jaffa well understood and, indeed, emphasized the distinction between the principles of American government and the principles of the Constitution. In the essay, Jaffa analyzes at great length the 1825 Virginia Board of Visitors resolution and the background correspondence between Madison and Jefferson, quoting liberally from each of the documents. Jaffa's examination of the documents was occasioned by Martin Diamond's argument that the Declaration, although " indispensable [as a] source of the feelings and sentiments of Americans and of the spirit of liberty in which their institutions were conceived . . . is devoid of guidance as to what those institutions should be." Citing Madison's statement to Jefferson that the Declaration, like the works of Sidney and Locke, provides "no aid in guarding our Republican Charters against constructive violations," Diamond asserted: "The Declaration, Madison is saying and Jefferson cheerfully agrees, offers no guidance for the construction of free government and hence offers no aid in protecting the American form of government under the Constitution." *Id*. at 94. Jaffa took sharp issue with Diamond's reading of Madison's letter, correctly pointing out that Madison's reference to the Declaration did not pertain to "the construction of free government"—that is, what American governmental "institutions should be"—but rather referred to "constructive violations" of the Constitution. *Id*. at 99. Indeed, Jaffa noted that the Declaration and the works of Sidney and Locke could not have aided in preventing misconstructions of the Constitution, for they "were all produced before our 'Republican Charters,' meaning before our national or state constitutions existed. . . . On the question of the proper . . . mode of constitutional interpretation. . . . it would have been, of course, impossible to find any single 'guide' or 'guard' written before 1787." *Id*. Jaffa further noted that, while Madison objected to requiring an "unqualified conformity" to any of the suggested texts because none of them provided perfect guidance on the principles of the Virginia and federal governments, "neither Madison nor Jefferson seems to have hesitated for a moment in affirming that among the works which may be called 'the *best guides*' to the 'distinctive principles of government of our State and of that of the United States,' the *first* was the Declaration of Independence." *Id*. at 104. Thus, in answering Diamond, Jaffa painstakingly parsed the language of the 1825 Board of Visitors resolution and the background correspondence between Madison and Jefferson, and correctly interpreted them to say that the Declaration is a fine guide on the principles of American government, but a poor one on the meaning of the American Constitution. In light of his 1978 book, his subsequent description in *Original Intent* of the Board of Visitors resolution as

Indeed, Jaffa says that Madison and Jefferson turned to the Declaration before the *Constitution itself* for guidance on the principles of the Constitution. On its face this assertion is, well, silly, so one need not actually go to the trouble to check Jaffa's sources to know that Madison and Jefferson did not truly entertain it. Having gone to the trouble, however, of reviewing the 1825 Virginia Board of Visitors resolution and background correspondence, we see that when Madison and Jefferson looked beyond the Constitution itself for guidance on the "principles of the Constitution," they turned first to *The Federalist*.[25] Only in unusual cases of constitutional construction would they turn for guidance to the Declaration.

But there is more in the resolution that resists Jaffa's reading of it. Were Jaffa's understanding of the interpretative significance of the Declaration as "canonical" to the Founders as he says, one would expect to find this view expressed often by them, either explicitly in their descriptions of the judicial function in interpreting the Constitution, or implicitly in their own written opinions interpreting the Constitution. Jaffa can cite no such support. To the contrary, the other three documents listed in the resolution contain strong internal evidence against Jaffa's thesis.

The Federalist is devoted almost exclusively to explaining the meaning of the words and phrases that comprise the Constitution's text, yet nowhere do its authors attach interpretative significance to the Declaration, let alone equate the principles of the Declaration with the principles of the Constitution. To the contrary, Hamilton's classic statement in *The Federalist* No. 78 of the judicial function in constitutional adjudication does not even refer to the Declaration.

Similarly, the Virginia Resolutions of 1799 addressed one of the most serious constitutional issues of the period: the constitutionality of the Alien and Sedition acts. Madison, as a member of the Virginia House of Delegates, authored a lengthy committee report defending the resolutions. Madison's attack on the constitutionality of the Sedition Act is

---

equating the principles of the Declaration with the principles of the Constitution is startling.

[25] The absurdity of Jaffa's claim is captured vividly when one attempts to conceive of language that actually says what Jaffa attributes to the 1825 Board of Visitors resolution. It is difficult, to say the least, to imagine Madison and Jefferson offering the following resolution: "And on the distinctive principles of the Constitution of the United States, the best guides are to be found in—1. The Declaration of Independence. 2. The Constitution of the United States. 3. The book known by the title of 'The Federalist'."

among the finest examples of constitutional interpretation—of originalism—as there is to be found. He opens his report with a concise
statement of the originalist creed: "[T]he compact ought to have the interpretation plainly intended by the parties to it."[26] In his search for the
intended meaning of the compact, Madison painstakingly analyzed the
language, structure, and history of each of the relevant constitutional
provisions. He looked to the proceedings in the conventions of the framers and the ratifiers, the arguments advanced in *The Federalist*, the
framing of the First Amendment in the First Congress—in short, "everything from which aid [could] be derived," in Chief Justice Marshall's
famous phrase. He did not mention the Declaration.[27]

Finally, President Washington's specific references to the Constitution in his Farewell Address are wholly at odds with Jaffa's thesis that
the Constitution is subordinate in authority to the Declaration's natural
law principles. In particular, Washington said this of the Constitution:

> Respect for its authority, compliance with its laws, acquies-
> cence in its measures, are duties enjoined by the fundamental
> maxims of true liberty. The basis of our political systems is the
> right of the people to make and to alter their constitutions of
> government. But the constitution which at any time exists till
> changed by an explicit and authentic act of the whole people is
> sacredly obligatory upon all. The very idea of the power and
> the right of the people to establish government presupposes the
> duty of every individual to obey the established government.[28]

Washington made no reference to the Declaration of Independence.

Thus, on reading the Board of Visitors resolution and the related correspondence between Madison and Jefferson, it is clear that we do not
truly "have Madison's and Jefferson's word that the principles of the
Constitution . . . are those of the Declaration of Independence." To the
contrary, we have only Jaffa, inventing a new and radical Constitution

---

[26] James Madison, Report of 1800, Jan. 7, 1800, in 17 *The Papers of James Madison*
(David B. Mattern et al. eds., 1991).
[27] Madison rejected the claim that the whole "common or unwritten law" had somehow
been incorporated into the Constitution, noting that the whole genius of the Constitution,
as reflected in its history and text, was to substitute a written constitution and a government of expressly limited legislative powers for the common-law alternative of England.
[28] Washington's Farewell Address, Sept. 17, 1796, in *Documents of American History*
169, 171-72 (Henry Steele Commager ed., 1973).

and, in Posner's words, "presenting himself as the passive agent of the sainted Founders."

V

Although it is difficult to imagine a better example of bad originalism than Jaffa's treatment of the Virginia Board of Visitors resolution, Taney's opinion in *Dred Scott* comes close. As discussed earlier, however, Jaffa's attack on Bork, Rehnquist, and Meese is based in large part on his claim that Taney's opinion in *Dred Scott* is a flawless example of Borkian originalism. Jaffa makes this claim in full view of statements by Bork, Rehnquist, and Meese denouncing *Dred Scott* not just as judicial activism, but as the original sin of judicial activism—the birthplace of "substantive due process."

Now the importance to Mr. Jaffa of this assertion—that Taney did precisely what Bork, Rehnquist, and Meese would have him do—simply cannot be overstated. For if a faithful search for the intended meaning of the Constitution's provisions yields the conclusion that Taney was wrong—that the Missouri Compromise's territorial prohibition on slavery was a valid exercise of Congress's delegated constitutional powers—there is simply no necessity for Jaffa to produce the same result through an appeal to the Declaration's (and therefore, says Jaffa, the Constitution's) principle of the natural equality of all men.

No later than the third paragraph of the opening page of his book, Mr. Jaffa states that "no one, on or off the Court, has ever expounded the theory of original intent with greater eloquence or conviction than Chief Justice Taney in the case of *Dred Scott*." The point was made in response to Meese's observation, published in *Policy Review* in 1986, that Taney's opinion is an example of the "danger in seeing the Constitution as an empty vessel into which each generation may pour its passion and prejudice." To be sure, as Jaffa says, Taney's formulation of the doctrine was perfect in every respect. "If any of [the Constitution's] provisions are deemed unjust," said Taney, "there is a mode prescribed in the instrument itself by which it may be amended. . . .[But] so long as it continues in its present form, it speaks not only in the same words, but with the same meaning and intent with which it spoke when it came from the hands of its framers, and was voted on and adopted by the people of the United States" (pp. 13-14). Based upon Taney's self-certification as an originalist, and very little more, Jaffa concludes that "[w]hatever is wrong with [Taney's] opinion, it is not because [he] did not hold to the doctrine of original intent" (p. 15).

It is a sufficient answer to Jaffa to say, as Judge Bork did at his confirmation hearing when confronted with the same passage from *Dred Scott*, that even the Devil can quote Scripture. As Professor Lino Graglia has observed: "It is no argument against originalism . . . that even activist judges such as Taney . . . have claimed to be originalists. Their claims merely show their recognition that originalism is the only legitimate basis for judicial review."[29]

Jaffa was forced to elaborate his defense of Taney's fidelity to Borkian originalism, however, when Judge Bork published a critique of *Dred Scott* in his 1989 book *The Tempting of America: The Political Seduction of the Law*. The essential facts of the case can be briefly outlined. Dred Scott was a slave originally held in Missouri. His master took him first to the free state of Illinois, then to the Upper Louisiana Territory, where slavery had been outlawed by the Missouri Compromise, and then back to Missouri. Claiming to be a citizen of Missouri, Scott sued for his freedom on the theory that he became emancipated when he was taken by his master to jurisdictions in which slavery was outlawed. After concluding that the federal courts lacked jurisdiction over Scott's claim because no black, whether free or slave, could be a citizen of the United States, Taney nonetheless went on to decide the merits of the case, ruling that the prohibition on slavery in the Missouri Compromise violated the Due Process Clause of the Fifth Amendment.

In *Tempting*, Bork focuses his attention on Taney's determination to hold that the right of property in slaves was guaranteed by the Constitution. Taney began the critical portion of his analysis with the unremarkable observation that the limits placed by the Constitution on congressional power apply no less to laws pertaining to the territories than they do to any other laws. To illustrate this point, he noted: "[N]o one . . . will contend that Congress can make any law in a Territory respecting the establishment of religion, or the free exercise thereof, or abridging the freedom of speech or of the press."[30]

While this point is unobjectionable, Bork notes, "there is no similar constitutional provision that can be read with any semblance of plausibility to confer a right to own slaves."[31] (It is this statement by Bork that Jaffa disputes, as I shall discuss in a moment.) But this difficulty did not

---

[29] Graglia, *supra* note 10, at 1045.
[30] *Scott v. Sanford,* 60 U.S. (19 How.) 393, 449 (1856).
[31] Bork, *supra* note 9, at 30.

deter Taney, who discovered such a right in the Fifth Amendment's prohibition against the federal government depriving a person of property without due process of law. The critical sentence in Taney's opinion is this: "[A]n act of Congress which deprives a citizen of the United States of his liberty or property, merely because he came himself or brought his property into a particular Territory of the United States, and who had committed no offense against the laws, could hardly be dignified with the name of due process of law."[32]

With these words, a rule intended merely to ensure procedural regularity and fairness in the application of laws was transformed by Taney into a rule regulating the permissible substance of the laws. And as Bork notes, Taney's invention—substantive due process—has since then been used countless times, most notably in *Lochner* and *Roe*, "by judges who want to write their personal beliefs into a document that, most inconveniently, does not contain those beliefs."[33] Finally, Bork praised Justice Curtis's dissenting opinion in *Dred Scott*, which relentlessly demolished every facet of Taney's reasoning.

Jaffa charges that "Judge Bork makes his case against Taney only by the most shameless expurgating and bowdlerizing of the Constitution's text" (p. 300). Specifically, Jaffa takes issue with Bork's "amazing" and "fantastic" assertion that the right to own slaves is "'nowhere to be found in the Constitution.'" Jaffa rejoins that "the Constitution most assuredly recognizes such a right" in three places: (1) the Fugitive Slave Clause (Article IV, Section 2), which provides that a slave escaping into a free state shall not be emancipated under the laws thereof, "but shall be delivered up on claim of" the slave owner; (2) the Importation Clause (Article I, Section 9), which prohibited Congress until 1808 from exercising its commerce and naturalization powers to interfere with the slave trade; and (3) the Three-Fifths Clause (Article I, Section 2), which counts only three-fifths of the slaves for purposes of apportioning congressional representation and direct taxes. In light of these express constitutional provisions, Jaffa argues, "it was not unreasonable for [Taney] to conclude that it was unconstitutional to deprive a person of such valuable [property] merely because he took [it] with him into a United States Territory" (p. 300).

Jaffa is certainly correct that the original Constitution recognized a right to slave ownership. But Bork did not deny that the Constitution

---

[32] *Scott*, 60 U.S. at 450.
[33] Bork, *supra* note 9, at 31.

recognized a right to slave ownership; he said instead that the Constitution does not "confer a right" to slave ownership. While the distinction is, I trust, obvious, let me illustrate. The Fugitive Slave Clause recognizes both that the laws of some states permit the ownership of slaves and that the laws of the other states prohibit the ownership of slaves. In other words, the Constitution recognizes the right of freedom in all men guaranteed by some states no less than it recognizes the right of property in slaves guaranteed in other states. But the key point is that in either case the right being recognized in the Constitution is a right under state law. It is not a federal constitutional right. In contrast, the Second Amendment confers a federal constitutional right to keep (and thus presumably to own) arms. The federal government lacks power to legislate in a manner that infringes on this right. There is no similar constitutional provision conferring a right to keep slaves. Bork, in his critique of Taney's analysis, said no more, and no less, than this, as Jaffa well understands.[34]

---

[34] Jaffa recently made it difficult to indulge the assumption that his false and hyperbolic claim that Bork had bowdlerized the Constitution was attributable to an honest misunderstanding of the import of Bork's words, rather than a deliberate misreading of them. In a recent exchange between Bork and Jaffa in the pages of *National Review*, Bork responded to Jaffa's charge, noting the obvious distinction between the Constitution *guaranteeing* a right to own slaves (which he denied) and the Constitution recognizing a right to own slaves (which he did not deny): "The Constitution certainly recognized that slaves were held pursuant to the laws of some states, but the Constitution most emphatically did not guarantee such a right. *"National Review*, Feb. 7, 1994, at 62. Jaffa responded as follows:

> It bears repeating that in his book Judge Bork asserted categorically that *recognition* of a right of slave ownership was "nowhere to be found" in the Constitution. Now he admits that the Constitution of 1787 "certainly recognized" such a right. But he pours out his invective upon me for discovering his error.

National Review, Mar. 21, 1994, at 56 (emphasis added). Jaffa thus answers his enemy at the level of fact, and Bork either said it or he didn't. Here is what Bork actually says in his book: "How did Taney know that slave ownership was a constitutional right? Such a right is nowhere to be found in the Constitution. He knew it because he was passionately convinced that it *must* be a constitutional right." Bork, *supra* note 9, at 31 (emphasis in original). And this passage was introduced by Bork's observation that "Taney was determined to prove that the right of property in slaves was *guaranteed* by the Constitution." *Id.* at 30 (emphasis added). Thus, Bork said, plainly and unmistakably, that "a constitutional right" to "slave ownership" was "nowhere to be found in the Constitution." He did not say that a state-law right to slave ownership was nowhere recognized in the Constitution.

In any event, the Constitution's express recognition of a right in some states to property in slaves simply has no effect whatever on the due process analysis. The Due Process Clause embraces and protects all forms and types of property, regardless of whether it is "recognized" as property in some provision of the Constitution. Property in mining equipment, for example, is entitled to protection under the Due Process Clause even though such property is nowhere "recognized" in the Constitution. The slave property recognized by some states would be no less entitled to the protection of the Due Process Clause if there had been no Fugitive Slave Clause or other constitutional provisions "recognizing" such property. Thus, the question in *Dred Scott* was not whether slave property was entitled to due process protection by virtue of its "recognition" in the Fugitive Slave Clause; it was entitled to full due process protection quite apart from the Fugitive Slave Clause. The question, rather, was what did that due process protection entail?

On this question, as we have seen, Jaffa thinks that Taney got it right, as a matter of Borkian originalism, in concluding that a slaveholder was entitled under the Due Process Clause to take his slaves with him into a United States territory. This raises some difficult questions for Jaffa. Is Congress's plenary legislative authority over the territories similarly limited with respect to other substances or activities that are permitted in at least some of the states? Would Congress, for example, be barred by the Fifth Amendment from outlawing the possession and use of cocaine in the territories simply because some states had not outlawed it? If citizens of Utah, for example, enjoyed the freedom to practice polygamy, would Congress be prohibited under the Due Process Clause from outlawing the practice? Would a prostitute from Nevada be constitutionally entitled to engage in her profession in the territories? I think that the answer to these questions is quite plainly no.

Then is Jaffa's Borkian interpretation of the Due Process Clause limited to slave property? In other words, did those who framed and ratified the Due Process Clause of the Fifth Amendment intend it to be construed as though it provided, in the fashion of the Second Amendment, that "the right of the people to keep slaves shall not be infringed."

On its face, the proposition is farfetched, for if this is what the framers and ratifiers of the Fifth Amendment meant, then it would have been easy enough to say. But quite apart from this difficulty, it is clear that the Due Process Clause was not intended to establish a federal constitutional right to own slaves, or to create any other substantive right. It was designed to afford *procedural* protection, requiring that government proceed according to written laws as interpreted and applied by judicial tribunals. The protection of due process of law descended from the Magna Carta and was included in every state constitution, free states and slave states alike. And no one suggested that it comprehended a right to own slaves.

The Fugitive Slave Clause, far from supporting Taney's interpretation of the Fifth Amendment, actually cuts against Taney. For on its face it shows that its framers saw no irreconcilable conflict between the freedom of a state (and thus presumably a territory[35]) to ban slavery and the constitutional obligation to return a fugitive slave to his owner in a slave state.

In a similar vein, the Northwest Ordinance provides a particularly serious obstacle to Taney's due process analysis, and thus to Jaffa's defense of it. At the same time that the First Congress framed the Due Process Clause of the Fifth Amendment, it enacted the Northwest Ordinance to govern the vast territory ceded to the United States by Virginia. Now we should note that Jaffa elsewhere has stated that "the living Constitution generated" by the founders included not only the Bill of Rights, but the Northwest Ordinance, whose "importance as one of our fundamental political arrangements is incalculable."[36] The Northwest Ordinance banned the institution of slavery from the territory, and also provided for the return of any fugitive slave who had escaped from one of the original states. It seems unlikely, to say the least, that the First Congress intended at once to enact a territorial ban on slavery and to frame and propose a constitutional amendment that would invalidate the enactment. Indeed, the Northwest Ordinance had its own due process clause!

Finally, Jaffa himself provides the most telling refutation of Taney's analysis of the original intent of the Fifth Amendment's Due Process Clause. Throughout his writing on this subject, he characterizes the slavery provisions of the Constitution as a "bundle of compromises" of the

---

[35] The Fugitive Slave Clause is expressly limited in scope to states and state laws; later in Article IV (Section 3, clause 2), the Constitution gives Congress plenary authority to pass federal law for the territories. This provides a powerful "expressio unius" argument against Taney (and Jaffa): when the framers wanted to require slaves to be returned to their masters, they knew how to do it, and they provided no such requirement in the context of territories (the issue, of course, in *Dred Scott*).

[36] Harry V. Jaffa, *How To Think about the American Revolution* 79 (1978). Indeed, Jaffa says that "the Northwest Ordinance, which was a Jeffersonian document, was—unlike the Constitution—uncompromising in its attempt to seek equal rights for all." *Id.* at 82. This claim seems somewhat exaggerated in light of the fact that the Northwest Ordinance included its own Fugitive Slave Clause.

Declaration's (and thus the Constitution's) principle of natural human equality. The compromises represented the greatest good attainable at the time. Is it possible that the Fifth Amendment would have been submitted by the First Congress to the states, or ratified by the requisite number thereof, were it understood and intended to disable Congress from prohibiting slavery in the territories? Then how can it *honorably* be said, as Taney said, that the rule of law to which the people consented in ratifying the Fifth Amendment established a federal constitutional right to own slaves?

Jaffa declines to deal with any of these points. I say "declines" because they are not new, and he must be aware of them. All of them, or at least most of them, were made by Justice Curtis in a dissenting opinion that has few equals in the United States Reports as an exemplar of judicial craftsmanship and of originalism. According to Judge Bork, as I mentioned earlier, Justice Curtis "destroyed Taney's reasoning, and rested his own conclusions upon the original understanding of those who made the Constitution."[37] Yet, in advancing the claim that Taney was an originalist in the Borkian mold, Jaffa does not deign even to mention Curtis's name, let alone to treat with the arguments that palpably reveal Taney for the dishonest activist—the bad originalist—that he was.

Earlier I suggested that Jaffa's urgent defense of Taney against the claims of the Borkian originalists was driven by his commitment to the idea that the right result in *Dred Scott*—the constitutionality of the Missouri Compromise—could be reached only through an appeal to the transcendent natural right of equality that he says is made binding on all constitutional interpretation by the Declaration of Independence. But Jaffa needs Taney for another reason. Jaffa offers a hypothetical case in which the antebellum Congress has enacted a slave code for the territories. He says that Lincoln, and therefore we may presume Jaffa, would not have hesitated in striking down the statute as a violation of the Due Process Clause of the Fifth Amendment (p. 272). Jaffa returns to the point at the end of *Original Intent*, arguing that because "the moral question involved in the slavery question was more fundamental than the legal or constitutional question," neither he nor Lincoln "would have objected, if the Taney Court had been antislavery and had declared a federal law unconstitutional because it extended slavery to virgin territories" (p. 396). Thus, Taney's illegitimate invention—substantive due

---

[37] Bork, *supra* note 9, at 33.

process—is no less central to Jaffa's constitutionalism than it was to Taney's. Jaffa has no problem with Taney's methodology, just with his moral values and, hence, his result. But Justice Curtis's originalist response to Taney's substantive due process analysis is no less dispositive of Jaffa's.

In sum, Jaffa's claim that the constitutionalism of Bork, Rehnquist, and Meese is the constitutionalism of Taney is false. It is Harry Jaffa who speaks with Taney's voice.

Appendix

Letter from Thomas Jefferson to an unknown addressee,
in *The Writings of Thomas Jefferson* 397
(H.A. Washington ed., 1854)

Dear Sir, —Although our Professors were, on the 5th of December, still in an English port, that they were safe raises me from the dead, for I was almost ready to give up the ship. That was eight weeks ago; they may therefore be daily expected.

In most public seminaries text-books are prescribed to each of the several schools, as the *norma docendi* in that school; and this is generally done by authority of the trustees. I should not propose this generally in our University, because I believe none of us are so much at the heights of science in the several branches, as to undertake this, and therefore that it will be better left to the Professors until occasion of interference shall be given. But there is one branch in which we are the best judges, in which heresies may be taught, of so interesting a character to our own State and to the United States, as to make it a duty in us to lay down the principles which are to be taught. It is that of government. Mr. Gilmer being withdrawn, we know not who his successor may be. He may be a Richmond lawyer, or one of that school of quondam federalism, now consolidation. It is our duty to guard against such principles being disseminated among our youth, and the diffusion of that poison, by a previous prescription of the texts to be followed in their discourses. I therefore enclose you a resolution which I think of proposing at our next meeting, strictly confiding it to your own knowledge alone, and to that of Mr. Loyall, to whom you may communicate it, as I am sure it will harmonize with his principles, I wish it kept to ourselves, because I have always found that the less such things are spoken of beforehand, the less obstruction is contrived to be thrown in their way. I have communicated it to Mr. Madison.

Letter from James Madison to Thomas Jefferson, Feb. 8, 1825,
in 17 *The Papers of James Madison* 218-21
(David B. Mattern et al. eds., 1991)

DEAR SIR . . . .

. . . .

I have looked with attention over your intended proposal of a text book for the Law School. It is certainly very material that the true doctrines of liberty, as exemplified in our Political System, should be inculcated on those who are to sustain and may administer it. It is, at the same time, not easy to find standard books that will be both guides & guards for the purpose. Sidney & Locke are admirably calculated to impress on young minds the right of Nations to establish their own Governments, and to inspire a love of free ones; but afford no aid in guarding our Republican Charters against constructive violations. The Declaration of Independence, tho' rich in fundamental principles, and saying every thing that could be said in the same number of words, falls nearly under a like observation. The "Federalist" may fairly enough be regarded as the most authentic exposition of the text of the federal Constitution, as understood by the Body which prepared & the Authority which accepted it. Yet it did not foresee all the misconstructions which have occurred; nor prevent some that it did foresee. And what equally deserves remark, neither of the great rival Parties have acquiesced in all its comments. It may nevertheless be admissible as a School book, if any will be that goes so much into detail. It has been actually admitted into two Universities, if not more—those of Harvard and Rh:Island; but probably at the choice of the Professors, without any injunction from the superior authority. With respect to the Virginia Document of 1799, there may be more room for hesitation. The' corresponding with the predominant sense of the Nation; being of local origin & having reference to a state of Parties not yet extinct, an absolute prescription of it, might excite prejudices against the University as under Party Banners, and induce the more bigoted to withhold from it their sons, even when destined for other than the studies of the Law School. It may be added that the Document is not on every point satisfactory to all who belong to the same Party. Are we sure that to our brethren of the Board it is so? In framing a political creed, a like difficulty occurs as in the case of religion tho' the public right be very different in the two cases. If the Articles be in very general terms, they do not answer the purpose; if in very particular terms, they divide & exclude where meant to unite & fortify. The best that can be done in our case seems to be, to avoid the two extremes, by referring to selected Standards without requiring an unqualified conformity to them, which indeed might not in every instance be possible. The selection would give them authority with the Students, and might controul or counteract deviations of the Professor. I have, for your consideration, sketched a modification of the operative passage in your draught, with a view to relax the absoluteness of its injunction, and added to your list of Documents the Inaugural Speech and the Farewell Address of President Washington. They may help down what might be less readily swallowed, and contain nothing which is not good; unless it be the laudatory reference in the Address to the Treaty of 1795 with G. B. which ought not to weigh against the sound sentiments characterizing it.

After all, the most effectual safeguard against heretical intrusions into the School Politics, will be an Able & Orthodox Professor, whose course of instruction will be an example to his successors, and may carry with it a sanction from the Visitors.

Affectionately yours.

Sketch.

And on the distinctive principles of the Government of our own State, and of that of the U. States, the best guides are to be found in —1. The Declaration of Independence, as the fundamental act of Union of these States. 2. the book known by the title of the "Federalist," being an Authority to which appeal is habitually made by all & rarely declined or denied by any, as evidence of the general opinion of those who framed & those who accepted the Constitution of the U. States on questions as to its genuine meaning. 3. the Resolutions of the General Assembly of Virg.[a] in 1799, on the subject of the Alien & Sedition laws, which appeared to accord with the predominant sense of the people of the U. S. 4. The Inaugural Speech & Farewell Address of President Washington, as conveying political lessons of peculiar value; and that in the branch of the School of law which is to treat on the subject of Gov.[t], these shall be used as the text & documents of the School.

The Writings of Thomas Jefferson 459-66

(Andrew A. Lipscomb editor-in-chief, 1904)

At a special meeting of the Board of Visitors of the University, called by George Loyall, Chapman Johnson and Joseph C. Cabell, while attending the last session of the legislature, and held at the University March 4, 1825.

Present, Thomas Jefferson, rector, James Madison, George Loyall, John H. Cocke and Joseph C. Cabell.

. . . .

A resolution was moved and agreed to in the following words:

Whereas, it is the duty of this Board to the government under which it lives, and especially to that of which this University is the immediate creation, to pay especial attention to the principles of government which shall be inculcated therein, and to provide that none shall be inculcated which are incompatible with those on which the Constitutions of this State, and of the United States were genuinely based, in the common opinion; and for this purpose it maybe necessary to point out specially where these principles are to be found legitimately developed:

Resolved; that it is the opinion of this Board that as to the general principles of liberty and the rights of man, in nature and in society, the doctrines of Locke, in his "Essay concerning the true original extent and end of civil government," and of Sidney in his "Discourses on government," may be considered as those generally approved by our fellow citizens of this, and the United States, and that on the distinctive principles of the government of our State, and of that of the United States, the best guides are to be found in, 1. The Declaration of Independence, as the fundamental act of union of these States. 2. The book known by the title of "The Federalist," being an authority to which appeal is habitually made by all, and rarely declined or denied by any as evidence of the general opinion of those who framed, and of those who accepted the Constitution of the United States, on questions as to its genuine meaning. 3. The Resolutions of the General Assembly of Virginia in 1799 on the subject of the alien and sedition laws, which appeared to accord with the predominant sense of the people of the United States. 4. The valedictory address of President Washington, as conveying political lessons of peculiar value. And that in the branch of the school of law, which is to treat on the subject of civil polity, these shall be used as the text and documents of the school.

. . . .

And the Board adjourned without a day.

TH. JEFFERSON

March 5, 1825.

About the Author

Established in 1978, The Claremont Institute sponsors research, writing, teaching, and discussion to illuminate the principles and promote the practice of free government. In addition to the Center for the Study of the Natural Law, it incorporates the Center for the American Constitution, the Golden State Center for Policy Studies, and the Asian Studies Center.

Harry V. Jaffa is Professor Emeritus of Political Philosophy at Claremont McKenna College and a Distinguished Fellow at The Claremont Institute. Among his many books are *Crisis of the House Divided: An Interpretation of the Lincoln-Douglas Debates; How to Think about the American Revolution; The Conditions of Freedom; and Original Intent and the Framers of the Constitution: A Disputed Question.*

Professor Lino A. Graglia is A. Dalton Cross Professor of Law at the University of Texas Law School. He has written widely in constitutional law—especially on judicial review, constitutional interpretation, race discrimination, and affirmative action—and also teaches and writes in the area of antitrust. He is the author of *Disaster by Decree: The Supreme Court Decision on Race and the Schools* (Cornell, 1976) as well as many articles.

Charles Cooper is a partner in the Washington, D.C., law firm of Cooper Carvin & Rosenthal, PLLC. From 1985 to 1988, Mr. Cooper served as the Assistant Attorney General for the Office of Legal Counsel in the United States Department of Justice. He has spoken and written extensively on the subject of constitutional interpretation.

The Claremont Institute
250 West First Street, Suite 330
Claremont, California 91711

Telephone (909) 621-6825
Fax (909) 626-6724
www.claremont.org ▪ www.founding.com

167